Lecture Notes in Computer Science 9001

Commenced Publication in 1973
Founding and Former Series Editors:
Gerhard Goos, Juris Hartmanis, and Jan van Leeuwen

More information about this series at http://www.springer.com/series/7409

Ivana Podnar Žarko · Krešimir Pripužić
Martin Serrano (Eds.)

Interoperability and Open-Source Solutions for the Internet of Things

International Workshop, FP7 OpenIoT Project
Held in Conjunction with SoftCOM 2014
Split, Croatia, September 18, 2014
Invited Papers

 Springer

Editors
Ivana Podnar Žarko
University of Zagreb
Zagreb
Croatia

Krešimir Pripužić
University of Zagreb
Zagreb
Croatia

Martin Serrano
National University of Ireland
Galway
Ireland

ISSN 0302-9743   ISSN 1611-3349 (electronic)
Lecture Notes in Computer Science
ISBN 978-3-319-16545-5   ISBN 978-3-319-16546-2 (eBook)
DOI 10.1007/978-3-319-16546-2

Library of Congress Control Number: 2015933506

LNCS Sublibrary: SL3 – Information Systems and Application, incl. Internet/Web, and HCI

Springer Cham Heidelberg New York Dordrecht London

Printed on acid-free paper

Springer International Publishing AG Switzerland is part of Springer Science+Business Media (www.springer.com)

Preface

This volume contains the proceedings of the Workshop on Interoperability and Open-Source Solutions for the Internet of Things held in Split, Croatia, on September 18, 2014. The workshop was organized by the OpenIoT project with support from the European Commission under the 7th Framework Programme and in conjunction with the conference SoftCOM 2014: The 22nd International Conference on Software, Telecommunications, and Computer Networks.

The Internet of Things (IoT) can be seen as the next evolutionary step in the Internet lifecycle, with already more than 10 billion connected devices in 2013. However, to enable wide adoption and proliferation of IoT services, further development is needed in the area of interoperability and standardization as well as the convergence of the Web and IoT standards in the M2M space, e.g., W3C SSN, and OneM2M. We are also witnessing the emergence of open-source solutions targeting the IoT and cloud integration, which can further drive innovation and provision of utility-driven IoT services. The aim of the workshop was to address the aforementioned challenges by bringing together researchers and practitioners from industry and academia to showcase their practical work, exchange ideas and experiences, as well as discuss future developments in the area of interoperability and open-source solutions for the IoT.

The workshop featured two invited keynote talks, an invited presentation of the OpenIoT platform, 10 oral presentations of original scientific papers, and a demo session closely aligned to the workshop main topics. The original scientific papers presented at the workshop and accepted for publication in this volume underwent a rigorous two-step review process and acquired a total of three reviews, where two reviews were authored by the Technical Program Committee members from academia and one Technical Program Committee member from industry. There were 15 papers initially registered for presentation at the workshop and in the end of the review procedure 10 papers were selected for oral presentation at the workshop and publication in this volume of the workshop proceedings.

The main highlights in the Workshop Program were two keynote talks given by two distinguished speakers and a hands-on session demonstrating IoT solutions built on top of the Open-Source OpenIoT platform. Bill Weinberg, Senior Director from Open-Source Strategy Consulting at Black Duck Software, USA, presented his view on open-source strategies for driving the IoT, while Markus Weinberger, Director of Bosh IoT Lab, Switzerland discussed business ecosystems for IoT. Extended abstracts of keynote talks are included in this volume. The volume includes selected papers presenting open-source solutions targeting the IoT and cloud integration as well as implementations of IoT-related standards. Furthermore, it includes an invited overview paper introducing the OpenIoT platform and selected use cases in the area of IoT built on top of the OpenIoT platform. Since the papers included in this volume address topics that are highly related to a wide adoption and proliferation of IoT services, we hope that it will contribute to further drive innovation and provision of utility-driven IoT services.

We would like to express our thanks to the keynote speakers, Mr. Bill Weinberg and Dr. Markus Weinberger for their inspiring talks. The Chairs' special thanks go to the Technical Program Committee members for their valuable efforts in the review process. We cordially thank all the authors for their contributions, workshop participants for their interest and active involvement in the Workshop Program, as well as the organizers of the SoftCOM 2014 for providing an excellent workshop venue in Split, Croatia. Thank you all for making this workshop a valuable experience.

December 2014

Ivana Podnar Žarko
Martin Serrano

Organization

The workshop was organized by the OpenIoT project with support from the European Commission under the 7th Framework Programme.

Program Committee Co-chairs

Martin Serrano   National University of Ireland Galway, INSIGHT
                              Centre, Ireland
Ivana Podnar Žarko   University of Zagreb Faculty of Electrical
                              Engineering and Computing, Croatia

Publication Chair

Krešimir Pripužić   University of Zagreb Faculty of Electrical
                              Engineering and Computing, Croatia

Publicity Chair

Johan E. Bengtsson   AcrossLimits, Malta

Web Master

Keith Spiteri   AcrossLimits, Malta

Local Organization Chair

Tihana Sesar   University of Zagreb Faculty of Electrical
                              Engineering and Computing, Croatia

Technical Program Committee

Karl Aberer   EPFL, Switzerland
Payam Barnaghi   University of Surrey, UK
Vedran Bilas   University of Zagreb, Croatia
Jean-Paul Calbimonte   EPFL, Switzerland
Gino Carrozzo   Nextworks, Italy
Oscar Corcho   Universidad Politécnica de Madrid, Spain

Jorge Cuellar	Siemens, Germany
Philippe Cudré-Mauroux	University of Fribourg, Switzerland
Panos Dimitropoulos	SENSAP, Greece
Dimitrios Georgakopoulos	CSIRO, Australia
Armin Haller	CSIRO, Australia
Manfred Hauswirth	Fraunhofer – FOKUS, Germany
Reinhard Herzog	Fraunhofer IOSB, Germany
Darko Huljenić	Ericsson Nikola Tesla, Croatia
Prem Jayaraman	CSIRO, Australia
Ignac Lovrek	University of Zagreb, Croatia
Arndt Marylin	Orange, France
Patricia Martigne	Orange Labs, France
Maja Matijašević	University of Zagreb, Croatia
Cosmin-Septimiu Nechifor	Siemens, Romania
Omar Elloumi	Alcatel-Lucent, France
Mirko Presser	Alexandra Institute, Denmark
Enrico Scarrone	Telecom Italia, Italy
John Soldatos	Athens Information Technology, Greece
Joerg Swetina	NEC Europe, Austria
Tajana Šimunic Rosing	University of California, USA
Thomas Usländer	Fraunhofer IOSB, Germany

Contents

IoT Applications

The Internet of Things and Open Source (Extended Abstract)

Bill Weinberg[✉]

Black Duck Software, 8 New England Executive Park,
Burlington, MA 01803, USA
bweinberg@blackduck.com

Abstract. This paper explores divergent visions for the evolution of Internet of Things (IoT) technology and business models, and the ecosystem that exists around them. In particular, it examines the role and reach of open source software (OSS) in building and sustaining the IoT, from infrastructure to applications and other value-added device content. Specifically, it explores how OSS can support competing and complementary architectures and meet looming IoT challenges, including security and privacy on this new digital frontier.

Keywords: IoT · Open-source software · Evolution · Business models · Ecosystem · Architecture · Challenges

1 Introduction

The build out of the Internet of Things (IoT) is advancing at a tremendous rate, by all accounts outpacing desktop and mobile computing. By 2020, over 50 billion intelligent devices will connect to and exchange information over the Internet according to Cisco, while Gartner projected 7.3 billion tablets, smartphones and PCs with an economic impact of nearly US$2 trillion. This huge cohort of "things" comprises staggering diversity, from recognizable computers to infrastructure devices to sensors, light switches, and thermostats. The impact of the IoT will span the gamut of industries and applications, including medical, agriculture, manufacturing, consumer electronics, transportation, and energy. And, like the existing Internet, the emerging IoT will rely upon and instigate adoption of open source technologies and open standards.

2 Competing Visions for IoT

The IoT engenders great excitement and inspires sweeping optimistic statements about its potential. Monetization of the IoT, especially of the open source software that will support that build out, will be subject to competing technical and financial models.

There are two prevalent views of the architecture and make-up of the IoT. We call them *Many Peers* and *Many Leaves*. With *Many Peers*, the IoT is effectively an extension of the current connected universe, while *Many Leaves* envisions an extension of the M2M (machine to machine) paradigm, with a vast cohort of relatively simple end-point systems, deployed with deeply embedded real-time operating systems. These two visions

© Springer International Publishing Switzerland 2015
I. Podnar Žarko et al. (Eds.): FP7 OpenIoT Project Workshop 2014, LNCS 9001, pp. 1–5, 2015.
DOI: 10.1007/978-3-319-16546-2_1

are not incompatible and devices implementing both paradigms are already populating the nascent IoT. They differ principally in terms of who promotes which: *Many Leaves* is the logical province of semiconductor suppliers and embedded software vendors, as well as adherents to the maker movement. *Many Peers* is the darling of systems vendors and enterprise software suppliers.

There are dozens of ways to monetize open source in general – no two companies working in or around open source are alike in the mix of tactics they employ. At a conceptual level, OSS business models fit into the following four major categories: building OSS, building with OSS, building for OSS and building on OSS.

A stark distinction exists between vertical integration and horizontal diversity which are two approaches to populating the different technical tiers of the IoT. These approaches have important implications for collaboration and interoperability. There already exists a range of silos of IoT devices and protocols, but do not interoperate with nearly identical devices from other vendors. With a single IoT tier, there also exist less ambitious and more open suppliers. These companies offer fewer devices and device types but strive to interoperate with similar gear from other vendors and with third-party infrastructure devices as well. To achieve quality interoperability, vendors across tiers must implement using open IoT standards vs. enabling interoperation only with their own devices.

3   The Roles of Open Source in the IoT Build Out

While open source is and will continue to be instrumental to the IoT, its presence and utility is not uniform across all elements of the network as shown in Table 1.

Table 1. Open source in the IoT stack

	IoT End Points	IoT Infrastructure	Internet Infrastructure	Cloud & Data Center	Client Devices
Applications	possibly	possibly	possibly	possibly	possibly
Frameworks	possibly	most likely	most likely	most likely	possibly
Enabling M/W	possibly	most likely	most likely	most likely	possibly
OS	possibly	most likely	most likely	probably	probably
Firmware	possibly	probably	probably	no	probably
Dev Tools	most likely	most likely	most likely	most likely	most likely
Hardware	possibly	no	no	no	no

In practice, end points belong to one of the following categories: passive nodes, simple end points and peer-level end points. The role of OSS in the *passive nodes* lies not in the RFID tags and slugs themselves but in the equipment that energizes and scans them, and in supporting the applications that act upon the data. The role of OSS in *simple end points* is tactical and not guaranteed. OEMs may choose to use an open source RTOS (e.g., TinyOS, eCOS or FreeRTOS) or a closed source executive (from over 300 commercial/proprietary options) to manage resources and simplify value-added applications programming. Developers will surely use OSS tools to create leave node devices, and semiconductor suppliers will provide open source device drivers and other elements to support them, but the applications running on them will likely remain closed (as are many other types of device software). The *peer-level end points* are by definition multi-function devices and have the potential (or the necessity) of deploying enterprise-peer OSes – Linux, BSD, versions of Windows, etc. These devices represent more interesting opportunities for OSS, from system software (especially Linux and Android) up through middleware and applications frameworks, as well as routing software. Additionally, with fewer resource limitations and constraints on bills-of-material (BoM) costs, these types of devices are easier to build and accessible to "home brewing" and the creativity of the maker movement.

In discussion of open source for the IoT, we should examine two distinct types of infrastructure – routers, gateways, and aggregators that bridge between the existing Internet and IoT end points, vs. access points, LAN router and edge routers, backbone and core switches, and routers that constitute the Internet. The former infrastructure provide ample opportunities for OSS deployment and for the evolution of new open source implementations: embedded Linux provides a flexible platform with native IP networking, IP routing software, and standardized local file systems. New IoT frameworks are almost universally first hosted on Linux, as are most popular programming languages and tool kits. The latter infrastructure, from local wireless networks to broadband and mobile baseband access, to edge and core networking, is already teeming with open source software.

As with Internet infrastructure, the cloud is substantially built on open source software components – Linux, virtualization platforms, orchestration and management software, application support libraries and other types of cloud middleware, and the tools and frameworks developers use to write and deploy code – all open source. That is not to say that all cloud software is open (e.g., Microsoft Azure), nor that software that implements IaaS and PaaS is readily available as open source (e.g., the code behind Amazon Web Services or Rackspace Cloud Hosting). And, while code that implements (or will implement) IoT applications and IoT-centric SaaS solutions leverages OSS, there is no impetus for that code to be open source itself.

As with the existing marketplaces of mobile apps and the even broader universe of web applications, IoT end-user apps certainly benefit from the existence of open source development tools and middleware, but have no particular impetus towards being open source themselves. Reasons include small audiences for niche apps unlikely to engender and support communities; mostly traditional per-unit business models; freeware with revenue from advertising or in-app purchases that don't accrue additional benefit from the "frictionless" distribution model of OSS; strong affinity with a particular brand/company who regards their end-user apps as conferring proprietary advantage.

Across all nodes and tiers, developers of course rely on development tools to build and debug the software they create and deploy. Today, it is no exaggeration to say that most development tools derive from OSS projects or simply are open source.

The varied types of devices that populate the IoT – both end points and infrastructure nodes – fall into the category of embedded systems. Manufacturers of so-called connected "intelligent devices" have been incrementally embracing open source for two decades. Starting with a shift from proprietary compilers and debuggers in the 1990s, device developers went on to embrace embedded Linux through the 2000s, and over the last five years they have begun to build (non-mobile) devices with Android. In the same time period, device manufacturers have shifted their source code control and build engines from legacy proprietary solutions to SVN, GIT, Github, Chef, Puppet and "hot" OSS projects and technologies.

4 Meeting Key IoT Challenges with OSS

The IoT presents the following security and privacy challenges: physical attacks to end-point devices and various physical interfaces, spoofing of local wireless/mesh networks, vulnerabilities from poorly implemented interfaces and authentication, and lack of security updates due to deployment type. None of these challenges is insurmountable, but there exist no magic bullets either. The most ubiquitous "things" on the Internet today are mobile phones and tablets, which stand out as a morass of security problems.

While surely key in innovating solutions to IoT security challenges, open source is just one factor in any comprehensive IoT security and privacy paradigm. Equally important are best development practices and development tools to augment and enforce those practices. What does make OSS more amenable to security remediation is its very openness. Beyond "many eyes making bugs shallow", readily available source code and published OSS project information (e.g., on GitHub and from Black Duck OpenHub) enable automation of otherwise tedious and technically-challenging activities related to identifying security vulnerabilities, out-of-date versions, inactive or poorly maintained projects, assessing and remediating components with known vulnerabilities and monitoring IoT device and application codebases to ensure future security.

5 Conclusion

That open source software will help drive the IoT build-out is obvious, but dominance in IoT technologies is not a foregone conclusion. Open source does sustain and indeed dominate large swaths of intelligent device, networking, network infrastructure, and cloud platform software. For that strong position to translate into IoT dominance, developer communities will still have to cross key gaps and implement technologies essential to the IoT:

- Scalable (downward) system software that meets the needs of myriad end-point device types, especially on lower-end silicon.
- Open source implementations of mesh networking drivers and mesh network management middleware, utilities, and tools.

- Quality, portable open source implementations of IoT protocols/protocol stacks.
- Frameworks and tool kits for IoT application development on infrastructure nodes and in the cloud.
- Lightweight security mechanisms suitable for leaf nodes but robust enough to survive sophisticated cracking, and a provisioning and update paradigm matched to the IoT.

While OSS used the ubiquitous PC/AT architecture as a springboard for Linux and other software, the IoT won't have the luxury of a relatively homogeneous system architecture. The good news is that with over two million OSS projects launched to date and tens of millions of active OSS developers, meeting the unique and emerging needs of the IoT will be all in a day's work for OSS and the communities that create and comprise it.

References

LinuxPundit Weblog. http://linuxpundit.wordpress.com/
deCosta, F.: Rethinking the Internet of Things: A Scalable Approach to Connecting Everything. Apress, New York (2013). ISBN 1430257407
Evans, D.: The Internet of things: how the next evolution of the Internet is changing everything. A White paper by Cisco Systems (2011)
Harvey, C.: 35 Open Source Tools for the Internet of Things. Datamation, 14 August 2014
Merrit, R.: 10 Embedded Design Trends. Electronic Engineering Times, 21 April 2014
Weinberg, W.: The Internet of Things and Open Source. The Open Source Delivers Blog – Black Duck Software, 11 April 2013
Weinberg, W.: Machine to Machine - Intelligent Devices Talking to Each Other. RTC Magazine, September edition (2011)

Business Models and the Internet of Things (Extended Abstract)

Elgar Fleisch[1], Markus Weinberger[2(✉)], and Felix Wortmann[1,3]

[1] ETH Zürich and University of St. Gallen, Dufourstrasse 40a,
9000 St. Gallen, Zürich, Switzerland
efleisch@ethz.ch, felix.wortmann@unisg.ch
[2] Bosch Software Innovations GmbH, Dufourstrasse 40a,
9000 St. Gallen, Zürich, Switzerland
markus.weinberger@bosch-si.com
[3] University of St. Gallen, Dufourstrasse 40a,
9000 St. Gallen, Zürich, Switzerland

Abstract. In this extended abstract we aim on providing an overview on business models based on the Internet of Things for assisting companies that are currently focused on non-digital industries. In the first section the role of the Internet as an innovation driver for business models is reflected, secondly it is shown how business model patterns from digital industries are becoming relevant to physical industries as well. General business model logic patterns for the Internet of Things are shown and the challenges of implementing such patterns in hybrid business models are addressed.

1 The Influence of the Internet on Business Models to Date

In Today's market information technology (IT) has impacted business model innovation. In [4] more than 300 cases of companies have been studied, that broke with the established logic in their industries and in the process permanently changed it. Gillette, IKEA, Nespresso and Pixar are well-known examples of such companies. Out of these case studies a set of 55 business model patterns could be identified. A business model pattern is defined "as a definite configuration of four core elements (who are the customers? What is being sold? How is it produced? How is revenue earned?) that have proven successful in different companies and industries."

It is striking that since the 1990s, IT has been extremely significant in many case studies, even though there continue to be business model patterns that manage to transform an industry without IT. On the one hand, this is not surprising since IT first became widely used throughout the business world in the 1990s. On the other hand, the concentration of IT-driven cases is impressive. A large share of the newer case studies relies in particular on digital business model patterns.

Many of the IT-influenced business model patterns – regardless of the technology wave from which they emerged – follow three overarching trends:

This article has previously been published as a Whitepaper of the Bosch Internet of Things and Services Lab, a Cooperation of HSG and Bosch (2014) – www.iot-lab.ch.

I. Podnar Žarko et al. (Eds.): FP7 OpenIoT Project Workshop 2014, LNCS 9001, pp. 6–10, 2015.
DOI: 10.1007/978-3-319-16546-2_2

- *Integration of users and customers.* IT enables companies to increasingly integrate their customers in their value-creation chain. In other words, IT allows companies to delegate some tasks to their customers. Examples can be found in the *User Designed, E-Commerce, Open Source* (content) and *Mass Customization* business model patterns.
- *Service orientation.* Run time services and/or after-sales digital contact with customers are on the rise. Using IT-based services, IT allows companies to maintain and make use of customer relationships even after the sale. Exemplary business model patterns for this include *Rent instead of Buy, Subscription, Freemium, Razor and Blade* and *Add on.*
- *Core competence analytics.* Precise collection and analysis of transaction and use data are increasingly valuable and represent a key skill for product design, pricing, and sales structuring. Examples can be found in the *Subscription, Flat Rate, Freemium, Pay per Use* and *Performance-based Contracting* business model patterns.

IT is used today to upgrade value in business model patterns. When the Hidden Revenue pattern is applied by companies like Google or Facebook, however, which are part of digital industries, IT is by definition constitutive. IT not only revives old business model patterns and generates new business model patterns; it has also facilitated the emergence of an entirely new digital industry and redefined old business model patterns in that industry.

Many digital business model patterns, such as Freemium, have been applied exclusively in the digital world until now. In manufacturing industries, the Internet has mainly been used to simplify processes – and thus reduce costs while increasing quality and the variety offered. The Internet has been responsible for big breakthroughs in digital industries, as Google, Facebook, PayPal, eBay, YouTube, and others prove.

2   The Economic Power of the Internet of Things

This section outlines the formative power of the Internet of Things within the economy. A broader and more well-grounded analysis of the economic perspective on the Internet of Things can be found in [1, 2].

The digital world – and that includes its various industries – differs in multiple dimensions from the physical world and its industries, for instance in the areas of marginal costs in production, transport, and storage, in transport and production speeds, and in the ability to abstract and simulate.

Digitalization leads to high resolution management because the marginal costs of measuring (in the control process) and the actuating elements (in the controller) are almost zero, while interventions can be made with almost the speed of light.

The Internet of Things is now applying this logic step by step to the physical world. It represents the vision that every object and location in the physical world can become part of the Internet. Objects and locations are generally equipped with mini-computers so they become smart objects that can take in information about their environment and communicate with the Internet and other smart objects. These minicomputers are usually barely visible or completely invisible, so the physical dimension of the object remains people's most important interface.

Smart things are hybrids, composed of elements from both the physical and digital worlds. That means that, when used, they unite the principles of both worlds and in doing so, introduce high resolution management into the physical world, too [1].

Should a fastening equipment manufacturer operating an electronic Kanban system at its customers' plants provide information on the consumption to his customers free of charge or use the freemium model? Or service-for-pay integrated with physical delivery right from the start? And who owns the data? The customer whose warehouse is the source of the data, or the supplier; after all, he owns the smart containers that generate the data. Can and should the data – anonymized, across the entire customer base – reveal valuable, real-time developments in the industry and be capitalized as part of the Leverage Customer Data business model pattern? Whichever is chosen, the Freemium and Leverage Customer Data models are both examples of how business model patterns that have been confined to digital industries can suddenly become relevant for classic physical industries.

3 Business Model Patterns in the Internet of Things

The application-driven goal of this article is to derive well-grounded assistance, both theoretical and practical, for developing Internet of Things business models. These models should be inspiring and provided on a level of abstraction that will facilitate their application across industries, while remaining concrete enough to be actionable for innovators in business and society at large.

To accomplish this, we analyzed the 55 business model patterns from Gassmann [4] and many Internet of Things applications with regard to their value-creating steps and high resolution management. It is the latter that embody both the opportunities and limitations of the Internet of Things' technical capacities. The results of this analysis can be represented as six-components for business model patterns for the Internet of Things: Physical Freemium, Digital Add-on, Digital Lock-in, Product as Point of Sales, Object Self-Service, Remote Usage and Condition Monitoring. Based on their power and their kinship – all of them facilitate digital services for physical products – we merge them all together in a new business model pattern specific to the Internet of Things, *Digitally Charged Products*. On the other hand, the concept of *Sensor as a Service* is so novel and so powerful that we suggest that it is itself a new business model pattern. Further details on these components and new business model patterns can be found in [3].

4 Entrepreneurial Challenges in Implementing Internet of Things Business Models

Generating new ideas is not the biggest hurdle in establishing a new business model. The capabilities of an Internet of Things reignite the discussion regarding the optimal mix of product versus service in a business model.

One feature of the Internet of Things is the fact that the service portion of the business models outlined here is always digital in nature. This has two consequences:

First, the theory and practice of service orientation must be critically examined and expanded as needed against the backdrop of the characteristics of digital services. Second, digitalization that extends into the product itself (in contrast to digital support in the value-creation process) must of necessity lead to an additional service orientation.

The differing characteristics of physical and digital products are particularly noticeable in product development. In a world where a bug can be repaired with an update at almost no cost, even in an installed base running in the millions, and where right from the start high growth is required due to network effects, speed, early customer contact, and aesthetics are of utmost importance in development. In the hardware business, however, and in the world of embedded computing as well, other terms apply. Here, for example, an error in a product that has already been sold usually results in an extremely costly, image-damaging recall action. These differences conditioned by technology and economics have meant that divergent cultures arose in hardware compared to those governing Internet software departments and have shaped putatively incompatible organizational units.

Small units that can and must operate in the tradition of lean startups [5] are advantageous in addressing another challenge. Their leanness itself forces them to work on development together within a network of partners – which include their customers. This implies not only a lead user approach [6] but encompasses an entire ecosystem as facilitator. In the digital world, the one who brings the most developers to its platform wins. In most instances, hybrid solutions mean that the party offering them must have access to data that is constantly generated from application of the solution. This is new for classic production companies and brings with it both many opportunities as well as risks.

5 Summary and Outlook

The goal of this essay is to inspire innovators from business and society at large to develop business models leveraging the Internet of Things. It analyzes the role that the Internet has played in business models to date, documents the specific economic energy of the Internet of Things, and derives from that the general product/service logic serving as the foundation for specific components and patterns of Internet of Things business models. Finally, it indicates some of the key challenges involved in its implementation that will confront in particular companies with a successful history in manufacturing industries.

Maybe this essay raised more questions than it answers. But hopefully some can now be more specifically formulated. The Internet of Things remains an academically and economically fascinating and rewarding phenomenon.

Acknowledgements. The Bosch Internet of Things and Services Lab provided major funding to HSG for this project. We thank Prof. Oliver Gassmann, Ass. Prof. Karolin Frankenberger, Kristina Flüchter and Stefanie Turber for invaluable discussions and for their support.

References

1. What is the Internet of Things? An Economic Perspective, Auto-ID Labs White Paper WP-BIZAPP-053, ETZ Zürich & University of St. Gallen, January 2010. http://www.im.ethz.ch/education/HS10/AUTOIDLABS-WP-BIZAPP-53.pdf
2. Fleisch, E., Christ, O., Dierkes, M.: Die betriebswirtschaftliche Vision des Internets der Dinge. In: Fleisch, E., Friedemann, M. (eds.): Das Internet der Dinge, pp. 3–37. Springer, Berlin (2005)
3. Fleisch, E., Weinberger, M., Wortmann, F.: Business Models and the Internet of Things, Whitepaper of the Bosch Internet of Things and Services Lab, a Cooperation of HSG and Bosch (2014). www.iot-lab.ch
4. Gassmann, O., Frankenberger, K., Csik, M.: Geschäftsmodelle entwickeln: 55 innovative Konzepte mit dem St. Galler Business Model Navigator. Hanser Verlag, Munich (2013)
5. Ries, E.: The lean startup: How Today's Entrepreneurs Use Continuous Innovation to Create Radically Successful Businesses. Crown Business (2011)
6. von Hippel, E.: Lead users. A source of novel product concepts. Manage. Sci. **32**, 791–805 (1986)

OpenIoT Platform

OpenIoT: Open Source Internet-of-Things
in the Cloud

John Soldatos[1], Nikos Kefalakis[1], Manfred Hauswirth[2],
Martin Serrano[2], Jean-Paul Calbimonte[3], Mehdi Riahi[3], Karl Aberer[3],
Prem Prakash Jayaraman[4], Arkady Zaslavsky[4],
Ivana Podnar Žarko[5(✉)], Lea Skorin-Kapov[5], and Reinhard Herzog[6]

[1] Athens Information Technology, 0.8 Km Markopoulo Ave.,
P.O. Box 68, 19002 Peania, Greece
{jsol,nkef}@ait.gr
[2] INSIGHT@ National University of Ireland, Galway, IDA Business Park,
Lower Dangan, Galway, Ireland
{manfred.hauswirth,serrano}@deri.org
[3] EPFL IC LSIR, École Polytechnique Fédérale de Lausanne, Station 14,
1015 Lausanne, Switzerland
{jean-paul.calbimonte,mehdi.riahi,karl.aberer}@epfl.ch
[4] CSIRO Digital Productivity Flagship, Building 108 North Road,
Acton, Canberra 2617, Australia
{prem.jayaraman,arkady.zaslavsky}@csiro.au
[5] Faculty of Electrical Engineering and Computing, University of Zagreb,
Unska 3, 10000 Zagreb, Croatia
{ivana.podnar,lea.skorin-kapov}@fer.hr
[6] Fraunhofer IOSB, Fraunhoferstr. 1, 76131 Karlsruhe, Germany
Reinhard.Herzog@iosb.fraunhofer.de

Abstract. Despite the proliferation of Internet-of-Things (IoT) platforms for
building and deploying IoT applications in the cloud, there is still no easy way
to integrate heterogeneous geographically and administratively dispersed sensors and IoT services in a semantically interoperable fashion. In this paper we
provide an overview of the OpenIoT project, which has developed and provided
a first-of-kind open source IoT platform enabling the semantic interoperability
of IoT services in the cloud. At the heart of OpenIoT lies the W3C Semantic
Sensor Networks (SSN) ontology, which provides a common standards-based
model for representing physical and virtual sensors. OpenIoT includes also
sensor middleware that eases the collection of data from virtually any sensor,
while at the same time ensuring their proper semantic annotation. Furthermore,
it offers a wide range of visual tools that enable the development and deployment of IoT applications with almost zero programming. Another key feature of
OpenIoT is its ability to handle mobile sensors, thereby enabling the emerging
wave of mobile crowd sensing applications. OpenIoT is currently supported by
an active community of IoT researchers, while being extensively used for the
development of IoT applications in areas where semantic interoperability is a
major concern.

Keywords: Internet-of-Things · Open source · Semantic interoperability

© Springer International Publishing Switzerland 2015
I. Podnar Žarko et al. (Eds.): FP7 OpenIoT Project Workshop 2014, LNCS 9001, pp. 13–25, 2015.
DOI: 10.1007/978-3-319-16546-2_3

1   Introduction

We are nowadays witnessing the convergence of the Internet-of-Things (IoT) and the cloud computing paradigms, which is largely motivated by the need of IoT applications to leverage the scalability, performance and pay-as-you-go capabilities of the cloud. During recent years several efforts towards IoT/cloud convergence have been undertaken both in the research community (e.g., [1]) and in the enterprise (e.g., Xively.com). A common characteristic of these efforts is their ability to stream data to the cloud in a scalable and high performance way, while at the same time providing the means for managing applications and data streams. Nevertheless, these architectures do not essentially provide semantic interoperability [2] across IoT applications which have been developed/deployed independently from each other. Therefore, there is still no easy way to combine data streams and services from diverse IoT applications that feature incompatible semantics (e.g., units of measurement, raw sensor values and points of interest).

This paper presents an overview of the FP7-287305 OpenIoT project (co-funded by the European Commission), which has provided a middleware platform enabling the semantic unification of diverse IoT applications in the cloud. OpenIoT uses the W3C Semantic Sensor Networks (SSN) ontology [3] as a common standards-based model for semantic unification of diverse IoT systems. OpenIoT offers a versatile infrastructure for collecting and semantically annotating data from virtually any sensor available. OpenIoT exploits also the Linked Data concept [4] towards linking related sensor data sets. Furthermore, OpenIoT provides functionalities for dynamically filtering and selecting data streams, as well as for dealing with mobile sensors. It comes with a wide range of visual tools, which enable the development of cloud based IoT applications through minimal programming effort.

OpenIoT is currently available as an open source project (https://github.com/OpenIotOrg/openiot/). As of June 2014, it consists of nearly 400.000 lines of code, while it also integrates libraries of the popular Global Sensor Networks (GSN) open source project [5]. Recently, OpenIoT received an award from Black Duck, as being one of the top ten open source project that emerged in 2013 [6]. The rest of the paper is devoted to the presentation of the main technical developments of the project. The structure of the paper is as follows: Sect. 2 provides an overview of the OpenIoT platform, including an illustration of its architecture. Section 3 is devoted to the presentation of the main functionalities of the platform and how they can be used towards developing IoT applications. Section 4 provides an overview of real-life IoT applications, which have been developed based on OpenIoT. Section 5 concludes the paper.

2   OpenIoT Platform Overview

2.1   Achitecture Overview

The OpenIoT architecture comprises seven main elements [7] as depicted in Fig. 1.

- **The Sensor Middleware** (Extended Global Sensor Networks, X-GSN) collects, filters and combines data streams from virtual sensors or physical devices. The Sensor Middleware is deployed on the basis of one or more distributed instances

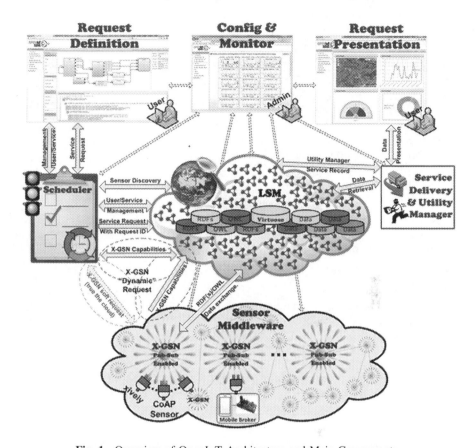

Fig. 1. Overview of OpenIoT Architecture and Main Components

(nodes), which may belong to different administrative entities. The OpenIoT prototype implementation uses X-GSN (Extended GSN), an extended version of the GSN middleware [5]. Furthermore, a mobile broker (publish/subscribe middleware) is used for the integration of mobile sensors.

- **The Cloud Data Storage** (Linked Stream Middleware Light, LSM-Light) acts as a cloud database which enables storage of data streams stemming from the sensor middleware. The cloud infrastructure stores also metadata required for the operation of OpenIoT. The OpenIoT prototype implementation uses the Linked Stream Middleware (LSM) [8], which has been re-designed with push-pull data functionality and cloud interfaces.

- **The Scheduler** processes requests for on-demand deployment of services and ensures their proper access to the resources (e.g. data streams) that they require. It discovers sensors and associated data streams that can contribute to a given service. It also manages a service and activates the resources involved in its provision.

- **The Service Delivery & Utility Manager** (SD&UM) combines data streams as indicated by service workflows within the OpenIoT system in order to deliver the requested service (typically expressed as an SPARQL query). The SD&UM acts also as a service metering facility which keeps track of utility metrics for each service.
- **The Request Definition** component enables on-the-fly specification of service requests to the OpenIoT platform. It comprises a set of services for specifying and formulating such requests, while also submitting them to the Scheduler. This component is supported by a GUI (Graphical User Interface).
- **The Request Presentation** component is in charge of the visualization of the outputs of a service. This component selects mash-ups from an appropriate library in order to facilitate service presentation.
- **The Configuration and Monitoring** component enables visual management and configuration of functionalities over sensors and services that are deployed within the OpenIoT platform.

2.2 OpenIoT Ontology for Semantic Interoperability and Linked Data Integration

The OpenIoT ontology represents a universally adopted terminology for the convergence of sensed data with the semantic web. It enhances existing vocabularies for sensors and Internet Connected Objects (ICOs), with additional concepts relevant to IoT/cloud integration such as terms to annotate units of measurement, raw sensor values and points of interest at some specific levels of granularity. In particular, the OpenIoT ontology is extending the W3C SSN ontology, which supports the description of the physical and processing structure of sensors. Sensors are not constrained to physical sensing devices: rather a sensor is anything that can estimate/calculate the value of a phenomenon. Thus, either a device or computational process or a combination of them could play the role of a sensor. The representation of a sensor in the ontology links together what it measures (the domain phenomena), the physical sensor (the device) and its functions and processing (the models).

The OpenoT ontology is available as a single OWL file, and provides the means for a semi-automatically generated documentation. Additional annotations have been added to split the ontology into thematic modules. The implementation of the ontology and its integration in the OpenIoT architecture are realized through the LSM middleware. LSM transforms the data from virtual sensors into Linked Data stored in RDF (Resource Description Format), which is de facto queried using SPARQL. In the context of IoT applications in general and LSM in particular, such queries refer typically to sensor metadata and historical sensor readings. The SPARQL endpoint of LSM provides the interface to issue these types of queries. The RDF triple store deployed by LSM is based on OpenLink Virtuoso and provides a Linked Data query processor that supports the SPARQL 1.1 standard. While SPARQL queries are executed once over the entire collection and discarded after the results are produced, queries over Linked

Stream Data are continuous. Continuous queries are first registered in the system, and continuously executed as new data arrives, with new results being output as soon as they are produced. LSM provides a wide range of interfaces (wrappers) for accessing sensor readings such as physical connections, middleware APIs, and database connections. Each wrapper is pluggable at runtime so that wrappers can be developed to connect new types of sensors into a live system when the system is running. The wrappers output the data in a unified format, following the data layout described in the OpenIoT ontology.

2.3 Mobile Broker and Publish/Subscribe Middleware

OpenIoT offers support for discovering and collecting data from mobile sensors (e.g., wearable sensors, sensors built-in mobile devices). This is achieved through a publish/subscribe middleware titled CloUd-based Publish/Subscribe middleware for the IoT (CUPUS) which integrates: (1) A cloud-based processing engine for sensor data streams based on the publish/subscribe principles and (2) A mobile broker running on mobile devices for flexible data acquisition from mobile ICOs. In the OpenIoT architecture, CUPUS interfaces to the Cloud Database via X-GSN which annotates the data collected from mobile devices. Hence, data streams from mobile ICOs are annotated and stored in the OpenIoT cloud via X-GSN, similar to the way data streams from stationary sensors are announced via the X-GSN sensor middleware.

CUPUS supports content-based publish/subscribe processing, i.e., stateless Boolean subscriptions with an expressive set of operators for the most common data types (relational and set operators, prefix and suffix operators on strings, and the SQL BETWEEN operator), and continuous top-k processing over sliding windows i.e. a novel publish/subscribe operator which identifies k best-ranked data objects with respect to a given scoring function over a sliding window [9]. It facilitates pre-filtering of sensor data streams close to data sources, so that only data objects of interest, value and relevance to users are pushed into the cloud. The filtering process is not guided locally on mobile devices, but rather from the cloud based on global requirements. Moreover, CUPUS distributes in near real-time push-based notifications from the cloud to largely distributed destinations, e.g., mobile devices, based on user information needs.

As depicted in Fig. 2, a Mobile Broker (MB) running on a mobile device can connect to and disconnect from a publish/subscribe processing engine running within the cloud. On the one hand, a device with attached sensors acts as a data source: The MB announces the type of data it is able to contribute to the platform and adds the sensor to the Cloud Data Storage. On the other hand, mobile phone users can define continuous requests for data in the form of subscriptions. Based on existing requests for sensor data expressed through subscriptions by either mobile device users or the OpenIoT platform, the MB receives subscriptions from the publish/subscribe processing engine which become data filters to prevent potential data overload within the cloud. This mechanism ensures that only relevant data is transmitted from mobile

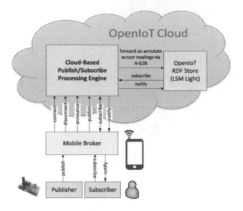

Fig. 2. High-level OpenIoT Publish/Subscribe Architecture

devices into the platform to be annotated and stored in the RDF repository, and sub-sequently to be transmitted in near real-time to adequate mobile devices.

Since the load of the publish/subscribe processing engine is generated by a varying number of publishers and subscribers with changing joint publication rate, the engine offers elastic real-time computation. It processes many subscriptions in parallel, which minimizes the processing overhead and optimizes the usage of cloud resources under varying load.

3   OpenIoT Platform Capabilities

3.1   Sensors and Data Streams Registration, Deployment and Discovery

OpenIoT manages the registration, data acquisition and deployment of sensors and interconnected objects, through X-GSN. X-GSN is an extension of the GSN that supports semantic annotation of both sensor data and metadata. The core fundamental concept in X-GSN is the virtual sensor, which can represent not only physical devices, but in general any abstract or concrete entity that observes features of any kind. A virtual sensor can also be an aggregation or computation over other virtual sensors, or even represent a mathematical model of a sensing environment.

In order to propagate its data to the rest of the OpenIoT platform, each virtual sensor needs to register within the LSM, so that other applications and users can discover them and get access to their data. The sensor is registered through X-GSN by posting a semantically annotated representation of its metadata. In order to associate metadata with a virtual sensor, a simple metadata descriptor is used. X-GSN takes care of creating the semantic annotations in RDF, according to the OpenIoT ontology, and posting them to the LSM cloud store repository.

```
sensorName=weather
source="Brussels netatmo"
sourceType=weather
sensorType=weatherType
information=Weather sensors in Brussels
author=openiot
feature="http://lsm.deri.ie/OpenIoT/BrusselsFeature"
fields="airtemperature"
field.airtemperature.propertyName="http://lsm.deri.ie/OpenIoT/AirTemperature"
field.airtemperature.unit=C
latitude=46.529838
longitude=6.596818
```

Listing 1. Sample metadata file for a X-GSN virtual sensor

Listing 1 illustrates the descriptor of a virtual sensor, which contains the location and the fields exposed by the virtual sensor. The descriptor includes the mapping between a sensor field (e.g., airtemperature) and the corresponding high-level concept defined in the ontology (e.g. the URI http://lsm.deri.ie/OpenIoT/AirTemperature).

```
@prefix : <http://sensordb.csiro.au/id/> .
@prefix rdf: <http://www.w3.org/1999/02/22-rdf-syntax-ns#> .
@prefix DUL: <http://www.loa-cnr.it/ontologies/DUL.owl#> .
@prefix ssn: <http://purl.oclc.org/NET/ssnx/ssn#> .
@prefix aws: <http://purl.oclc.org/NET/ssnx/meteo/aws#> .
@prefix prov:<http://purl.org/net/provenance/ns#> .
@prefix wgs84: <http://www.w3.org/2003/01/geo/wgs84_pos#> .
@base <http://sensordb.csiro.au/id/> .
<sensor/5010> rdf:type aws:CapacitiveBead,ssn:Sensor;
              rdfs:label "weather";
              ssn:observes aws:air_temperature ;
              ssn:onPlatform <site/narrabri/Pweather> ;
              ssn:ofFeature <site/narrabri/sf/sf_narrabri> ;
              prov:PerformedBy "SensorSource";
              DUL:hasLocation <place/location1>.
<place/location1> rdf:type DUL:Place;
              wgs84:lat 52.3;
              wgs84:long 98.2.
<site/narrabri/Pweather>  rdf:type ssn:Platform ;
              ssn:inDeployment <site/narrabri/deployment/2013> .
```

Listing 2. Sample RDF snippet of a sensor annotation, in Turtle format

After the sensor has been registered, the corresponding RDF triples (Listing 2) are stored in LSM, and the sensor is available for discovery and querying from the upper layers of the OpenIoT architecture. Data acquisition for each virtual sensor is achieved based on wrappers that collect data through serial port communication, UDP

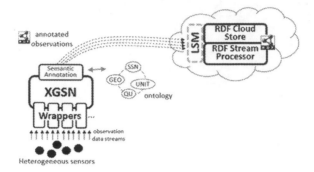

Fig. 3. Semantic annotation of observations in X-GSN

connections, HTTP requests, JDBC database queries, and more. X-GSN implements wrappers for these data providers, and allows users to develop custom ones. Virtual sensors and wrapper settings are specified in configuration files, which provide internal details of the data to be exposed. Data are represented as streams of data tuples which can be consumed, queried or analyzed on-line. In OpenIoT this processing includes the annotation of sensor observations as soon as they arrive to X-GSN, as depicted in Fig. 3. Note that virtual sensors can be built on top of other virtual sensors, providing different layers of information. For example, one can imagine a set of thermometers that send their data into X-GSN. Then all those data streams can feed an aggregating virtual sensor that averages received values over predefined time windows, annotates average values semantically and stores them in the LSM cloud store. The described example is realized by editing only a few XML files. In general, the effort needed to deploy a new sensor in OpenIoT is typically in the range of few man-hours.

3.2   Authenticated and Authorized Access to Resources

The diversity of applications interacting in an IoT ecosystem calls for non-trivial security and access-rights schemes. Conventional approaches (e.g., creating distinct user accounts for each application and granting access rights to each user) are not scalable as the number of applications and user accounts grows. OpenIoT adopts a flexible and generic approach for authentication and authorization. User management, authentication, and authorization are performed by the privacy & security module and its CAS (Central Authentication Service) service. Users are redirected to a centric login page the first time they try to access a restricted resource where they provide their username and password to the central authentication entity. If authentication is successful, the CAS redirects the user to the original web page and returns a token to the web application. Tokens represent authenticated users, have a predefined expiration time and are valid only before they expire. The token is forwarded from a service to the next one in a request chain, e.g., from the user interface to LSM. Services can check if the token is valid, or use the token to check if the user represented by this token has the necessary access rights.

In terms of implementation, OAuth2.0 enabled Jasig CAS has been extended for the OpenIoT needs. In particular, we added the end point permissions for retrieving authorization information from CAS. Authorization information includes user roles/ permissions. Permissions are textual values that define actions or behaviors and are defined per service. A wildcard permission format (Apache Shiro) is used. Permissions can consist of multiple levels delimited by colons, and levels can be defined by each application following a predefined pattern. For example, the permission string "admin: delete_role:SERVICE_NAME" has three levels: "admin" means that the permission is for administrative tasks, "delete_role" is the action, and "SERVICE_NAME" is the name of the service for which the action is permitted.

3.3 Zero-Programming Application Development

OpenIoT provides an integrated environment (i.e. OpenIoT IDE (Integrated Development Environment)) for building/deploying and managing IoT applications. OpenIoT IDE comprises a range of visual tools (Fig. 4) enabling: (a) Visual definition of IoT services in a way that obviates the need to master the details of the SPARQL language; (b) Visual discovery of sensors according to their location and type; (c) Configuration of sensor metadata as needed for their integration within the X-GSN middleware; (d) Monitoring of the status of the various IoT services, including the volumes of data that they produce and the status of the sensors that they comprise; (e) Visualization of IoT services on the basis of Web2.0 mashups (i.e. maps, line/bar charts, dashboards and more). These tools accelerate the process of developing IoT applications. In several cases simple applications can be developed with virtually zero programming.

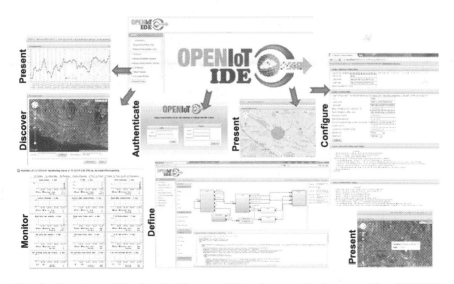

Fig. 4. Overview of the OpenIoT Integrated Development Environment (OpenIoT IDE)

3.4   Handling of Mobility with Quality Driven Sensor Management

As mobile crowd sensing applications generate large volumes of data with varying sensing coverage and density, there is a need to offer mobility management of ICOs and quality-driven mobile sensor data collection to satisfy global sensing coverage requirements while taking into account data redundancy and varying sensor accuracy [10]. CUPUS provides the means for collecting data from mobile ICOs, whose geographical location potentially changes while providing data to the cloud. As mobile brokers running on mobile devices announce the type of data that can be provided by their currently available publishers, they are configured so as to announce their available data sources each time they enter a new geographic area. Moreover, an X-GSN virtual sensor is created on demand for each new geographic area and is used to both push and annotate the data generated by all mobile sensors currently residing within its geographical area.

CUPUS addresses quality requirements (e.g., energy efficiency, sensing data quality, network resource consumption, latency), through smart data acquisition mechanisms. Firstly, by deploying mobile brokers on mobile devices, data can be selectively collected from external data sources attached to the mobile device and transmitted to the cloud only when required. Mobile brokers running in geographical areas where there are no currently active subscriptions will suppress data collection and refrain from sending unnecessary data into the cloud. Secondly, CUPUS is integrated with a centralized quality-driven sensor management function, designed to manage and acquire sensor readings to satisfy global sensing coverage requirements, while obviating redundant sensor activity and consequently reducing overall system energy consumption. Assuming redundant data sources in a certain geographic area, a decision-making engine is invoked to determine an optimal subset of sensors which to keep active in order to meet data requests while considering parameters such as sensor accuracy, trustworthiness, and battery level.

4   Proof-of-Concept Applications

4.1   Phenonet Experiment

Phenonet uses sensor networks to gather environmental data for crop variety trials at a far higher resolution than conventional methods and provides high performance real-time online data analysis platform that allows scientists and farmers to visualize, process and extract both real time and long-term crop performance information from the acquired sensor measurements. Figure 5 provides an example of a Phenonet experiment with two types of sensors (1) Gypsum block soil moisture sensors (GBHeavy) at various depths (e.g., 20, 30 and 40 cm) and (2) Canopy temperature measurement sensor.

The goal of the experiment is to monitor the growth and yield of a specific variety of crop by analyzing the impact of root activity, water use (soil moisture) and temperature. Information about crop growth obtained in real time effectively helps plant scientist researchers to provide estimates on the potential yield of a variety. OpenIoT facilitates the processes of real-time data collection, on-the-fly annotation of sensed data, data cleaning, data discovery, storage and visualization.

4.2   Urban Crowdsensing Application

This is a mobile application for community sensing where sensors and mobile devices jointly collect and share data of interest to observe and measure air quality in real-time. Volunteers carrying wearable air quality sensors contribute sensed data to the OpenIoT platform while moving through the city. Citizens are able to consume air quality information of interest to observe it typically in their close vicinity. Figure 6 shows air quality sensors measuring temperature, humidity, pressure, CO, NO2 and SO2 levels which communicate with the mobile application running on an Android phone via a Bluetooth connection. Users can declare interest to receive environmental data (e.g., temperature, CO levels) in their close vicinity and in near real-time. Moreover, they can express interest to receive the readings portraying poorest air quality for an area over time, or average readings within specific areas as soon as they are available.

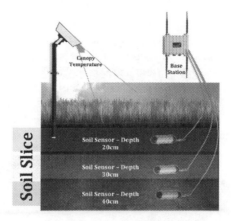

Fig. 5. Phenonet Experiment Illustration

Fig. 6. Air Quality Sensors and Mobile Application

4.3   Smart Campus Application

The smart campus application brings information about interactions among people and things within typical campus situations into one Common Information Model (CIM). This model combines observations from sensors with mobile applications and static structural information into one cyber-physical context managed by OpenIoT. In the prototype the used sensors are QR-code or NFC based scanners to detect and confirm the presence of persons and to identify assets and topics. The mobile applications are used for booking workplaces and for discussions. The structural information describes campus assets like buildings, rooms and workplaces, as well as teaching material. OpenIoT supports the stream oriented processing of events as well as context reasoning on the CIM.

5   Conclusions

OpenIoT has provided an innovative platform for IoT/cloud convergence which enables: (a) Integration of IoT data and applications within cloud computing infrastructures; (b) Deployment of and secure access to semantically interoperable applications; (c) Handling of mobile sensors and associated QoS parameters. The semantic interoperability functionalities of OpenIoT are a key differentiating factor of the project when compared to the wide range of other IoT/cloud platforms. These functionalities provide a basis for the development of novel applications in the areas of smart cities and mobile crowd sensing, while also enabling large scale IoT experimentation.

Acknowledgments. This work has been carried out in the scope of the OpenIoT project (http://openiot.eu). The authors acknowledge contributions from all partners of the project.

References

1. Hassan, M.M., Song, B., Huh, E.-N.: A framework of sensor-cloud integration opportunities and challenges. In: Proceedings of the 3rd International Conference on Ubiquitous Information Management and Communication (ICUIMC 2009), pp. 618–626. ACM, New York (2009)
2. Blair, G.S., Paolucci, M., Grace, P., Georgantas, N.: Interoperability in complex distributed systems. In: Bernardo, M., Issarny, V. (eds.) SFM 2011. LNCS, vol. 6659, pp. 1–26. Springer, Heidelberg (2011)
3. Compton, M., et al.: The SSN ontology of the W3C semantic sensor network incubator group. J. Web Semant. **17**, 25–32 (2012). Elsevier
4. Heath, T.: Linked data - welcome to the data network. IEEE Internet Comput. **15**(6), 70–73 (2011). IEEE Press, New York
5. Aberer, K., Hauswirth, M., Salehi, A.: Infrastructure for data processing in large-scale interconnected sensor networks. In: International Conference on Mobile Data Management (MDM 2007), pp. 198–205. IEEE Press, New York (2007)
6. Black Duck Software: Black Duck Announces Open Source Rookies of the Year Winners, Press Release, January 2013

7. Serrano, M., Hauswirth, M., Soldatos, J.: Design principles for utility-driven services and cloud-based computing modelling for the internet of things. Int. J. Web Grid Serv. **10**(2–3), 139–167 (2014). Inderscience Publishers, Geneva
8. Le Phuoc, D., Nguyen-Mau, H.Q., Parreira, J.X., Hauswirth, M.: A middleware framework for scalable management of linked streams. J. Web Semant. **16**, 42–51 (2012). Elsevier
9. Pripužić, K., Podnar Žarko, I., Aberer, K.: Top-k/w publish/subscribe: a publish/subscribe model for continuous top-k processing over data streams. Inf. Syst. **39**, 256–276 (2014). Elsevier
10. Antonić, A., Rožanković, K., Marjanović, M., Pripužić, K., Podnar Žarko, I.: A mobile crowdsensing ecosystem enabled by a cloud-based publish/subscribe middleware. In: 2014 International Conference on Future Internet of Things and Cloud (FiCloud), pp. 107–114. IEEE Press, New York (2014)

A Visual Paradigm for IoT Solutions Development

Nikos Kefalakis[1]([⊠]), John Soldatos[1], Achilleas Anagnostopoulos[2],
and Panagiotis Dimitropoulos[2]

[1] Athens Information Technology, 0,8 Km Markopoulo Ave.,
P.O. Box 68, 19002 Peania, Greece
{nkef, jsol}@ait.gr
[2] SENSAP Microsystems AE, Hydras 2, 18346 Moschato, Greece
{aanag, pdimi}@sensap.eu

Abstract. Despite the proliferation of Internet-of-Things (IoT) applications and services, there are still very few tools and techniques for developing IoT solutions in a visual fashion through minimal (or even) zero programming. In this paper we introduce a novel approach for developing IoT solution through visual development tools. The presented approach presents several advantages, in particular: (a) It leverages standards-based semantic models for sensors and IoT context (notably the W3 SSN ontology), (b) It is based on popular/mainstream web-based technologies (i.e. SPARQL, REST), (c) It provides a basis for integrated development of IoT services on the basis of a W3C SSN based Model Driven Architecture (MDA), (d) It is implemented as open source software as part of the OpenIoT open source project.

Keywords: Internet-of-Things (IoT) · Visual tools · Cloud computing · Sensors · Open source

1 Introduction

The Internet-of-Things (IoT) (Sundmaeker 2010) is gradually becoming one of the most prominent technologies that underpin our society, through enabling the orchestration and coordination of large numbers of physical and virtual Internet-Connected-Objects (ICO) towards human-centric services in a variety of sectors including logistics, trade, industry, smart cities and ambient assisted living (Smith 2012). Nowadays, more than ten years after the introduction of the term IoT (Internet-of-Things) (Ashton 2009), we have witnessed the emergence of several IoT architectures and related technical standards, which have paved the ground for the first wave of scalable, intelligent and interoperable IoT applications. Prominent examples of such IoT architectures are those promoted by standardization organizations, such as the Open Geospatial Consortium (OGC) (http://www.opengeospatial.org), the W3C (through its W3C Semantic Sensor Networks (SSN) incubator group) and the EPCglobal (http://www.gs1.org/epcglobal/). These architectures are in most cases supported by middleware platforms, which facilitate development and integration of (compliant) IoT applications. For example, the Fosstrak open source platform (http://www.fosstrak.org) (Floerkemeier et al. 2007)

© Springer International Publishing Switzerland 2015
I. Podnar Žarko et al. (Eds.): FP7 OpenIoT Project Workshop 2014, LNCS 9001, pp. 26–45, 2015.
DOI: 10.1007/978-3-319-16546-2_4

eases the development and deployment of EPCglobal compliant RFID applications, while the Linked Sensor Middleware (LSM) platform (Lephuoc 2011) facilitates the integration of applications that leverage the Semantic Sensor Networks (SSN) (Compton 2012) ontology towards modeling ICOs. Apart from middleware platforms that support standards-based development of IoT applications, there are also several platforms that provide proprietary middleware services to IoT applications. Prominent examples including the Global Sensor Networks (GSN) open source middleware (Aberer 2007) for WSN, as well as the WinRFID platform for RFID applications (Prabhu 2006). In addition to these examples, numerous methodologies and platforms for building multi-sensor IoT applications have been also introduced (Chatzigiannakis 2007).

Despite the emergence of the above platforms, less emphasis has been paid into the provision of easy to use tools for the development of IoT applications. Indeed, most of the above-listed platforms are not accompanied by comprehensive development environments that could essentially facilitate developers and solution providers in the complex task of building, testing and deploying IoT applications. In several cases the above-listed platforms come with simple tools for configuring solutions, which are not however integrated and do not support all the phases of the software development lifecycle. Also, with only few exceptions (e.g., (Patel 2011)), these tools are con-strained to particular types of applications (e.g., RFID or WSN applications) and cannot support the full range of physical and visual ICOs that comprise the IoT par-adigm. Hence, they are not suitable for supporting an integrated development envi-ronment for IoT applications based on Model-Driven-Architecture (MDA) concepts (Kleppe 2003). Furthermore, most of the available tools provide poor configurability and require application developers to write significant amounts of code even for simple solutions. We strongly believe that visual integrated tools for IoT development can greatly facilitate the production of IoT applications, thereby reducing their develop-ment and deployment costs. Furthermore, such tools could boost the proliferation of the currently rising community of IoT developers.

In this paper we introduce a range of tools for the visual development of IoT applications and services, as well as for the visual presentation of their results. These tools can serve as a basis for an integrated development environment, which could support the round-trip engineering of IoT applications across all the phases of their software engineering lifecycle. The presented environment relies on a blueprint cloud-based IoT architecture, which leverages the W3C SSN ontology for modeling sensors, ICOs and entities. This architecture is briefly presented and discussed in the paper, in order to facilitate the understanding of the middleware platform that underpins the introduced visual environments. Due to the use of W3C SSN as an underlying model for sensors and ICOs, the presented tools are used to construct semantic queries/ services (i.e. SPARQL based queries) over the various sensors and ICOs. Furthermore, they provide the means for validating the services, as well as for enacting them over the underlying IoT middleware platform. Overall the presented tools provide a first-of-a-kind effort towards the integrated standards-based (i.e. W3C SSN based) development of IoT applications with minimal (and in some cases zero) programming. In this context, the work described in the paper complements recent efforts for integrated IoT development (e.g., (Patel 2013)), which are however based on proprietary ontologies for modeling sensors and IoT resources. It is also noteworthy that our visual environment for modeling and developing IoT applications is available as open source software as part of the OpenIoT open source project (available at: https://github.com/OpenIotOrg/openiot). This provides the IoT open source community with imminent opportunities for using and extending the presented approach.

The rest of the paper is structured as follows: In Sect. 2 we position our work against related efforts. As part of this positioning we illustrate the limitations of existing environments and tools, and accordingly illustrate the novelty of our approach. Section 3 discussed the middleware architecture and platform that underpins the operations of our IoT visual development paradigm. Specifically, we introduce the use of W3C SSN for modeling sensors, as well as the use of SPARQL language as a means of defining IoT services. Section 4 presents the tools that enable visual definition/construction of IoT applications and services, while also discussing a range of visual (mashup-based) tools for the presentation of the results of IoT services. Finally, Sect. 5 concludes the paper and summarizes its main contributions.

2 Related Work

Several middleware platforms for RFID and WSN applications come with companion development and/or deployment tools. In the area of RFID applications the Fosstrak (Floerkemeier et al. 2007) project provides tools for browsing/managing RFID data residing within EPC-IS repositories, as well as tools for editing business rules transforming raw tag streams to business semantics. Similarly, the AspireRFID project (http://wiki.aspire.ow2.org) has provided a wide range of tools for building EPC-IS compliant RFID applications over the Fosstrak middleware platform. These include visual tools for editing/managing filters, as well as tools for managing data over EPC-IS repositories. Furthermore, AspireRFID has defined a process language for RFID applications (Kefalakis 2011) (i.e. the APDL (Aspire business Process Description Language), which enables the definition and configuration of complete RFID solutions. APDL is a Domain Specific Language (DSL), which is amenable by a customized workflow management tool. The latter tool enables the visual definition, configuration and enactment of complete RFID solutions. Beyond EPCGlobal compliant initiatives, there have also been other efforts enabling visual development of RFID applications such as Rifidi (www.rifidi.org) (Palazzi 2009), which enables the visual configuration, simulation and testing of RFID solutions. Note that Rifidi has been recently enhanced towards supporting IoT applications, but it is still RFID focused. Furthermore, in (Anagnostopoulos 2009) the authors have defined a simple DSL for collection, filtering and generation of events from RFID tag streams. While all these solutions facilitate the development of RFID applications, they are not sufficient when it comes to dealing with broader IoT applications comprising sensor networks, actuators, as well as virtual sensors and data streams. Moreover, most the above works are focused on parts of RFID solution development (e.g., RFID data collection and filtering, data management, device management) and do not support holistic integrated development of RFID applications.

In addition to RFID development tools, there have also been tools facilitating the development of RFID applications. A prominent example is the GSN (Global Sensor

Networks) platform, which defines a virtual sensor concept and provides the means for almost zero-programming WSN application development (Aberer 2007). Another example is the work described in (Mostafizur 2010), which includes a framework for modeling, simulation and code generation of complete WSN applications. Also, (Ghica 2008) illustrates an environment for the design, modeling and development of integrated WSN applications. The above list of development environments and tools is non exhaustive, given that most WSN middleware platforms (e.g., those listed in (Chatzigiannakis 2007)) come with some sort of tooling support for sensor applications. However, similar to the case of RFID oriented development environments, these tools are overly focused on WSN aspects. Hence, they tend to deal with the low-level details of sensor applications (e.g., sensor nodes communication, sensor data collection, data filtering, and data fusion) rather than with their higher level composition into IoT applications. Furthermore, they ignore in several cases key aspects of IoT applications, such as virtual sensors and data streams, as well as the need to model non-trivial sensors and contexts.

Recently, software engineering solutions for the integrated development of general IoT applications have also emerged (e.g., (Cassou 2010; Patel 2011)). These solutions leverage semantic models that capture the main elements of IoT applications (Patel 2013), such as sensors, actuators, and techniques for abstracting and modeling context in IoT applications. Note that context abstraction is an essential element of pervasive and context-aware computing (Dey 2001), and therefore an indispensable part of any development environment for pervasive computing applications (Dimakis 2008). In addition to context abstraction, the separation of programming concerns has been also identified as a key ingredient of integrated development environments for IoT applications (Patel 2013). The above efforts towards integrated development of IoT applications rely on proprietary models for sensors and context modeling, which is a set-back to their wider adoption. Furthermore, they do not take advantage of recent efforts towards accessing the low-level functionalities of the sensors through high level Web-based interfaces (such as CoAP (Constrained Application Protocol) (Colitti 2011)). The use of web based interfaces is a trend for most on-line IoT platforms, notably those enabling streaming of IoT data in cloud computing infrastructures. Prominent examples are the Xively (https://xively.com/) and Thingspeak (http://www.thingspeak.com) platforms, which provide Web based interfaces for accessing IoT data feeds in the cloud. Nevertheless, these platforms provide very simplistic non-interoperable models and formats for sensors and context, while they do not provide common semantics for interoperable representations of sensors. Therefore their associated visual development capabilities are generally limited to very simple IoT applications.

One of the main benefits of the approach that is suggested in this paper is that it relies on semantic models and ontologies under standardization (Serrano 2014), such as the W3C Semantic Sensor Networks (SSN) (Taylor 2011), which provides the means for abstracting/virtualizing virtually any sensor. In addition to general purpose descriptions of sensors and observations, the SSN ontology provides the means for modeling/abstracting the context of multi-sensor applications in order to facilitate processes such as dynamic discovery of sensor data and metadata, as well as tasking and programming in multi-sensor applications. In addition to its semantic power and expressiveness, the W3C SSN ontology enables the use of web based technologies and techniques for accessing and linking both sensor data and metadata, thereby giving rise to the web-of-things (Pfisterer 2011). The use of web-based technologies in IoT applications is expected to facilitate the engagement of large masses of web and mobile applications developers in the creation of innovative IoT based ideas and services. The approach introduced in coming section is in-line with this direction.

3 OpenIoT Middleware Platform – Foundations for an IoT Services Visual Development Paradigm

Our approach to visually designing, implementing and deploying IoT application hinges on the OpenIoT middleware platform, which is available as open source software. The OpenIoT platform, as shown in Fig. 1, provides the means for representing sensor data and metadata according to the W3C SSN ontology, but also for persisting the data within cloud infrastructures. Furthermore, the OpenIoT platform defines the notion of IoT services as SPARQL queries, which enables the dynamic discovery of sensor data and metadata, along with the execution of queries over arbitrary large numbers of geographically and administratively distributed sensors. At the same time, OpenIoT provides the means for collecting data streams from physical and virtual sensors and accordingly for transforming them to W3 SSN compliant data streams. Overall, the main elements of the OpenIoT platform are:

- **The Sensor Middleware,** which collects, filters and combines data streams stemming from virtual sensors (e.g., signal processing algorithms, information fusion algorithms and social media data streams) or physical sensing devices (such as temperature sensors, humidity sensors and weather stations). This middleware acts as a hub between the OpenIoT platform and the physical world, since it enables access to information stemming from the real world. Furthermore, it facilitates the interfacing to a variety of physical and virtual sensors such as IETF CoAP compliant sensors (i.e. sensors providing RESTful interfaces), data streams from other IoT platforms (such as https://xively.com) and social networks (such as Twitter). Among the main characteristics of the sensor middleware is its ability to stream W3 SSN compliant sensor data in the cloud. The Sensor Middleware is deployed on the basis of one or more distributed instances (nodes), which may belong to different administrative entities. The prototype implementation of the OpenIoT platform uses an enhanced/extended version of the GSN middleware (Aberer 2007) (namely X-GSN, which is currently as a module of the OpenIoT open source project). However, other sensor middleware platforms could be also used in alternative implementations and deployments of the OpenIoT architecture.
- **The Cloud Computing Infrastructure,** which stores data streams stemming from the sensor middleware thereby acting as a cloud database. The cloud infrastructure stores also metadata for the various IoT services, which are made available to the visual development tools of the following section. Note that the cloud infrastructure could be either a public infrastructure (such as the Amazon Elastic Compute Cloud (EC2)) or a private infrastructure (e.g., a private cloud deployed based on Open Stack (http://www.openstack.org/)). The cloud infrastructure can be

characterized as a sensor cloud, given that it primarily supports storage and management of sensor data streams (and of their metadata).

- **The W3 SSN Directory Service,** which keeps information about all the sensors that are available in the OpenIoT platform. It also provides the means (i.e. services) for registering sensors with the directory, as well as for the look-up (i.e. discovery) of sensors. The architecture specifies the use of semantically annotated descriptions of sensors as part of its directory service. The OpenIoT open source implementation is based on an enhanced version of the W3C SSN ontology, which is integrated as part of the LSM (Linked Sensor Middleware) (Lephuoc 2011). As a result of this implementation technology, semantic Web techniques (such as SPARQL and RDF (Resource Description Format)) and ontology management systems (e.g., Virtuoso) are used for querying the directory service. Furthermore, the exploitation of semantically annotated sensors enables the integration of data streams within the Linked Data Cloud, thereby empowering Linked Sensor Data.
- **The Scheduler,** which processes all the requests for on-demand deployment of services and ensures their proper access to the resources (e.g., data streams) that they require. This component undertakes the task of parsing the service request and

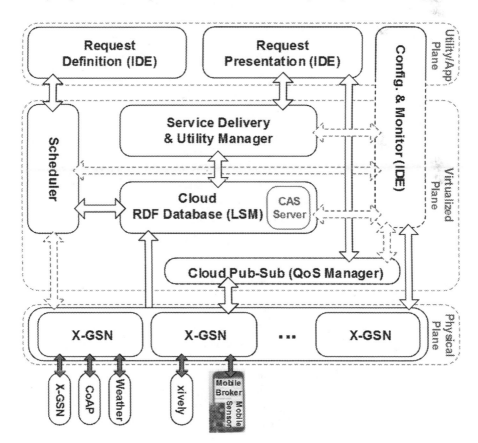

Fig. 1. Software components of the OpenIoT architecture

accordingly discovering the sensors that can contribute to its fulfillment. It also selects the resources, i.e., sensors that will support the service deployment, while also performing the relevant reservations of resources.

- **The Service Delivery & Utility Manager (SD&UM),** which performs a dual role. On the one hand, it combines the data streams as indicated by service workflows within the OpenIoT system, in order to deliver the requested service. To this end, this component makes use of the service description and the resources identified and reserved by the (Global) Scheduler component. On the other hand, this component acts as a service metering facility, which keeps track of utility metrics for each individual service.
- **The Pub-Sub server (QoS Manager),** which is the component which monitors over time the global demand for sensor data generated by MIOs and manages the data acquisition process from MIOs to achieve a desired sensing coverage while optimising parameters such as energy and bandwidth consumption, sensor trustworthiness and/or data propagation latency.
- **The Security module (CAS server),** which is based on Jasig CAS (http://www.jasig.org/cas) and provides OAuth2.0 authentication and authorization for all other OpenIoT modules.
- **The Request Definition tool,** which enables the specification of service requests to the OpenIoT platform. It comprises a set of services for specifying and formulating such requests, while also submitting them to the Global Scheduler. This tool features a GUI (Graphical User Interface), which resides at the heart of the visual IoT development paradigm that is introduced in the following sections.
- **The Request Presentation component,** which is in charge of the visualization of the outputs of an IoT service. This component selects mashups from an appropriate library in order to facilitate service presentation. Service integrators and solution providers have the option to enhance or override the functionality of this component towards providing a presentation layer pertaining to their solution.
- **The Configuration and Monitoring component,** which enables management and configuration functionalities over the sensors and the IoT services that are deployed within the platform. It is also supported by a GUI.

The delivery of IoT services according to the OpenIoT architecture relies on the following information flows and interactions between the various elements:

- X-GSN nodes are "announcing" the available virtual sensors to the Directory Service and start to publish their data in SSN compliant RDF format based on each X-GSN local configuration.
- Users request from the Scheduler all the available sensor/ICOs types that satisfy specific attributes (e.g., coordinates, radius) by using the Request Definition UI. The request is sent to the Scheduler service, which queries the Directory Service for the ICOs that fulfill the criteria set in the request.
- The Scheduler executes a combination of queries (SPARQL-based) according to the previously user specified request.
- The Directory Service retrieves the data and replies back to the Scheduler with the available sensor types.

- The reply is forwarded to the Request Definition UI from the Scheduler and the retrieved information is provided to the user of the visual development environment.
- The user, with the help of Request Definition UI, defines the request by implementing rules, provided by the tool, over the reported sensor types. Following paragraphs illustrate the structure of the visual tools and the nature of the rules that can be specified. The information about the IoT request (including execution and service presentation preferences) is pushed to the Scheduler.
- The Scheduler analyses the received information and sends the request to the Directory Service.
- After having configured the request for an IoT service, the user is able to use the Request Presentation UI for visualizing the data of a registered IoT service.
- With the help of SD&UM the Request Presentation retrieves all the registered applications/services related to a specific user.
- For any given/selected service, a user can request to retrieve the results related to it. Accordingly, the SD&UM requests and retrieves from the Directory Service all related information for the specific Service.
- The SD&UM analyses the retrieved information and forwards the included SPARQL script (created through the Request Definition UI and stored by the Scheduler) to the Directory Service SPARQL interface.
- The result is sent from the Directory Service to the SD&UM, which forwards it to the Request Presentation. The latter component includes all the needed information on how the data of the IoT service should be visualized.

In the sequel we illustrate our visual development paradigm for IoT applications based on the above architecture. As already outlined, this paradigm is primarily supported by the 《Request Definition》 and 《Request Presentation》 components. Note that the detailed presentation of other components and features of the architecture (such as accounting and resource optimization) are beyond the scope of this paper and described in (Serrano 2014).

4   Visual Design and Presentation of IoT Services

4.1   Request Definition Module Overview: Visual Definition of IoT Services

The request definition module is a web application that allows end-users to visually model their OpenIoT-based services using a node-based WYSIWYG (What-You-See-Is-What-You-Get) UI (User Interface). Modeled service graphs are grouped into "applications" which are called OAMOs (OpenIoT Application Model Object). These applications are able to group a collection of different services, which are called OS-MOs (OpenIoT Service Model Objects), that comprises/describes a real life application (e.g., weather reports). This enables end-users to manage (i.e. describe/register/edit/update) different (unrelated) applications from a single entry point. As already outlined, the metadata of all modeled services are persisted by the OpenIoT Scheduler and are automatically loaded whenever a user accesses the web application.

Figure 2 illustrates the main user interface components of the web application:

- The menu bar provides commands for creating new applications, opening existing applications for editing, extracting defined applications in XML format, loading applications from XML format, validating a new design and saving it to the cloud.
- The central pane serves as the workspace area for modeling services.
- The node toolbox (left pane) contains the list of nodes that can be dragged into the workspace. Nodes are grouped by functionality.
- The properties pane (right pane) provides access to any selected node's properties.
- The console pane (bottom pane) provides workspace validation information (problems/warnings) as well as a debug preview of the generated SPARQL code for the designed service.

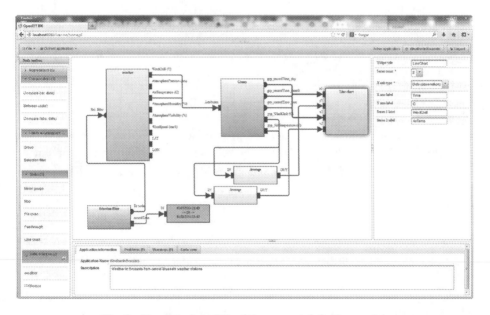

Fig. 2. User Interface (UI) of the request definition module

4.2   Applications Management

The tool provides a range of functionalities for managing IoT applications. In particular:

- A ≪reset applications≫ option is provided in order to clear all applications and services, while a ≪reload applications≫ option reloads all available applications.
- A ≪new applications≫ option allows for the creation of a new application through providing a name and a description. The new application appears as blank application and is available for editing.
- An ≪edit existing application≫ option is provided to allow for opening an application for further editing.

4.3   Modeling of IoT Application and Services

An IoT application is represented through a graph, which can be modeled visually. A service graph describing a particular application can be created by dragging nodes from the node-toolbox into the application workspace, setting them up and wiring them together. Each graph node is color-coded to indicate its function and provides input and output endpoints to facilitate connections. Each endpoint belongs to one or more scopes while its position on the rendered node is dictated by its function (inputs on the left, outputs on the right). The system allows only connections between endpoints that have common scopes. Connections between nodes may be established by clicking on an output endpoint and dragging a connection to another node's input endpoint. While a connection is dragged, the system will automatically highlight the endpoints that can serve as the connection's destination.

A service graph visualizes the information flow from a source (typically a sensor type) to a sink (a visualization widget). Therefore, all service graphs should contain at least one source node and one sink node. Other node types can be injected between the source and the sink to manipulate the data (i.e. perform an aggregation or filtering function). The available node types are described in following paragraphs.

Data Source Nodes. Data source nodes model the sensor types available for querying via the OpenIoT middleware platform. In order to populate the list of available sensors, a sensor discovery query has to be performed. By clicking the search button in the node toolbox, a sensor discovery dialog appears (Fig. 3), which enables search for sensors

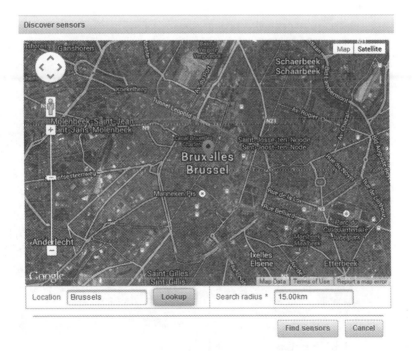

Fig. 3. Sensor discovery dialog

within a specific area. As soon as the sensors are found the node toolbox is updated with the list of available sensor types (classes) that match the search criteria.

Each sensor node represents all the sensor instances of a particular sensor type that are available at a specific location. When dragged into the workspace, the node encodes the search criteria that were used for locating it into its embedded properties. By dragging the appropriate sensor nodes into the workspace one can model graphs that process similar data from different locations. A sensor node example and its properties are shown on Fig. 4. All available sensor attributes appear as output endpoints. The node provides an additional input endpoint for connecting a selection filter node. The functions of this special node are described in the following paragraph.

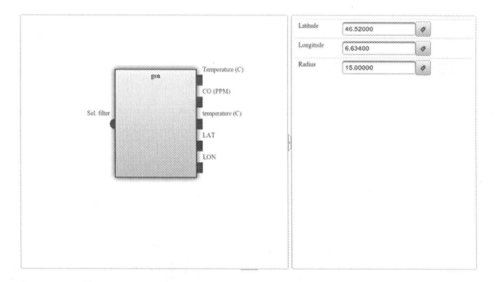

Fig. 4. A sensor node and its properties

Selection Filter Nodes. In IoT applications it is sometimes desirable to process data within a specific time window. The selection filter node allows one to limit the data records that will be processed using time-based criteria. Once connected to a sensor node, the selection filter node will expose its «recordTime» endpoint. This endpoint can be connected to a comparator node that describes filter parameters.

Comparator Nodes. Comparator nodes can be connected to a selection filter node to define a time-based filter. Each node's filter parameters are exposed as node properties. The following nodes are provided:

- **Between (date):** Ensures that the processed records fall between two specific dates.
- **Compare (abs. date):** Ensures that the processed records satisfy the condition "recordTime operator userDate", where operator is a user-selected operator (less, less or equal, equal, greater or equal, greater) and userDate a user-selected date.
- **Compare (rel. date):** Ensures that the processed records satisfy the condition "(NOW - recordTime) operator value timeUnit", where operator is a

user-selected operator, value is a numeric value used for the comparison and timeUnit is a user-selected time unit (`seconds`, `minutes`, `hours`, `months`, `years`). Figure 5 shows an example where the node is used to select data recorded within the last five (5) hours.

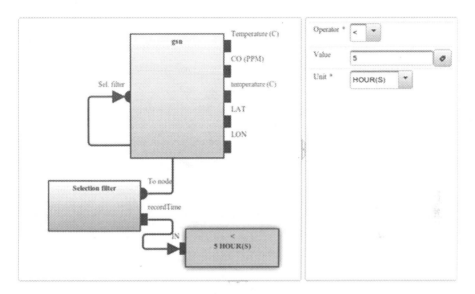

Fig. 5. Relative time filtering example

Group Nodes. Group nodes allow users to partition the sensor data into time buckets using each observation's record time. A group node is setup by connecting each attribute that should be grouped to the group node's input endpoint. Once a connection is made, a new output endpoint appears on the right side of the group node. The new endpoint represents partitioned time buckets and may be connected to an aggregation node or directly to a compatible sink node.

In order to define the observation's record time that will be used for grouping, a grouping options dialog has been implemented (Fig. 6). Through this dialog the component that will be used for grouping can be selected. In this case an additional endpoint for each selected group field appears at the right side of the group node in the tool (Fig. 7). For each attribute, the node generates an output tuple of the form: (`grp_recordTime1`, ..., `grp_recordTimeN`, `valueSet`).

Aggregation Nodes. Aggregation nodes apply an aggregation function to their inputs. The following aggregation functions are supported: `min`, `max`, `count`, `average`, `sum`. These nodes accept as input the outputs of sensor, groups or aggregation nodes.

Sink Nodes. Sink nodes serve as the termination endpoint of a service graph. All service graphs should have at least one sink node connected in order to pass the service graph validation check. While a standard set of sink nodes is provided, additional sink nodes can be defined depending on the application. The following sink nodes are supported:

Fig. 6. Grouping options dialog

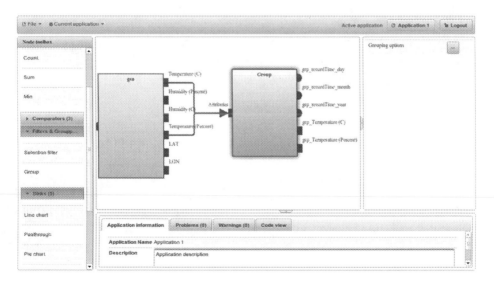

Fig. 7. Grouping an attribute by record time

- **Line chart sink node:** Line chart sink nodes render a line chart widget that supports up to five (5) data series. To setup the line chart, the number of series should be selected first. Depending on the number of series selected, additional inputs (y_i) will appear on the node for connecting each series' Y axis data. Then the type of data that will be plotted on the X axis is selected. Three types of data are supported for the X axis:
  - **Number:** The X axis will plot a numeric field. In this case, additional inputs (x_i) will appear on the node for connecting each series' X axis data. All X axis inputs only accept a single connection.

- **Date (result set):** In this mode, the X axis value will be automatically set to the system's timestamp when the query results arrive. In this case, no inputs for the X axis are available.
- **Date (observation):** This mode is designed to work together with a group node. In this case, additional inputs (x_i) will appear on the node for connecting each series' X axis timestamp data. These inputs accept multiple connections from a group node's `grp_recordTime` fields. Depending on which time fields where connected, the system will automatically generate a timestamp for the X axis while it processes incoming data. Figure 8 shows an example scenario where a line chart plots the max temperature for every day.
- **Pie chart sink node:** This type of node renders a pie chart and supports up to ten (10) series. The first step to setting up a pie chart involves the selection of the number of series. Depending on the number of series selected, additional inputs (y_i) appear on the node for connecting each series' value.
- **Meter gauge sink node:** This node will render a gauge with a dial indicating its current value. In order to setup the gauge, one has to provide its measure unit label and accordingly its minimum and maximum values. The node exposes a single input endpoint for connecting the gauge's value.
- **Map sink node:** The map sink node renders a map containing markers indicating the location of sensors and optionally renders circle overlays to indicate the magnitude of a specific attribute from each sensor. To set up this node one needs to setup the map widget parameters. To this end, the latitude, longitude and zoom level properties must be filled in. Then the type of overlays that should be rendered must be selected. The following overlay modes are supported:
  - **Markers only:** Renders a marker at each sensor's location.
  - **Circles only:** Renders a circle at each sensor's location with a radius equal to the connected property's value scaled by the "max value" property. The max value scaling factor defaults to one (1) and can be used to tweak the size of the generated circles.
  - **Markers and circles:** This mode combines the previous two modes.
- **Passthrough sink node:** The passthrough sink node is a special node designed to be used by applications that need to bypass the request presentation layer and perform their own custom processing on the service data. This node provides a simple sink with N inputs. The number of inputs is selected by editing the attribute count property of the node. Once the property is modified, the node will the appropriate number of input endpoints (`attr1`, ..., `attrN`) depending on the property value. Once the service has been registered, the application needs to manually invoke the SDUM to get the service results. When used via the request presentation layer, the bound attributes are rendered in tabular form.

Using Variable Property Values. Some application scenarios involve queries where some of the parameters are not known a priori during service design. For example, a service that reports the availability of a specific resource (like a room) near a mobile user depends on the user's location which is only known when the query is to be executed. To support such scenarios, provide a mechanism for converting node properties into variables is provided. This mechanism is supported for all nodes except

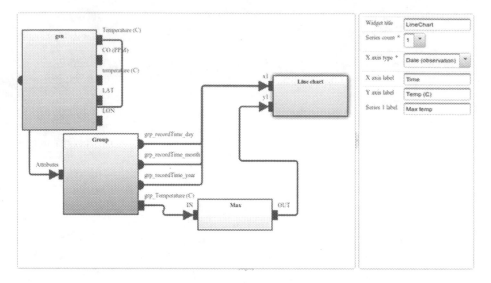

Fig. 8. A service that plots the max temperature per day

the sink nodes. Applications referencing services which contain variables should supply their values when they invoke the SD&UM. In case a variable value is not specified, it is automatically set to the default value.

4.4   Workspace Validation – SPARQL Generation and Service Deployment

Prior to saving an application, the tool audits the modeled graphs within the workspace against the following validation tests:

- No unconnected nodes exist.
- All required (mandatory) node properties have been filled in.
- All required node endpoints have been connected.
- The service graph contains no closed loops.

In addition to the above checks, some node-specific checks are also performed. The output of the workspace validation process is a list of problems (if any) and a set of warnings. The validation results appear in the console pane. By clicking on a problem or warning, the system highlights its location on the service graph in order to facilitate its fix. Validation runs automatically before saving an open application but it can also be manually invoked by the end user of the tool.

The «Request Definition» tool can automatically generate the SPARQL code, which corresponds to the modeled graph(s) (see Fig. 9 below). Accordingly, it can ensure its deployment over the OpenIoT middleware infrastructure and according to the operations' workflow described in the previous section.

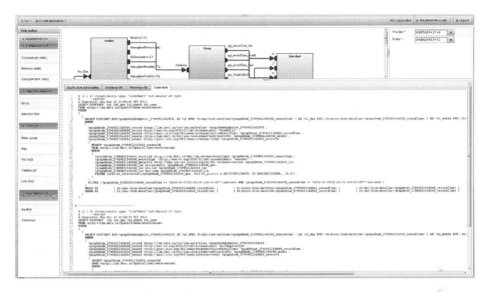

Fig. 9. Validation – SPARQL automatic generation

4.5   The Request Presentation Module: Presentation of IoT Services

The Request Presentation module is a Web application that provides end users with a visual interface to services created using the Request Definition Web application. When a user accesses the Web application, all the applications that have been modeled by the user are automatically loaded. Each application contains one or more visualization widgets. The Request Presentation layer parses the application metadata and generates a self-updating widget dashboard (see Fig. 10)). Note that the supported widgets are those described in the previous section (i.e. line charts, pie charts, maps, meter gauges).

Dashboards refresh automatically every 30 seconds. However, the user may manually trigger an update by clicking on the current application menu and selecting the "Manual data refresh" option. To clear the data of a specific widget, click on the "Clear data" button on its top-right corner.

4.6   Validation of the OpenIoT Visual Development Paradigm

The presented framework has been validated in the development of several IoT applications. In particular a set of sample IoT services are bundled within the open source implementation of the framework. These sample services (such as weather service) are simple and aim at demonstrating the functionalities of the ≪Request Definition≫ and ≪Request Presentation≫ modules. In addition to the sample services, the visual tools have been used to support the development and deployment of three IoT use cases in the areas of smart cities, manufacturing and crop management. Each of these use cases comprises several IoT services, which have been developed in a visual fashion. Note that the implementation and integration of these use case has illustrated the practical use of the visual tools in the scope of non-trivial applications. In particular,

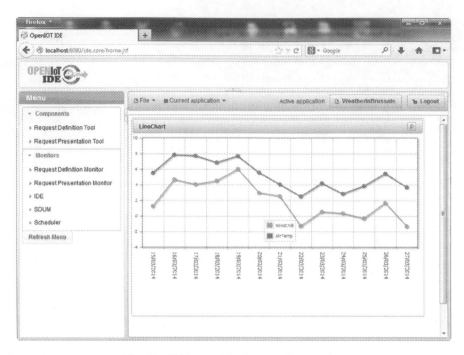

Fig. 10. Widgets of the Request Presentation

it has shown that developers can use the presented tools for creating a baseline service, which they can further enhance through additional coding/development outside of the scope of the visual tools.

5 Conclusions

Despite the emergence and proliferation of middleware frameworks for developing and deploying IoT applications, nowadays there are still only a limited number of environments and tools for the visual development of IoT applications. These environments are typically focused on certain low-level aspects of IoT applications such as nodes connectivity in WSN and the management of RFID devices. Hence, they are not suitable for supporting the development and deployment of integrated IoT applications, which leverage data from the wide range of physical and virtual sensor sources that comprise the IoT paradigm. In this paper we have introduced a visual environment, which facilitates the development of IoT applications with minimal (almost zero) programming effort. The visual environment operates over the OpenIoT architecture, which uses the W3C SSN ontology as its main semantic model for describing sensors and related IoT context. Modeling IoT services using the presented tool is based on the specification of a graph, which corresponds to an IoT application. The nodes of the graph correspond to (sensor) data sources, processing components, as well as presentation components. Every graph can be validated through the tool and accordingly the code for IoT services can be generated and enacted over the OpenIoT middleware platform.

Our visual paradigm for the modelling, development and deployment of IoT services presents several distinct advantages. First it leverages standards-based semantic models for sensors and IoT context, which boosts its wide adoption and technological longevity. Second, it is based on web-based technologies (i.e. SPARQL, REST) thereby opening up the exciting field of IoT services development to the large pool of web application developers. Third, it provides a basis for integrated development of IoT services on the basis of an MDA realized based on W3C SSN. The production of an integrated development environment for IoT applications is in progress as part of the OpenIoT project. Another advantage of the presented paradigm is that it is implemented as open source software as part of the OpenIoT open source project. The availability of this open source implementation is expected to encourage community developers to enhance our visual paradigm on the basis of new features, functionalities and development tools for IoT services. Several such enhancements are already part of the implementation roadmap of the OpenIoT open source project.

Acknowledgments. Part of this work has been carried out in the scope of the OpenIoT project (FP7-287305) (http://openiot.eu). The authors acknowledge help and contributions from all partners of the project.

References

Aberer, K., Hauswirth, M., Salehi, A.: Infrastructure for data processing in large-scale interconnected sensor networks. In: Proceedings of the 2007 International Conference on Mobile Data Management (MDM), pp. 198–205 (2007)

Aberer, K., Hauswirth, M., Salehi, A.: Invited talk: zero-programming sensor network deployment. In. International Symposium on Applications and the Internet Workshops (SAINTW'07), saint-w, p. 1 (2007)

Anagnostopoulos, A., Soldatos, J., Michalakos, S.G.: REFiLL: A lightweight programmable middleware platform for cost effective RFID application development. Pervasive Mob. Comput. 5(1), 49–63 (2009)

Ashton, K.: That 'Internet of Things' Thing. RFID Jurnal, June 2009. http://www.rfidjournal.com/articles/view?4986

Cassou, D., Bruneau, J., Mercadal, J., Enard, Q., Balland, E., Loriant, N., Consel, C.: Towards a tool-based development methodology for sense/compute/control applications. In Proceedings of the ACM International Conference Companion on Object Oriented Programming Systems Languages and Applications Companion, pp. 247–248. ACM (2010)

Chatzigiannakis, I., Mylonas, G., Nikoletseas, S.E.: 50 ways to build your application: a survey of middleware and systems for wireless sensor networks. In: IEEE Conference on ETFA, pp. 466–473 (2007)

Colitti, W., et. al.: REST enabled wireless sensor networks for seamless integration with web applications. In: Proceedings of the 8th IEEE International Conference on Mobile Adhoc and Sensor Systems (MASS), October 2011

Compton, M., Barnaghi, P.M., Bermudez, L., Garcia-Castro, R., Corcho, Ó., Cox, S., Graybeal, J., Hauswirth, M., Henson, C.A., Herzog, A., Huang, V.A., Janowicz, K., Kelsey, W.D., Phuoc, D.L., Lefort, L., Leggieri, M., Neuhaus, H., Nikolov, A., Page, K.R., Passant, A., Sheth, A.P., Taylor, K.: The SSN ontology of the W3C semantic sensor network incubator group. J. Web Sem. **17**, 25–32 (2012)

Dey, A., Abowd, G., Salber, D.: A conceptual framework and a toolkit for supporting the rapid proto-typing of context-aware applications. Human-Comput. Interact. **16**(2–4), 97–166 (2001)

Dimakis, N., Soldatos, J., Polymenakos, L., Fleury, P., Curín, J., Kleindienst, J.: Integrated development of context-aware applications in smart spaces. IEEE Pervasive Comput. **7**(4), 71–79 (2008)

Floerkemeier, C., Roduner, C., Lampe, M.: RFID application development with the accada middleware platform. IEEE Syst. J. **1**(2), 82–94 (2007)

Ghica, O., Trajcevski, G., Scheuermann, P., Bischof, Z.S., Valtchanov, N.: SIDnet-SWANS: a simulator and integrated development platform for sensor networks applications. In: Proceedings of the 6th International Conference on Embedded Networked Sensor Systems, SenSys 2008, Raleigh, NC, USA, 5–7 November 2008

Kefalakis, N., Soldatos, J., Konstantinou, N., Prasad, N.R.: APDL: a reference XML schema for process-centered definition of RFID solutions. J. Syst. Softw. **84**(7), 1244–1259 (2011)

Kleppe, A., Warmer, J., Bast, W.: MDA Explained: The Model Driven Architecture. Practice and Promise. Addison-Wesley, Reading (2003)

Mozumdar, M.M.R., Lavagno, L.: Rapid application development for wireless sensor networks. In: Silvestre-Blanes, J. (ed.) Factory Automation. InTech, Rijeka (2010). doi:10.5772/9514. ISBN: 978-953-307-024-7

Palazzi, C., Ceriali, A., Dal Monte, M.: RFID emulation in Rifidi environment. In: Proceedings of the International Symposium on Ubiquitous Computing (UCS 2009), Beijing, China, August 2009

Patel, P., Pathak, A., Teixeira, T., Issarny, V.: Towards application development for the internet of things. In: Proceedings of the 8th Middleware Doctoral Symposium, p. 5. ACM (2011)

Patel, P., Pathak, A., Cassou, D., Issarny, V.: Enabling high-level application development in the internet of things. In: Zuniga, M., Dini, G. (eds.) S-Cube. LNICST, vol. 122, pp. 111–126. Springer, Heidelberg (2013)

Pfisterer, D., Römer, K., Bimschas, D., Kleine, O., Mietz, R., Truong, C., Hasemann, H., Kröller, A., Pagel, M., Hauswirth, M., Karnstedt, M., Leggieri, M., Passant, A., Richardson, R.: SPITFIRE: toward a semantic web of things. IEEE Commun. Mag. **49**(11), 40–48 (2011)

Phuoc, D.L., Quoc, H.N.M., Parreira, J.X., Hauswirth, M.: The linked sensor middleware: connecting the real world and the semantic web. In: 9th Semantic Web Challenge Co-located with 10th International Semantic Web Conference – ISWC 2011, Bonn, Germany, 23–27 October 2011

Prabhu, S., Su, X., Ramamurthy, H., Chu, C., Gadh, R.: WinRFID –a middleware for the enablement of radio frequency identification (RFID) based applications invited chapter. In: Shorey, R., Choon, C.M., Tsang, O.W., Ananda, A. (eds.) Mobile, Wireless and Sensor Networks: Technology, Applications and Future Directions. Wiley, New York (2006)

Serrano, M., Hauswirth, M., Soldatos, J., Kefalakis, N.: Design principles for utility-driven services and cloud-based computing modelling for the internet of things. Int. J. Web Grid Serv. **10**, 139–167 (2014). Inderscience Publishers Ltd

Smith, I.G., Vermesan, O., Friess, P., Furness, A.: The Internet of Things 2012 New Horizons. ISBN: 978-0-9553707-9-3, http://www.internet-of-things-research.eu/pdf/IERC_Cluster_Book_2012_WEB.pdf

Sundmaeker, H., Guillemin, P., Friess, P., Woelfflé, S. (eds): Vision and Challenges for Realising the Internet of Things. European Union, March 2010. doi:10.2759/26127. ISBN: 978-92-79-15088-3

Taylor, K.: Semantic sensor networks: the W3C SSN-XG ontology and how to semantically enable real time sensor feeds. In: 2011 Semantic Technology Conference, San Francisco CA, USA, 5–9 June (2011)

The OpenIoT Approach to Sensor Mobility with Quality-Driven Data Acquisition Management

Ivana Podnar Žarko$^{(\boxtimes)}$, Aleksandar Antonić, Martina Marjanović,
Krešimir Pripužić, and Lea Skorin-Kapov

Faculty of Electrical Engineering and Computing, University of Zagreb,
Unska 3, 10000 Zagreb, Croatia
`ivana.podnar@fer.hr`

Abstract. Given the prominence of IoT applications integrating mobile Internet-connected objects (ICOs), e.g., wearable sensors and mobile devices with built-in sensors, novel solutions are required to discover and collect data from mobile sensors producing data streams from varying locations, while taking into account sensor accuracy, energy-efficiency, and potential data redundancy. The OpenIoT platform offers support for mobile sensors by means of its publish/subscribe middleware solution entitled CloUd-based Publish/Subscribe middleware for the IoT (CUPUS). The CUPUS publish/subscribe component is used to collect data from mobile ICOs in a flexible and energy-efficient manner and to provide preprocessed data into the OpenIoT cloud. Moreover, CUPUS in collaboration with a Quality of Service (QoS) Manager component enables mobility management of ICOs and quality-driven data acquisition from mobile sensors to satisfy the global sensing coverage requirements while taking into account data redundancy and ICO battery lifetime.

Keywords: Internet of things (IoT) · Mobile sensors · Publish/subscribe middleware

1 Introduction

The proliferation of wearable sensors and mobile devices with built-in sensors creates new challenges for the Internet of Things (IoT) platforms which need to address specific requirements pertaining to a mobile context, whereby challenges arise due to the uncontrolled mobility of sensors and mobile end user devices. To support mobile crowdsensing applications [3] which naturally generate large volumes of data with varying sensing coverage and density, both in space and time, there is a need to offer mobility management of ICOs and quality-driven data acquisition from mobile sensor to satisfy global sensing coverage requirements. Moreover, challenges arise with respect to data redundancy and varying sensor accuracy, as well as managing sensor data in an energy- and bandwidth-efficient manner.

© Springer International Publishing Switzerland 2015
I. Podnar Žarko et al. (Eds.): FP7 OpenIoT Project Workshop 2014, LNCS 9001, pp. 46–61, 2015.
DOI: 10.1007/978-3-319-16546-2_5

The OpenIoT platform which is developed within the FP7 OpenIoT project co-funded by the European Commission under contract FP7-287305, offers support to discover and acquire data from mobile sensors by means of a publish/subscribe middleware solution CloUd-based Publish/Subscribe middleware for the IoT (CUPUS)[1] designed to offer context-aware and quality-driven mobile sensor data collection. To address the challenges of meeting the quality requirements of mobile IoT-based applications in terms of energy efficiency, sensing data quality, network resource consumption, and latency, the CUPUS middleware supports several smart data acquisition mechanisms. Firstly, by deploying processing engines on mobile devices, data can be selectively collected from external data sources attached to the mobile device and transmitted to the cloud only when required by external applications. Secondly, the CUPUS middleware is integrated with a centralized quality-driven sensor management function, designed to smartly manage and acquire sensor readings to satisfy global sensing coverage requirements, while obviating redundant sensor activity and consequently reducing overall system energy consumption. Assuming redundant data sources in a certain geographic area, a decision-making engine is invoked to determine an optimal subset of sensors which to keep active in order to meet data requests while considering parameters such as sensor accuracy, level of trustworthiness, and available battery level.

In our previous work [8,11], we have introduced CUPUS as a component enabling context-aware and energy-efficient acquisition and filtering of sensor data in mobile environments. The CUPUS communication infrastructure is based on the principles of publish/subscribe, whereby data sources (referred to as *publishers*) disseminate data using a push-based mechanism to interested data destinations (*subscribers*). Users/applications generate data queries referred to as *subscriptions* [5]. In this paper we extend the work by introducing a centralized quality-driven sensor management function which enables quality-driven data acquisition and provide technical details regarding the architecture for sensor mobility and related communication protocols implemented within the scope of the OpenIoT project.

The paper is structured in the following way: Sect. 2 introduces the general architecture for quality-driven data acquisition from mobile sensors. We present the details of the implemented publish/subscribe communication model in Sect. 3, while Sect. 4 introduces the quality-driven sensor management function. An application built on top of the presented solution is briefly presented in Sect. 5. We list related work in Sect. 6 and conclude the paper in Sect. 7.

2   The OpenIoT Architecture for Mobile ICOs

The OpenIoT solution for acquiring and processing sensor data produced by mobile ICOs is based on the publish/subscribe communication infrastructure and is centered around the following design objectives:

---

[1] The CUPUS and QoS Sensor Management Function source codes are available at the OpenIoT project's Github - https://github.com/OpenIotOrg/openiot/.

– Data acquisition from mobile ICOs needs to be flexible to enable pre-processing and filtering of sensor data on mobile devices while taking into account data needs expressed by an end application and its users.
– Since sensor data streams can be characterized as Big Data streams, the engine for continuous processing of such streams needs to be efficient and tailored to cloud environments to optimally use the available computing resources while adapting well to the processing load.
– The developed solution should enable delivery of notifications from the cloud to mobile devices in near real-time and in accordance with user information needs and context.
– The data acquisition process should be *context-aware* and *quality-driven*, and influenced by the following parameters: sensor accuracy, mobile ICO location and battery lifetime, and potential data redundancy/insufficiency.

The first three listed objectives can be achieved by use of the cloud-based publish/subscribe middleware CUPUS, while for the fourth objective we add an additional component, QoS Manager, capable to perform quality-driven data acquisition management for mobile ICOs. Naturally, the data produced by mobile ICOs is geotagged, either by an exact location measured by GPS or cell identifier (e.g., a mobile network cell identifier or MGRS[2] area). The QoS Manager leverages the publish/subscribe communication style to continuously monitor sensor locations, their status (e.g. battery level, accuracy) and produced data streams with the goal to make informed decisions regarding a subset of sensors to keep active to meet application sensing requirements. Of course, a selection can only be made for geographic areas with redundant sensors, while the QoS Manager can also identify areas with insufficient sensing coverage. For such areas, the QoS Manager may employ techniques such as data interpolation and estimation to meet a required sensing coverage, or even motivate volunteers by means of incentives to visit and acquire data for those areas.

A view of the OpenIoT architecture for mobile ICOs is given in Fig. 1. The central component is the Cloud-based Publish/Subscribe Processing Engine (CPSP Engine), responsible for acquiring data from external data sources (e.g., smartphones), processing the data to see if it matches any active subscriptions, and disseminating the data to external data consumers. It interacts with a Mobile Broker (MB), which is a data stream processing component running on mobile devices responsible for filtering and aggregating locally produced sensor data. The CPSP engine and MB build the CUPUS middleware. The QoS Manager interacts with the CPSP Engine to monitor both subscriptions and publications defined and acquired by the engine to make smart decisions regarding mobile ICO activation/deactivation. The QoS Manager also serves as a hub for pushing the data received by the CPSP Engine to the OpenIoT Cloud Database for permanent storage. This is achieved by use of the eXtended Global Sensor Network (X-GSN) component which annotates the data and creates RDF triples,

---

[2] The Military Grid Reference System (MGRS) is the geocoordinate standard used by NATO for locating points on the earth.

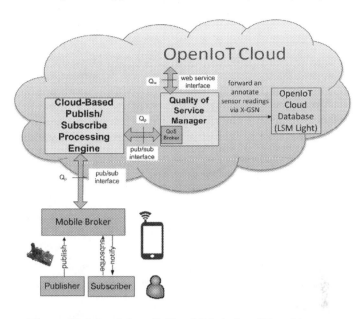

Fig. 1. High-level OpenIoT publish/subscribe architecture

as Linked Sensor Middleware (LSM-Light) integrates an RDF store to be used as the OpenIoT Cloud Database.

A Mobile Broker and the CPSP Engine running within the OpenIoT cloud interact over a publish/subscribe interface Q_p. The CPSP Engine and the QoS Manager also interact over the same interface Q_p by use of the following messages: *publish, subscribe, notify* and *announce*. In addition, the QoS Manager exposes a web service interface Q_w through which it offers services to other OpenIoT components. For example, if a user of the OpenIoT platform wants to locate available mobile data sources in his/her close vicinity, or average data readings acquired by mobile sensors for a specific area, he/she can access this information through the Q_w interface. Both interfaces are explained in more detail in Sects. 3 and 4.

2.1   Cloud-Based Publish/Subscribe Middleware (CUPUS)

CUPUS implements the standard *publish-subscribe-notify* communication pattern enhanced with an *announce* message to advertise the data types associated with mobile sensors and sensor locations. It has a hierarchical three-tier architecture with the CPSP Engine at the top layer, MBs running on mobile devices at the middle layer, and publishers and subscribers at the bottom layer. Publishers and subscribers typically also run on mobile devices and can also connect directly to the CPSP Engine. For example, a mobile device with attached sensors acts as both a data source (publisher) and data destination (subscriber) since device users can define continuous requests for data in the form of subscriptions.

An MB running on the device can announce the type of data it is able to contribute based on sensors attached to it and its current location. This information is transmitted to the CPSP Engine which thus knows the locations and characteristics of all available data publishers. The CPSP Engine answers to *announce* messages with subscriptions matching the defined data types which become data filters and prevent potential data overload within the CPSP Engine. This mechanism ensures that only relevant data is transmitted from mobile devices into the cloud, and further on to interested mobile users and other subscribers in near real-time.

An MB is a special processing engine running on mobile devices for filtering of sensor data close to data sources to suppress redundant sensing and related data transmissions to the CPSP engine. By doing so, it saves batteries of both sensors and end-user devices. The filtering is achieved by matching of locally generated publications with active subscriptions received from the CPSP engine so that only matching publications are forwarded to the CPSP engine. To save resources while performing the filtering on mobile devices, a special mechanism is needed to maintain the minimal set of appropriate subscriptions. Such a set of subscriptions contains only a subset of CPSP subscriptions that can potentially match locally generated publications. A detailed description of MB design and implementation together with evaluation of its processing performance on mobile devices is available in [11].

CUPUS supports content-based publish/subscribe processing, i.e., stateless Boolean subscriptions with an expressive set of operators for the most common data types (relational and set operators, prefix and suffix operators on strings, and the SQL BETWEEN operator), and continuous top-k processing over sliding windows, a novel publish/subscribe operator which identifies k best-ranked data objects with respect to a given scoring function over a sliding window of size w [9]. It facilitates pre-filtering of sensor data streams close to data sources, e.g., on mobile devices, so that only data objects of interest, value and relevance are pushed into the OpenIoT cloud. The filtering process is not guided locally on mobile devices, but rather from the cloud based on global data requirements. Moreover, CUPUS distributes in near real-time push-based notifications from the cloud to largely distributed destinations, e.g., mobile devices, based on user information needs and context.

Since the load on the CPSP Engine running within the OpenIoT cloud is generated by a varying number of publishers and subscribers with changing joint publication rate, the engine needs to offer elastic real-time computation. In other words, it should be able to process many subscriptions in parallel while the processing overhead per publication is minimized. This is achieved through the splitting and merging of matcher components that compare incoming publications to the set of subscriptions to identify subscribers with matching subscriptions.

The CPSP engine implements a flat cloud broker architecture composed of independent matcher components running in parallel and the central coordinator responsible for matcher management. Both the splitting and merging are triggered by the idle time of a single process for the last N received and processed messages, where N, splitting threshold and merging threshold are parameters of the engine. The coordinator initiates the splitting and merging actions based on the observed idle time of a single process. The splitting of a matcher is initiated when idle time of the matcher process in the window of N last received messages is smaller than a given threshold, i.e., when the matching process is active throughout the time span of the window, expressed as the percentage of the total window time. If the idle time is smaller than the given splitting threshold, a splitting trigger is fired. Since the observed matcher is under high load, i.e., it takes too much time to process incoming messages, the subscription structure needs to be reduced. To reduce the load on the matcher, half of the subscription structure is forwarded to a newly created matcher. The merging of a matcher is initiated when the maximal processing time in the window of N last publication matching is smaller than a given threshold, i.e. when all publications in the window were processed in lower processing time than the defined threshold. This criterion is, like the splitting criterion, chosen for its robustness with regard to sudden spikes in processing times.

2.2 QoS Manager

While CUPUS architecture supports controlled data acquisition based on global data requirements, the CPSP engine does not provide further intelligent decision-making mechanisms aimed at optimizing sensing data quality and energy consumption while retaining a required sensing coverage. We envision cases when redundant sensed data is available in certain geographical locations (e.g., due to a large number of sensors generating data in a certain geographic area), whereby a subset of sensors may be requested to transmit data, while others may be deactivated. Decisions on determining an optimal subset of sensors which to keep active in order to meet subscription requirements can be made based on parameters such as sensor accuracy, level of trustworthiness, and available battery level.

The QoS Manager component adds support for intelligent QoS-based monitoring and management mechanisms in mobile IoT usage scenarios involving mobile devices with either built-in or wearable sensors as data sources. It is implemented as a stand-alone component which interfaces the CPSP engine and is further integrated with the OpenIoT platform in order to achieve the following goals: (1) context-aware sensing coverage and data quality management and (2) energy efficiency management.

1. **Context-aware sensing coverage and data quality management:** Ensure that the sensed data received by an end user meets his/her sensor data demands with established quality thresholds (in terms of accuracy, frequency of sensor readings) through support of context-aware data acquisition mechanisms, while maintaining energy efficiency. In other words, for a given geographic area and time interval, the goal is to acquire a sufficient number of sensor readings from activated sensors to satisfy the data quality requirements for all active end-user subscriptions in that area (i.e., global data requirements integrating individual data demands), thus effectively minimizing energy consumption.

2. **Energy efficiency management:** Effectively manage the energy/battery consumption of sensors/mobile devices in order to maximize battery lifetime and minimize energy consumption while maintaining a required level of data quality (in terms of frequency and accuracy of sensor readings within a certain geographical area).

The QoS Manager has to administrate the sensing process from various data sources in the system. For that purpose, it needs to monitor both subscriptions and publications received by the CPSP Engine. The QoS Manager maps active subscriptions and valid publications to geographical areas and also publishes processed readings (e.g., average sensor readings for particular areas if requested by users) through the CPSP Engine. Additionally, the QoS broker sends control messages to the CUPUS middleware based on the QoS Manager decisions. This way, the CPSP engine can turn them on/off when needed by forwarding subscriptions/unsubscriptions received from the QoS broker to them. The QoS Manager stores all received publications and subscriptions during their validity periods in memory for later use in the QoS logic component. To limit the amount of memory used for QoS Manager operation in practice, we limit the time window for publication storage to 30 min and calculate average sensor readings also for this time window.

The QoS Manager is responsible for three key functionalities: (1) QoS subscription monitoring and management, whereby the QoS Manager aggregates CUPUS subscriptions and determines global application requirements with respect to sensor data acquisition from mobile sources which are integrated through the CUPUS middleware; (2) QoS publication monitoring and management, whereby the QoS Manager aggregates monitored sensor data publications, and manages the sensor data acquisition in order to optimize energy and bandwidth consumption while meeting application requirements and (3) providing sensor data readings to the rest of the OpenIoT platform, as explained in Sect. 4. Based on reported mobile ICO battery levels, the QoS Manager decides about activation/deactivation of available data sources.

The QoS Manager web interface Q_w offers services for components requiring the request-reply interaction mechanism. It is used to retrieve active mobile ICOs within an area, provide average sensor readings for an area, or define a subscription over an area of interest. The data matching such subscription is stored in the OpenIoT Data Cloud for later usage.

3   Interactions Within the CUPUS Middleware

In this section we provide a detailed description of interactions between CUPUS components (the Q_p interface).

Connect and disconnect. The two methods are used by subscribers, publishers and MBs. The method *connect* adds subscriber/publisher/MB identifier into the list of connected components maintained by the CPSP engine, while the method *disconnect* removes them from the list. In case a subscriber or MB reconnect to the CPSP engine, the engine first delivers all publications that have been matched to their active subscriptions while they were disconnected.

Publish. The CPSP engine stores all received subscriptions through *subscribe* requests to a list of active subscriptions. When an MB receives a *publish* message from a mobile ICO (denoted as MIO in the following figures), it forwards the message to the CPSP engine only if it has previously received a matching subscription from the CPSP engine. Otherwise, the MB retains the publication since no one is obviously interested. The MB stores all subscriptions received from the cloud broker and local subscribers in a list of active subscriptions. Each publish event from an MIO is subsequently matched to the list of stored subscriptions. The matching process identifies whether a publication should be forwarded to the CPSP engine or not which in turn performs its matching to the subscription forest. A sequence diagram depicting the delivery of a new publication to an interested subscriber is shown in Fig. 2.

Announce. Figure 3 shows the sequence of events following a new *announce* message. When an MB receives a new external data source announcement from one of its MIOs, it announces a new publisher to the CPSP engine by sending the corresponding announce message. The CPSP engine then stores the announcement in a list of stored announcements and compares it with the list of stored active subscriptions. If there are interested subscribers with subscriptions matching the announcement, it may activate the publisher by forwarding the matching subscriptions to the MB in the corresponding subscribe message. Any publisher connected to an MB can *revoke* its previous announcement. When this happens, the CPSP engine just needs to delete the announcement from its list of stored announcements and unsubscribe messages to corresponding MBs. The revoke

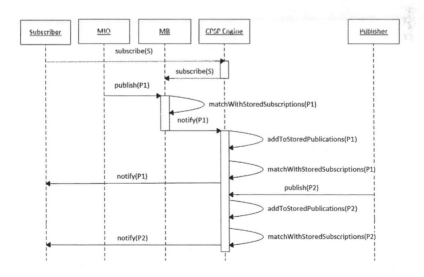

Fig. 2. Delivery of a new publication

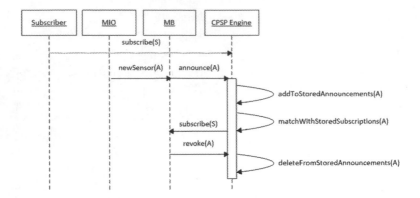

Fig. 3. Announcing a new publisher

event can be initiated by the MB (e.g., to save the battery when its level is low) or MIO. Additionally, if there are alternative publishers and matching subscriptions requesting this kind of information, the CPSP engine can activate alternative MBs and their publishers.

Unsubscribe. Clients usually unsubscribe when they are no longer interested in publications coming from certain areas. When the CPSP engine receives an *unsubscribe* message, either from a subscriber or MB, it needs to delete the subscription from the list of stored subscriptions. Additionally, if such a canceled subscription is the last one which is interested in publications announced by a specific publisher connected to an MB, the MB instructed to stop producing new publications by forwarding an unsubscribe message.

4   Interactions with the OpenIoT Cloud Database

The QoS Manager has been chosen as a point of integration with the rest of the OpenIoT platform since it monitors all the data acquired through the CPSP engine and can decide which data needs to be stored permanently in the OpenIoT RDF store. Thus users of the OpenIoT platform can search for mobile sensors in the same fashion as when searching for fixed sensors, and receive the data being produced by mobile sensors by using the OpenIoT Request Definition and Request Presentation components. Hereafter we describe the process of registering mobile sensors with the LSM-Light component to enable the OpenIoT Scheduler process to discover them and to retrieve data streams generated by mobile sensors.

4.1   Sending Data Through Virtual Sensors

The QoS Manager transmits all sensor readings which it received from the CPSP Engine through the X-GSN component to be stored in the LSM-Light RDF store. Since the X-GSN does not directly interact with real physical sensors but with

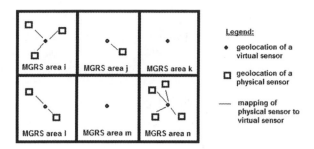

Fig. 4. Example assignment of virtual sensors to MGRS areas. All physical sensors in a given area are mapped to the corresponding virtual sensor.

their virtual sensor representations, the QoS Manager need to create and maintain virtual sensor instances that provide sensor data for the X-GSN component.

In order to link geographically close sensor data readings, each geographical area (in our implementation this is an MGRS area) is represented by one X-GSN virtual sensor, as shown in Fig. 4. When a mobile sensor is located inside a specific area, the QoS Manager component finds a corresponding virtual sensor which serves as a gateway to the X-GSN. In case this is the first mobile data source announced in an observed geographical area, the prerequisite for sending sensor data to the X-GSN is to register a new virtual sensor instance in the X-GSN, while the area center is defined as the location of the virtual sensor. All sensor data from mobile ICOs located within a geographical area covered by a virtual sensor are transmitted to the X-GSN component via this virtual sensor instance.

When a virtual sensor instance is successfully registered with the X-GSN, data readings from mobile data sources located in the virtual sensor area can be

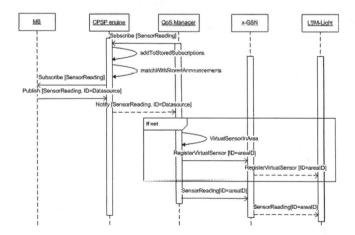

Fig. 5. Forwarding sensor readings to the OpenIoT platform

transmitted to the X-GSN. The QoS Manager simply pushes sensor data readings from mobile sensors to the adequate X-GSN virtual sensors immediately after receiving such readings. Apart from sensor data readings (e.g., temperature, humidity, pressure, etc.), we include the exact geolocation of a mobile sensor and send it the X-GSN. This way, if somebody is interested in data readings of a specific mobile sensor node, he/she can access those readings through the LSM-Light component.

4.2   Interaction with LSM-Light

Figure 5 depicts interactions between the QoS Manager component and LSM-Light. The CPSP engine provides sensor readings from mobile sensors to the QoS Manager and the rest of the OpenIoT platform. Moreover, as the engine does not include a permanent storage, but rather performs the matching and forwarding of mobile sensor data, the QoS Manager stores sensor data in memory only for a 30 min period. All sensor data requiring permanent storage are stored and maintained by LSM-Light.

To enable the forwarding of mobile sensor readings from the CPSP engine to the OpenIoT platform, the engine regards the QoS Manager as a general subscriber to all publications and forwards all sensor readings to the QoS Manager, as previously described in Sect. 2.2. When the QoS Manager receives a new sensor publication, it checks if in the observed area there exists a virtual sensor that is previously registered with the X-GSN component, and if not, the QoS Manager first registers a new virtual sensor with X-GSN. Afterwards, the QoS Manager forwards received sensor readings to the X-GSN through the virtual sensor instance in which the mobile sensor is currently located. The X-GSN component registers the virtual sensor and stores received data streams for the corresponding virtual sensor instance in the LSM-Light. All sensor readings for which there is current interest, either among subscribers of the CUPUS middleware or among the OpenIoT platform users, are forwarded to the OpenIoT platform. Otherwise, the readings from inactivated publishers are not forwarded to the OpenIoT platform. Note that a publisher on a mobile device is active if the mobile broker running on the device has received subscriptions matching publisher data from the CPSP engine, and the QoS Manager did not turn it off.

For a full integration of mobile sensors with the rest of the OpenIoT platform, mobile sensors mapped to virtual sensors need to be discovered by the OpenIoT platform and selected as resources for service provision. Thus, in case there is an OpenIoT service request which requires readings from mobile sensors, we need a mechanism which is initiated by the OpenIoT platform to activate adequate mobile publishers in a certain area. This can be achieved by sending an explicit subscription from the OpenIoT platform via a web interface of the QoS Manager to the CPSP engine, as depicted in Fig. 6. Since the OpenIoT platform does not know if these publishers are currently active or not, it has to request a new subscription over the area of interest. After receiving such instruction, the QoS Manager sends an explicit subscription to the CPSP engine which activates available mobile sensors. If there were no previously active sensor nodes in

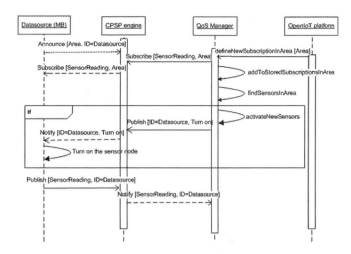

Fig. 6. Activating a new subscription from the OpenIoT platform

this area (i.e. a sensor was not producing data), the QoS Manager will make decisions with regards to turning on any required new sensor nodes and send them control messages via the CPSP engine to activate their sensing process. Mobile data sources will only start producing sensor data after receiving such instructions. The data is subsequently disseminated to the QoS Manager and stored in the Cloud Database, as depicted in Fig. 5.

5 Urban Air Quality Crowdsensing Use Case

To demonstrate the applicability of the CUPUS middleware with quality-driven data acquisition management, we have developed a mobile crowd-sensing application for air quality monitoring. The application integrates the data produced by low-cost wearable mobile sensors measuring pollutant gas concentrations and meteorological conditions, such as carbon monoxide, nitrogen dioxide, and sulfur dioxide, as well as temperature, relative humidity and atmospheric pressure. A wearable sensor communicates with the mobile device over a Bluetooth interface.

With our Android mobile application users can define personalized subscriptions to receive alerts regarding air quality in near real-time on their smartphones. They can subscribe to receive individual data readings of interest (e.g., temperature, pressure and SO2 levels) for their current MGRS area, or to received average data readings in the area. Furthermore, users can define subscriptions over an arbitrarily selected area. These subscriptions are relayed through the MB running on user mobile device to the CPSP engine, and further on to the QoS Manager which is responsible for activation/deactivation of sensor nodes which are currently located in the observed area and can meet user requirements. Selected sensors are invoked to start periodic readings (as shown in

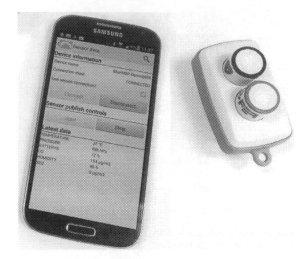

Fig. 7. Smartphone running the monitoring application connected to a wearable sensor

Fig. 7), while the mobile device transmits adequate readings to the CPSP engine to notifies interested end-users about received environmental data, as well as the QoS Manager which pushes received data into the OpenIoT Cloud Database.

Figure 8 shows the mobile device interface depicting a received air quality alert in the geographical area where the user is currently located. Figure 8(a) depicts a received sensor readings on a map, while Fig. 8(b) shows an average sensor reading for the current area. Users can change or cancel their subscriptions over time.

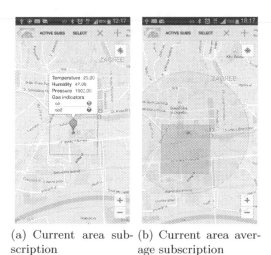

(a) Current area sub- (b) Current area aver-
scription   age subscription

Fig. 8. Air quality alerts in the geographical area where a user is currently residing

6   Related Work

Significant research effort is focused on IoT architectures integrating sensor data streams with cloud environments which address the issues of energy- and bandwidth-efficient data collection. In the work reported in [4] the authors propose a collaborative mobile sensing framework called Mobile Sensor Data EngiNe (MOSDEN), designed to operate on smartphones to capture and share sensed data between multiple distributed applications and users. The engine is designed so as to be compatible with the GSN (Global Sensor Network) middleware. By supporting processing and storage on end user smartphone devices, the platform aims to reduce the necessary data transmission to a centralized server, consequently achieving bandwidth and energy efficiency. In their subsequent work [7], the authors specifically address sensor discovery and configuration challenges and issues such as configuring sensor sampling rate to determine an optimal balance between user (application) requirements and energy consumption.

Specifically focusing on mobility aspects, Mobile Crowdsensing applications (MCS) take the advantage of a population of individuals to measure large-scale phenomena that cannot be otherwise measured by individuals [4]. The challenges of meeting resource limitations in the context of MCS applications are summarized in [3]. The authors further discuss resource allocation challenges in the case of multiple concurrent applications sampling various sensors on a single mobile device. Potential solutions include prioritizing applications that require sensor data, hence reducing or increasing the sampling rate of certain sensors while aiming to achieve efficient energy consumption of the mobile device. A discussion of different mobile crowdsourcing applications and optimizing smartphone related energy consumption is given in [1].

In general, model-driven approaches to data acquisition in sensor networks have demonstrated high-fidelity representation of real phenomena while requiring smaller amounts of live data to be collected [2]. In [6], the authors address the problem of energy efficiency in case of redundant sensor readings and present an approach for model-driven adaptive environmental sensing. Their approach is complementary to the techniques proposed in this paper since their solution requires that mobile devices maintain local models of expected sensor readings hence generating predictive readings, and push updates to the back-end server only in cases when predicted values do not match actual sensor readings. The authors in [10] provide an extensive overview of utility-driven data acquisition techniques for efficient collection of data in participatory sensing, whereby queries of different types (e.g., one-shot queries, continuous monitoring queries) may come from different applications. In the context of data acquisition, the proposed algorithms aim to achieve efficient sharing of sensor data among multiple queries that may be of different types, and is thus more general than the problem addressed in this paper.

While a number of aforementioned projects and approaches focus on mobile/ fixed sensing architectures and address the issues of energy- and bandwidth-efficient data collection, what is missing is a generalized solution for providing QoS support at different levels (physical level, network level, application level) and in terms of a number of metrics. While detailed utility functions and algorithms are discussed, this paper focuses on a proof-of-concept prototype implementation of a practical solution for quality-driven data acquisition from mobile sensors by means of the QoS Manager component built around a cloud-based publish/subscribe middleware. It has shown to be applicable in particular for mobile IoT application scenarios.

7   Conclusion

The paper presents the OpenIoT solution for integrating mobile sensors and managing data acquisition from such sensors in a quality-driven fashion. It provides an integrated view on the OpenIoT components providing support for mobile IoT environments, namely the CUPUS middleware and QoS Manager component. The design of a stand-alone QoS Manager component interfacing with the OpenIoT CUPUS middleware is presented. The QoS Manager enables improved energy-efficiency for mobile sensors while satisfying global application requirements for both sensing coverage and energy monitoring and management. Further on, details on the integration of the QoS Manager with the CUPUS middleware and the rest of the OpenIoT platform are provided to describe how the proposed solution can be used for optimized mobile sensing while taking into account sensor accuracy, energy-efficiency, and data redundancy. The paper further presents the prototype implementation and deployment of the QoS Manager interacting with CUPUS in the context of an Urban Crowdsensing case study focused on opportunistic sensing of air quality via mobile sensors and devices.

Future steps will focus on experimental testing of the proposed architecture in the scope of a real air quality monitoring field study.

Acknowledgments. This work has been partially carried out in the scope of the project ICT OpenIoT Project FP7-ICT-2011-7-287305 co-funded by the European Commission under FP7 program.

References

1. Chatzimilioudis, G., Konstantinidis, A., Laoudias, C., Zeinalipour-Yazti, D.: Crowdsourcing with smartphones. IEEE Internet Comput. **16**(5), 36–44 (2012)
2. Deshpande, A., Guestrin, C., Madden, S.R., Hellerstein, J.M., Hong, W.: Model-driven data acquisition in sensor networks. In: Proceedings of the Thirtieth International Conference on Very Large Data Bases. VLDB 2004, VLDB Endowment, vol. 30, pp. 588–599 (2004). http://dl.acm.org/citation.cfm?id=1316689.1316741
3. Ganti, R.K., Ye, F., Lei, H.: Mobile crowdsensing: current state and future challenges. IEEE Commun. Mag. **49**(11), 32–39 (2011). http://dx.doi.org/10.1109/mcom.2011.6069707
4. Jayaraman, P.P., Perera, C., Georgakopoulos, D., Zaslavsky, A.: Efficient opportunistic sensing using mobile collaborative platform mosden. In: 2013 9th International Conference Conference on Collaborative Computing: Networking, Applications and Worksharing (Collaboratecom), pp. 77–86. IEEE (2013)

5. Mühl, G., Fiege, L., Pietzuch, P.: Distributed Event-Based Systems. Springer, Heidelberg (2006)
6. Nikzad, N., Yang, J., Zappi, P., Rosing, T.S., Krishnaswamy, D.: Model-driven adaptive wireless sensing for environmental healthcare feedback systems. In: ICC, pp. 3439–3444 (2012)
7. Perera, C., Jayaraman, P.P., Zaslavsky, A., Christen, P., Georgakopoulos, D.: Sensor discovery and configuration framework for the internet of things paradigm (2013). arXiv preprint arXiv:1312.6721
8. Podnar Zarko, I., Antonic, A., Pripužic, K.: Publish/subscribe middleware for energy-efficient mobile crowdsensing. In: Proceedings of the 2013 ACM Conference on Pervasive and Ubiquitous Computing Adjunct Publication, pp. 1099–1110. UbiComp 2013 Adjunct, ACM, New York, NY, USA (2013). doi:10.1145/2494091.2499577
9. Pripužić, K., Žarko, I.P., Aberer, K.: Top-k/w publish/subscribe: a publish/subscribe model for continuous top-k processing over data streams. Inf. Syst. **39**, 256–276 (2014). http://www.sciencedirect.com/science/article/pii/S030643791200049X
10. Riahi, M., Papaioannou, T.G., Trummer, I., Aberer, K.: Utility-driven data acquisition in participatory sensing. In: Proceedings of the 16th International Conference on Extending Database Technology, pp. 251–262. ACM (2013)
11. Antonic, A., Rozankovic, K., Marjanovic, M., Pripuzic, K., Zarko, I.P.: A mobile crowdsensing ecosystem enabled by a cloud-based publish/subscribe middleware. In: 2014 International Conference on Future Internet of Things and Cloud, FiCloud 2014, Barcelona, Spain, August 27–29, 2014. pp. 107–114. IEEE (2014). http://dx.doi.org/10.1109/FiCloud.2014.27

Mapping the OGC SensorThings API onto the OpenIoT Middleware

Hylke van der Schaaf$^{(\boxtimes)}$ and Reinhard Herzog

Fraunhofer IOSB, Fraunhoferstr. 1, 76131 Karlsruhe, Germany
{hylke.vanderschaaf,reinhard.herzog}@iosb.fraunhofer.de

Abstract. The OGC SensorThings API is an OGC candidate standard for providing an open and unified way to interconnect IoT devices, data, and applications over the Web. The OpenIoT middleware, developed in the OpenIoT project, is an Open Source reference implementation to support IoT applications. Consequently the OpenIoT middleware is the perfect platform to implement the OGC candidate standard and to test its applicability.

This paper describes the approach to map the OGC data model to the OpenIoT data model and discusses the findings of this proof of concept experiment.

1 Introduction

The "Internet of Things" (IoT) is currently at the peak of inflated expectations [1] and as a result the number of available programming interfaces is increasing with a scary speed. With respect to interoperability this is one of the most critical obstacles for the acceptance of IoT solutions. As such a solution, the OpenIoT middleware [7] is facing the question how to make its services available to its users, without contributing to this API inflation. For a semantic oriented middleware the selection of SPARQL (SPARQL Protocol and RDF Query Language, [8]) was a quit strait forward decision, as it is the commonly used standard query language for semantic requests. Not so easy is the selection of an interface for a more simple and resource oriented application access. The main requirements for such an interface are simplicity, efficiency and availability. OpenIoT has decided to test the OGC SensorThings API [2] for that purpose.

The OGC SensorThings API is a standard which is designed to be applicable for resource-constrained devices. The concepts within the data model are simple and designed to provide easy to use abstraction of IoT resources. Moreover, the origins of this new standard are linked to the data model used in the OpenIoT middleware. The SensorThings API is based on the OGC Sensor Web Enablement (SWE, [6]) standards. On the other hand, the core of the OpenIoT middleware is the Semantic Sensor Network Ontology (SSN-Ontology, [9]) which was strongly influenced by SWE concepts. These common roots of the two data models imply that the OpenIoT middleware should be well prepared to support the OGC SensorThings API, so this proof-of-concept experiment was started to test this hypothesis.

© Springer International Publishing Switzerland 2015
I. Podnar Žarko et al. (Eds.): FP7 OpenIoT Project Workshop 2014, LNCS 9001, pp. 62–70, 2015.
DOI: 10.1007/978-3-319-16546-2_6

This paper reports on the mapping between the OpenIoT native data model, which is the SSN-ontology, and the OGC SensorThings API model. The challenge for this mapping is to bridge the complexity of SSN-Ontology to the simplicity of the OGC API while maintaining as much of the information as possible.

2 Conceptual Background

2.1 OpenIoT

The OpenIoT middleware is designed to provide an open interface to integrate heterogeneous sensor data into one common information model. This information model is based on the standard SSN-Ontology and the sensor data are semantically aligned in order to fit into this model. The main purpose is to have a semantically enriched description of the sensor data and the context to fit these data into a world model. The OpenIoT middleware provides services to schedule reasoning queries to analyse the data and it provides streaming mechanisms to feed semantically filtered live data to the client applications.

A simplified form of the data model is displayed in Fig. 1. At the core of the model is the observation. Each observation has an observation value containing the actual value of the observation, an observed property describing what is being measured, and a feature of interest, describing the object that is being monitored. Each observation is made by a given Sensor, which has a SensorType.

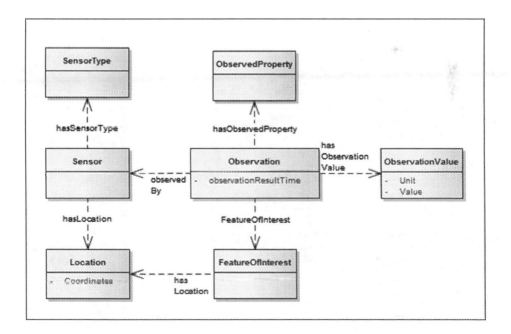

Fig. 1. Simplified OpenIoT data model

The concept SensorType was introduced by OpenIoT to ease the management of large numbers of sensors. Both the Sensor and the Feature of Interest have a Location, which is used to store where the object is.

Besides these defined relations, each of the above introduced objects can have custom defined relations and properties that fit the use-case for which the OpenIoT platform is being used.

2.2   SensorThings API

The OGC SensorThings API is an OGC candidate standard for providing an open and unified way to interconnect IoT devices, data, and applications over the Web. The OGC SensorThings API builds on Web protocols, the OGC Sensor Web Enablement standards and the observations and Measurements model [5], and applies an easy-to-use REST-like style. (see [2]). The RESTful web service interface provides the typical Create, Read, Update, and Delete (CRUD) actions on uniquely-identifiable resources. The OGC SensorThings API is specifically designed for the IoT but inspired by the OASIS Open Data Protocol (OData, [4]), which defines a general-purpose RESTful service interface.

It is the simplicity of the SensorThings API which makes it attractive for the OpenIoT middleware. OpenIoT provides strong reasoning and semantic streaming capabilities, but the typical clients for these kinds of services are devices with more available resources. A more light weight client might benefit from a simple resource based interface. Together with the fact that the OGC SensorThings API is a candidate standard, this API is expected to be a strong added value for the OpenIoT middleware.

The OGC SensorThings API consists of two parts based around the concepts thing and location. The Tasking Profile part deals with actuators (things that can accept commands) while the Sensing Profile deals with sensors. At the centre of the API (see Fig. 2) is the concept "Thing". Each thing can have a location indicating where the thing is, and multiple historical locations, each with a time property indicating when the thing was there.

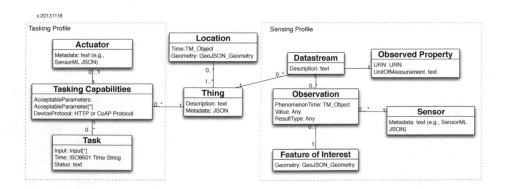

Fig. 2. The OGC SensorThings API data model. [3]

In the Sensing Profile, each thing can have multiple "Datastream" objects that are used to group observations together. The observations in a datastream all have the same observed property, but they can be made by different sensors on different features of interest. Each observation is associated with 1 datastream, 1 Sensor and 1 Feature of Interest.

The Sensor is what made the observation. It can be a hardware sensor, but also a piece of software or even a human. Sensors can be in-situ sensors, like the thermometer in an oven, or remote sensors, like a camera on a satellite. The Feature of Interest is the object on which the observation was made. It can be the thing itself, or any other identifiable object.

In the Tasking Profile part, each thing can have zero or more "Tasking Capabilities" objects. These function as a bridge between Actuators and Tasks on one side and the thing on the other. The OpenIoT platform currently does not describe actuators, therefore we can focus on the sensing profile part of the SensorThings API, and ignore the tasking profile.

3 Data Model Mapping

At first glance the data models of OpenIoT and the OGC SensorThings API are very similar. The most important difference is that the OpenIoT data model does not specify the concepts "Thing" and "Datastream".

3.1 Thing

SensorThings API defines "Thing" as:

> "a thing is an object of the physical world (physical things) or the information world (virtual things) which is capable of being identified and integrated into communication networks."

Things in the SensorThings API have a Location, described as a geometry object and a time, to support mobile things. Things also have a description and any arbitrary metadata.

In the SSN ontology, and thus in OpenIoT, "Thing" is simply the top-level concept for all that can be described. In SSN "Sensor" is a sub class of "Physical Object", which is a sub class of "Object", which is a sub class of "Entity", which is a sub class of "Thing". "Feature of Interest" is a direct sub class of "Thing" and an "Observation" is also eventually a sub class of "Thing". As a result, there is no nice mapping from a concept in OpenIoT onto the SensorThings API concept of Thing. OpenIoT does not define a class of "Things that can communicate". In the standard OpenIoT ontology the closest match for the SensorThings API concept "Thing" is actually the SSN concept "Feature of Interest". An advanced version could also allow the administrator to define the queries used to fetch and create things. This would allow for more freedom in the definition of things, since it enables the use of the custom ontology extensions that are created for a specific use case.

3.2   Feature of Interest

A feature of interest is defined as follows in SensorThings API:

> "Features or feature collections that represent the identifiable object(s)
> on which the sensor systems are making observations. In the case of an
> in-situ sensor or observations being attributes of the thing, the feature
> of interest could be the thing itself. For remote sensors, this may be the
> geographical area or volume that is being sensed."

This definition is the same in SSN and thus in OpenIoT. In the SensorThings
API the location of the feature of interest is encoded differently than the location
of a thing. For a thing the location is encoded in one or more Location objects,
each of which contain a Geometry object together with the time of when the
thing was in that location. Features of interest do not have a Location object,
but instead have a direct Geometry object. This means that a feature of interest
in the SensorThings API can't be mobile. This does not mean that the sensor
can not be mobile. Only for some use cases with mobile sensors this could be
a problem, for most use cases this is not a problem. An example of a mobile
sensor is for instance a sensor in a car, measuring the position and speed of
the car. In this case the sensor measures properties of the car, thus the feature
of interest is the car. However, since every measurement in a moving car is made
in a different location, it is not possible to both use a single feature of interest
for all measurements and encode the location of the feature of interest in the
geometry field. An example where a mobile sensor is used with static features
of interest is the case of a person or vehicle fitted with an air-quality sensor. In
this case the feature of interest is not the person or vehicle, but the street or
room where the person is, since the measurement is of the quality of the air in
this street or room.

3.3   Mapping OpenIoT FoI onto Thing and FoI

Since the SensorThings API concept thing is closest matched by the OpenIoT
concept Feature of Interest, we can map the OpenIoT concept Feature of Interest
to both the concepts thing and Feature of Interest in the SensorThings API. The
SensorThings API does not specify any limitations on how entity IDs are defined.
This means it is possible to use the same namespace for both entities of the type
thing and Feature of Interest. An implementation of the SensorThings API on
top of the OpenIoT platform can return a different view on the entity, depending
on how it is requested:

- http://server.eu/ST_Api/Things(EntityID)
- http://server.eu/ST_Api/FeaturesOfInterest(EntityID).

For non-moving entities this mapping would work well. The geometry information of the entity can be encoded in a Location object if the entity is requested
using the "Things" interface, and the same information can be encoded in the

geometry property if the entity is requested through the "FeaturesOfInterest" interface. For moving entities this mapping does cause problems, since the current SensorThings API data model for Feature of Interest does not support moving FoIs. This means that when a moving entity is requested through the "FeaturesOfInterest" interface only one of its locations can be encoded in the geometry field of the returned entity and all observations that have this entity as Feature of Interest would appear to be made in this location.

One feature that can not be supported using the standard OpenIoT ontology is having the feature of interest of an observation to be different from the thing that is associated with the observation. The observation in OpenIoT is only linked to a sensor, a property and a feature of interest, not to other things. In the SensorThings API the observation is also linked to a thing, though a datastream entity.

3.4   Datastream

In the SensorThings API the concept "Datastream" is used to group related observations together:

> "A datastream groups a collection of observations that are related in some way. The one constraint is that the observations in a datastream must measure the same observed property (i.e., one phenomenon)."

A datastream in the SensorThings API links a set of observations that have the same observed property, to a thing. In OpenIoT the concept "data streaming" is used in the context of getting continuously generated data from point A to point B in a continuous way that does not involve separate HTTP GET requests. As such, these similar sounding concepts in the two systems have nothing to do with each other.

In SSN each observation has a direct link to its Sensor, its Feature of Interest and its observed property and there is no further way to group observations. There is no concept in SSN that could be mapped to the SensorThings API concept datastream.

A SensorThings API implementation based on OpenIoT could offer virtual datastreams based on a SPARQL query. Several interesting queries would be possible:

- All observations for 1 observed property and 1 thing/feature of interest.
- All observations for 1 observed property and 1 sensor.
- All observations for 1 observed property, 1 sensor and 1 thing/feature of interest.

Of course a more advanced solution where a user can specify the query to be used for each individual datastream is also possible, as long as all observations returned by the query measure the same observed property. This would allow for even more powerful filtering since it can make use of the custom ontology extensions created for the use case. For instance, since features of interest in SSN can have geometric relations, it is possible to have a feature of interest for a building, containing features of interest for each floor, containing features of interest for each room. The building-feature could have an associated datastream listing all the observations in the entire building, while each floor has one listing the observations on that floor and so on. This set-up seems to be very much in the spirit of the idea behind datastreams, since the description of datastreams explicitly mentions having the same observed property being the only constraint, however the SensorThings API also specifies that each observation links to only 1 datastream and this set-up would have observations be in multiple datastreams. When an observation is requested the service could return only the datastream with the smallest semantic distance to the feature of interest of the observation.

Regardless of which query is used to implement the datastreams, when using virtual datastreams the creation of a new datastream through the SensorThings API is not possible. However, it might be possible to accept datastream-creation commands without actually creating new datastreams. When creating a new datastream through the SensorThings API, a client has to specify both a thing and an observed property. Since the server is free to assign an identifier to a newly created datastream, it can map this identifier to the identifier of one of the virtual datastreams, and return that. From the perspective of the client it would seem like the create command was successful.

The disadvantage of doing things this way with virtual datastreams is that when two clients both create a datastream for the same observed property and thing, they will receive the same datastream identifier, and will end up posting observations to the same datastream, even though they might not expect this. For read-only operation this implementation of virtual datastreams would work adequately.

3.5 Observations

There is little difference in the concept of observations as used in the OGC SensorThings API and in OpenIoT. In OpenIoT an observation is split into the concepts "Observation" and "ObservationValue", but since there is a 1-1 relationship between the two, this makes no difference for the mapping of the two data models.

There is a difference in that the OpenIoT observation has a direct relation to the observed property, while in the SensorThings API this relation goes over a datastream object. The SensorThings API specifies that when a client/sensor creates a new observation, it has to specify the datastream for this observation, but not an observed property. To store the observation in the OpenIoT data format, the server will have to connect the observation to an observed property. When using virtual datastreams one way to do this is to encode the identifier of the observed property into the identifier of the datastream. That way the server can deduce the observed property from the datastream-identifier that is specified when observation is created.

3.6 Sensors

The biggest difference in the data models regarding the sensor concept is that OpenIoT has split the concept into sensor and sensor type, to ease the management of large numbers of sensors. When requesting the properties of a sensor through the SensorThings API the properties of the sensor type could be merged into the properties of the sensor before the data is returned. However, when creating a new sensor through the SensorThings API this could create a problem, since it would be hard to determine the sensor type from the merged data. A better option could be to keep the sensor type as a separate, custom object type in the OpenIot SensorThings API implementation. That way each sensor can have a link to its sensor type.

4 Conclusions

In this paper we described the potential usage of the OGC candidate standard SensorThing on top of the OpenIoT middleware. The central question was: how can the simple REST-like API be mapped to the high-level semantic interfaces of the OpenIoT middleware? The answer is, surprisingly well. Surprisingly, because the data model of the SensorThing API is a very significant simplification of the OpenIoT data model. The Semantic Sensor Network (SSN) ontology, as the OpenIoT data model, is a quite powerful description framework of almost any kind of sensor observation. Unfortunately this comes with a price the SSN is not especially easy to apply. It allows a very comprehensive description of context for the "internet of things" which is required for the services the OpenIoT middleware is supposed to support. For simpler applications this type of service is probably not the best choice.

Fortunately the SensorThing data model is a very consistent and stringent simplification of the observation and measurement concept behind the SSN ontology. The naming of the concepts are not always a good indicator for the mapping between the two models, as shown with the example of the "Thing" concept. But looking at the meaning behind the names, it was always possible find an appropriate paring concept. The described mapping will give a consistent view to a subset of the OpenIoT data model. We believe that the implementation of the SensorThing API will be a major improvement for the OpenIoT middleware. It will give OpenIoT a standardized and truly easy to use interface to sensor values. This will complement the rich semantic reasoning services with a simple resource based interface. And the consistent data model mapping gives both a common context to describe the internet of things.

One notable proposed improvement of the OGC SensorThings API would be the support for mobility for the Feature of Interest. The simplest way to achieve this is to encode the geometry of the Feature of Interest in the same way as the geometry of a thing, with a list of Location objects, each containing a time and a geometry. That way any thing can be presented as a Feature of Interest without having to recode its Location. Both the OGC SensorThings

API and the OpenIoT platform are works-in-progress and therefore details of the specifications are subject to change.

Acknowledgments. This work was funded in part by the European Community in the framework of the OpenIoT FP7 project (Open Source blueprint for large scale self-organizing cloud environments for IoT applications) under contract number FP7-ICT-287305.

References

1. LeHong, H., Velosa, A.: Hype cycle for the internet of things, July 2014. https://www.gartner.com/doc/2804217
2. Liang, S.: The OGC sensorThings API, July 2014. http://ogc-iot.github.io/ogc-iot-api/
3. Liang, S.: The OGC sensorThings API - datamodel, July 2014. http://ogc-iot.github.io/ogc-iot-api/datamodel.html
4. OASIS: Oasis open data protocol (odata) technical committee, July 2014. https://www.oasis-open.org/committees/tc_home.php?wg_abbrev=odata
5. Open Geospatial Consortium: Observations and measurements model, July 2014. http://www.opengeospatial.org/standards/om
6. Open Geospatial Consortium: Sensor web enablement (swe), July 2014. http://www.opengeospatial.org/ogc/markets-technologies/swe
7. OpenIoT Consortium: Openiot - open source cloud solution for the internet of things, July 2014. http://www.openiot.eu/
8. Prud'hommeaux, E., Seaborne, A.: Sparql query language for RDF, March 2013. http://www.w3.org/TR/rdf-sparql-query/
9. W3C Semantic Sensor Network Incubator Group: Semantic sensor network ontology, July 2014. http://www.w3.org/2005/Incubator/ssn/ssnx/ssn

Open Platforms and Standards

An Open-Source Cloud Architecture for Big Stream IoT Applications

Laura Belli[1], Simone Cirani[1]([✉]), Luca Davoli[1], Lorenzo Melegari[1],
Màrius Mónton[2], and Marco Picone[1]

[1] Department of Information Engineering, University of Parma,
181/A, Viale G.P. Usberti, 43124 Parma, Italy
{laura.belli1,luca.davoli}@studenti.unipr.it, {simone.cirani,
marco.picone}@unipr.it, lorenzo.melegari@tlc.unipr.it
[2] WorldSensing, 383 4t Aragó, 08013 Barcelona, Spain
marius@worldsensing.com

Abstract. The Internet of Things (IoT) is shaping to a worldwide network of networks consisting of billions of interconnected heterogeneous sensor/actuator-equipped devices (denoted as *"things"* or *"smart objects"*), which are expected to exceed 50 billions by 2020. Smart objects, which will be pervasively deployed, are constrained devices with (i) limited processing power and available memory and (ii) limited communication capabilities, in terms of transmission rate and reliability. Future Smart-X applications, such as Smart Cities and Home Automation, will be fostered by the use of standard and interoperable IP-based communication protocols that smart objects are going to implement, by simplifying their development, integration, and deployment. Smart-X applications will significantly differ from traditional Internet services, in terms of: (i) the number of data sources; (ii) rate of information exchange; and, (iii) need for real-time processing. Because of these requirements, such services are denoted as "Big Stream" applications, in order to distinguish them from traditional Big Data applications. In this paper, we present an implementation of a novel Cloud architecture for Big Stream applications based on standard protocols and open-source components, which provides a scalable and efficient processing platform for IoT applications, designed to be open and extensible and to guarantee minimal latency between data generation and consumption. We also provide a performance evaluation based on experimentation in a real-world Smart Parking scenario, to assess the feasibility and scalability of the proposed architecture.

Keywords: Internet of things · Big stream · Cloud computing · Interoperability · Smart-X applications · Open source software

1 Introduction

In recent years, the forecast of a global worldwide network of heterogeneous networks is coming true. The Internet of Things (IoT) will involve billions of communicating heterogeneous devices, thus enabling new forms of interaction between

© Springer International Publishing Switzerland 2015
I. Podnar Žarko et al. (Eds.): FP7 OpenIoT Project Workshop 2014, LNCS 9001, pp. 73–88, 2015.
DOI: 10.1007/978-3-319-16546-2_7

things and people. The actors involved in IoT scenarios will have extremely heterogeneous characteristics, in terms of processing and communication capabilities, energy supply and consumption, availability, and mobility, spanning from constrained devices, also denoted as "smart objects," to smartphones and other personal devices, Internet hosts, and the Cloud. Shared and interoperable communication mechanisms and protocols are currently being defined and standardized, allowing heterogeneous nodes to efficiently communicate with each other and with existing Internet actors. The most prominent driver for interoperability in the IoT is the adoption of the Internet Protocol (IP), namely IPv6 [1,2]. An IP-based IoT will be able to extend and interoperate seamlessly with the existing Internet. Standardization institutions, such as the Internet Engineering Task Force (IETF) [3], and several research projects [4] are in the process of defining mechanisms to bring IP to smart objects, due to the need to adapt higher-layer protocols to constrained environments. However, not all objects will be supporting IP, as there will always be tiny devices that will be organized in closed/proprietary networks and rely on very simple and application-specific communication protocols. These networks will eventually connect to the Internet through a gateway/border router. In this context, with billions of nodes capable of gathering data and generating information, Big Data techniques address the need to process extremely large amounts of heterogeneous data for multiple purposes. These techniques have been designed mainly to deal with huge volumes (focusing on the data itself), rather than to provide real-time processing and dispatching. Cloud computing has found a direct application with Big Data analysis due to its scalability, robustness, and cost-effectiveness. Moreover, the processing and storage functions implemented by remote Cloud-based collectors are the enablers for their core business, which involve providing services based on the collected and processed data to external consumers.

IoT applications provide useful services to final users as a consequence of the processing work on the huge amount of data collected by smart objects. Moreover several reference IoT scenarios, such as industrial automation, transportation, networks of sensors and actuators, require real-time/predictable latency and could even change their requirements (e.g., in terms of data sources) dynamically and abruptly. This can be mistakenly considered only as a Big Data scenario, but is important to note that Smart-X services significantly differ from traditional Internet services, in terms of: (i) number of data sources; (ii) rate of information exchange; and (iii) need for real-time processing. The requirements listed above create a new need for Cloud architectures specifically designed to handle this kind of scenario and to guarantee minimal processing latency. Such systems are denoted as "Big Stream" systems. Big Data architectures generally use traditional processing patterns with a pipeline approach [5]. These architectures are based on a processing approach where the data flow goes downstream from input to output, to perform specific tasks or reach the target goal. Typically, the information follows a pipeline where data are sequentially handled, with a pre-defined processing tightly coupled sub-units (static data routing). The described paradigm can be defined as "process-oriented:" a central coordination point manages the execution of sub-units in a certain order and each sub-unit provides a specific processing output, which is created to be used only within the scope of its own process without the possibility to be shared among different processes. This approach represents a major deviation from traditional Service Oriented Architectures (SOAs), where the sub-units are external web services invoked by a coordinator process rather than internal services [6]. Traditional Big Data approaches might cause higher processing latencies since they are not optimized for real-time processing tasks.

Big Stream-oriented systems should react effectively to changes and provide smart behavior for allocating resources, thus implementing scalable and cost-effective Cloud services. Dynamism and real-time requirements are the reasons why Big Data approaches, due to their intrinsic inertia (i.e., Big Data typically works with batch-based processing), are not suitable for many IoT scenarios. The Big Stream paradigm allows to perform real-time and ad-hoc processing in order to link incoming streams of data to consumers, with a high degree of scalability, fine-grained and dynamic configuration, and management of heterogeneous data formats. In brief, while both Big Data and Big Stream deal with massive amounts of data, the former focuses on the analysis of data, while the latter focuses on the management of flows of data, as shown in Fig. 1. The main difference resides in the meaning of the term "Big": for Big Data it refers to volume of data while for Big Stream it refers to global information generation rate as generated by data sources. Additionally, for Big Data applications it is important to keep a history of sensed data in order to be able to perform any required computation, Big Stream applications might decide to perform data aggregation or pruning in order to minimize the latency in conveying the results of computation to consumers, with no need for persistence. Note that, as a generalization, Big Data applications might be consumers of Big Stream data flows.

In this paper, we present an implementation of a novel Cloud architecture for Big Stream applications based on standard protocols and open-source components, which provides a scalable and efficient processing platform for IoT applications. The architecture has been designed to be open and extensible and to decrease the latency between data generation and consumption. In order to assess

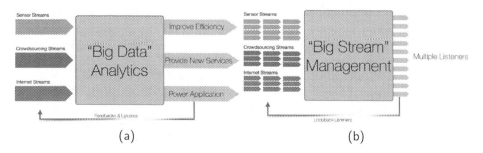

Fig. 1. (a) The volume of data analysis in Big Data systems. (b) The multiple data sources and listeners management in Big Stream system.

the feasibility, scalability, and the performance of the proposed architecture, the implementation has been evaluated through an experiment in a real-world Smart Parking scenario.

The rest of this work is organized as follows. In Sect. 2, the proposed architecture is presented and detailed. Section 3 presents the implementation details such as protocols and used components, while Sect. 4 describes the evaluation use case with real-world data. In Sect. 5, an overview of related works is presented. Finally, in Sect. 6, we draw our conclusions and discuss future research directions.

2   Architecture

The proposed architecture has been explicitly designed for the management of Big Stream applications targeting IoT scenarios. It aims at decreasing the latency in data dispatching to consumers and optimizing resource allocation. In this architecture, the data flow is "consumer-oriented," rather than being based on the knowledge of collection points (repositories) where data can be retrieved. In the proposed scenario, some consumer applications or processes might be interested in data generated by one or more deployed smart objects; the consumer, denoted as *listener*, registers its interest in receiving updates (either in the form of raw or processed data) that come from a streaming endpoint (i.e., Cloud service). On the basis of application-specific needs, each listener defines a set of rules, which specify what type of data should be selected and possible filtering operations. Besides end-users, Cloud services can also act as additional listeners processing the same data stream, applying different rules, and providing a new stream, which can be later consumed by others. The purpose of the proposed Big Stream architecture is to guarantee that, as soon as data are available, they will be dispatched to all the interested listeners, which are thus no longer responsible to poll data, in order to decrease latency and possibly avoiding unnecessary network traffic.

The listener-oriented communication model is optimal in terms of minimization of the time that a listener must wait before it receives data of interest [7]. Figure 2 shows the information flow in the listener-based Cloud architecture. This solution introduces a change of perspective compared to the typical delays chain of traditional architecture. The proposed Cloud Graph-based architecture is built on top of functional building blocks that are self-consistent and perform "atomic" processing on data, and are not directly linked to a specific task. In such a system, data flow is based on dynamic graph-routing rules determined only by the nature of the data and not by a centralized coordination unit. In the end of the flow, processed data are dispatched to external listeners, such as mobile applications, Big Data applications based on Data Warehouses (DW), customers that might have subscribed for a particular data stream, or a generic consumer that is willing to use processed data. This new approach allows the platform to be "consumer-oriented" and to effectively implement an optimal resource allocation mechanism. Without the need of a coordination process, data streams

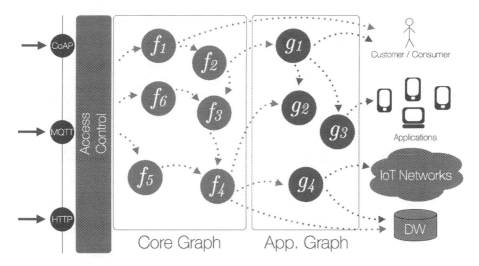

Fig. 2. The proposed listener-based Graph architecture. The nodes of the graph are listeners, the edges represent the dynamic flow of information data streams.

can be dynamically routed in the network by following the edges of the graph and allowing to switch-off nodes (if processing units are not required) and replicate nodes (if processing units are required by a significant number of listeners). Figure 3 illustrates the components defining the proposed system and the relationships between each element. The next subsections describe in detail all the building blocks. The complete architecture is shown in Fig. 4.

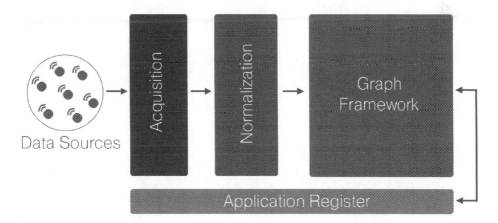

Fig. 3. Components of the proposed Graph Cloud architecture and relations between each element.

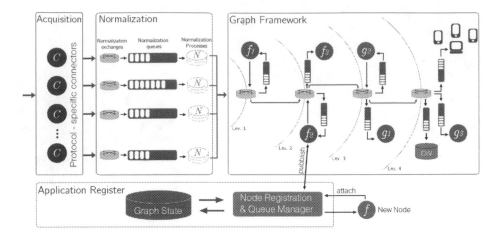

Fig. 4. The complete Graph Cloud Architecture with reference to the data stream flow between all building blocks, from IoT data sources to final consumers.

2.1   Acquisition Module

The *Acquisition Module* represents the entry point for external IoT networks of smart objects to the Cloud architecture. Its purpose is to collect raw data from different and heterogeneous data sources and make them available to the other functional blocks. It is important to underline that several application-layer protocols can be implemented by smart objects. For this reason, the Acquisition Module includes a set of different connectors in order to properly handle each protocol-specific incoming data stream.

2.2   Normalization Module

Raw data are generally application-dependent, thus a *Normalization Module* has been designed in order to normalize all the collected information and generate a representation suitable for processing. The normalization procedure is made by fundamental and atomic operation on data such as: (i) the suppression of useless information (e.g., unnecessary headers or meta-data); (ii) the annotation with additional information; and (iii) the translation of the payload to a suitable format. In order to handle the huge amount of incoming data efficiently, the normalization step is organized with protocol-specific queues and *Exchanges*. An *Exchange* works as a router in the system and dispatches incoming data to one or more output queues depending on dynamic routing rules. As shown in the normalization section of Fig. 4, the information flow originating from the Acquisition Module is handled as follows:

– all data streams relative to a specific protocol are routed to a dedicated protocol-specific exchange, which forwards them to a protocol-dedicated queue;

– a normalization process handles the input data currently available on the queue and performs all necessary normalization operations in order to obtain a stream of information units that can be processed by next modules;
– the normalized stream is forwarded to an output exchange;

The output of the Normalization block represents the entry-point of the first Graph Module *Exchange*, that pass it to all the interested listeners of the next levels. The main advantage of using Exchanges is that queues and normalization processes can be dynamically adapted to the current workload; for instance, normalization queues and processes could be easily replicated to avoid system congestion.

2.3 Graph Framework

The *Graph Framework* is composed of listeners. A listener is an entity (e.g., a processing unit in the graph or an external consumer) interested in the raw data stream or in the output provided by a different node in the graph [7]. Each listener represents a node in the topology. The connection of multiple listeners across all processing units define the routing of data streams from producers to consumers. The nodes are processing units performing some kind of computation on incoming data and edges represent the flow of information linking together processing units, which implement some complex behavior as a whole. All the nodes of the graph can be listeners for incoming data or outputs of other graph nodes. As shown in Fig. 2, the graph is divided in two stages: (i) in the *Core Graph* basic processing provided by the architecture (e.g., format translation, normalization, aggregation, data correlation, and other transformations) is performed; (ii) in the *Application Graph*, listeners that require data coming from the core or an inner graph level to perform custom processing on already processed data are defined. The Core and Application graph are organized in one or more concentric levels, in order to provide a set of commonly available functionalities and to dynamically extend the capabilities of the system. The complexity of processing is directly proportional to the number of levels that data have crossed and the flow of information is always directed to outer or external levels.

In the "Graph Framework", each level is accessible from a level-dedicated Exchange that forwards all data streams to nodes in its level. Each graph node i in a specific layer n can listen for incoming data stream on a dedicated queue managed by the Exchange of level n. If the node i, as well as being a consumer, it acts also as a publisher, then its computation results are delivered to the Exchange of level n, which is bounded with the Exchange of layer $n+1$. Therefore the Exchange in level $n+1$ can forward streams coming from level n to all nodes of level $n+1$ interested in this kind of data.

2.4 Application Register Module

The *Application Register Module* has the fundamental responsibility to maintain all the information about the current state of all graph nodes in the system, and to route data across the graph. In more detail, the application register module performs the following operations: (i) attach new nodes or consumer applications interested in some of the streams provided by the system; (ii) detach nodes of the graph that are no more interested in streaming flows and eventually re-attach them; (iii) handle nodes that are publishers of new streams; (iv) maintain information regarding topics of data, in order to correctly generate the routing-keys and to compose data flows between nodes in different graph levels. In order to accomplish all these functionalities, the Application Register Module is composed by two main components, as shown in Fig. 4. The first one is the *Graph State Database*, which is dedicated to store all the information about active graph nodes, such as their state, level, and whether they are publishers. The second one is the *Node Registration and Queue Manager* (NRQM), which handles requests from graph nodes or external process, and handles the management of queues and the routing in the system. When a new process joins the graph as a listener, it sends an attach request to the Application Register Module, specifying the kind of data to which it is interested. The NRQM module stores the information about a new process in the Graph State Database and creates a new dedicated input queue for the process, according to its preferences. Finally, the NRQM sends a reference of the queue to the process, which becomes a new listener of the graph and can read the incoming stream from the input queue. After this registration phase, the node can perform new requests (e.g., publish, detach, get status), which are detailed next.

The designed graph-based architecture allows to optimize resource allocation in terms of *efficiency*, by switching off processing units that have no listeners registered to them (enabling cost-effectiveness), and *scalability*, by replicating those processing units which have a large number of registered listeners. The combination of these two functionalities and the concept of listener allow the platform and the overall system to adapt itself to dynamic and heterogeneous scenarios by properly routing data streams to the consumers and add new processing unit and functionalities on demand. In Fig. 4, all the architecture modules with the complete flow of information through all steps described above are presented in detail.

3   Implementation

Three main modules concur in forming the entire system: (i) acquisition and normalization of the incoming raw data; (ii) graph management; (iii) application register entity. In this section, the details of the implementation of the proposed architecture by using standard protocols and open-source components are presented. The implementation has been carried out by deploying an Oracle VirtualBox®VM, equipped with Linux Ubuntu 12.04 64-bit, 2GB RAM, 2 CPU, 10GB HDD. Since the architecture is based on a queue-communication paradigm, an instance of RabbitMQ [8], an open-source queue server implementing the standard Advanced Message Queuing Protocol (AMQP) [9], was used. RabbitMQ provides a multi-language (Java, PHP, Python, C, ...) and platform-indipendent API. Next, the implementation of each fundamental building block is described in detail.

3.1   Acquisition Nodes and Normalization Nodes Implementation

The system needs an input block capable to handle external incoming raw data, through different application-layer protocols. Data must then be processed and structured, in order to be managed by the graph processes.

Acquisition Nodes. Considering the main and most widespread IoT application-layer protocols, the implementation supports: (i) HTTP [10]; (ii) CoAP [11]; and (iii) MQTT [12].

For the sake of scalability and efficiency, an instance of NGINX [13] has been adopted as HTTP acquisition node reachable via the default HTTP port. As a processing module, a dedicated PHP page has been configured to forward incoming data to the inner queue server. NGINX has been selected instead of the prevailing and well-known open source Apache HTTP Server Project [14] because it uses an event-driven asynchronous architecture to improve scalability and specifically aims to reach high-performances even in case of critical number of request.

CoAP acquisition node has been implemented using a Java process, based on a mjCoAP [15] server instance connected to the RabbitMQ queue server.

MQTT acquisition node is realized by implementing an ActiveMQ [16] server through a Java process, listening for incoming data over a specific input topic (*mqtt.input*). This solution has been preferred over other existing solution (e.g., the C-based server Mosquitto [17]), because it provides a dedicated API that allows a custom development of the component. The MQTT acquisition node is also connected to the architecture's queue server. In order to avoid potential bottlenecks and collision points, each acquisition protocol has a dedicated *Exchange* and a dedicated queue (managed by RabbitMQ), linked together with a protocol related routing key, ensuring the efficient management of incoming streams and their availability to the normalization nodes.

Normalization Nodes. Incoming raw data from the acquisition nodes may require a first optimization process, aiming at structuring them into a common and easily manageable format. Normalization processes extract raw data from dedicated incoming queues, leaving the routing key, which identifies the originator smart object protocol, unchanged. Each normalization node is implemented as a Java process, which processes incoming raw data extracted from a queue identified through a protocol-like routing key (e.g., *<protocol>.event.in*). Received data are fragmented and encapsulated in a new JSON structure, which provides an easy-to-manage format. At the end of the processing chain, each normalization node forwards the new data chunk to its next Exchange, which connects the normalization block to the first Graph layer Exchange (Fig. 5).

3.2   Graph Management Implementation

Incoming messages are stored into active queues, connected to each Graph Layer's Exchange. Queues can be placed into the *Core Graph*, for basic computation, or into *Application Graph*, for enhanced data treatment. Layers are

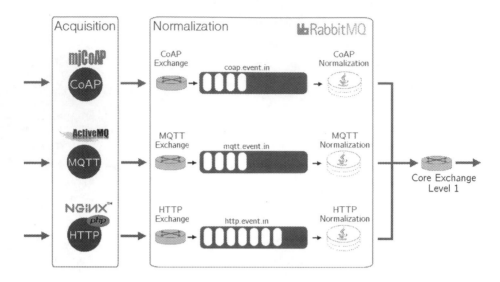

Fig. 5. Acquisition and normalization blocks.

connected with one-way links with their own successor Exchange by using the
binding rules allowed by queue manager, ensuring proper propagation of data
flows and avoiding loops. Each graph layer is composed by Java-based Graph
Nodes dedicated to process data provided by the Graph layer's Exchange. Such
processes can either be *Core Nodes*, if they are dedicated to simple and primitive
data processing, or *Application Nodes*, if they are oriented to a more complex
and specific data management. Messages, identified by a routing key, are first
retrieved from the layer's Exchange, then processed, and finally sent to the target Exchange, with a new work-related routing key, as depicted in Fig. 6. If the
outgoing routing key belongs to the same incoming graph layer, data object or
stream stay within the same Exchange and becomes available for other local
processes. If the outgoing routing key belongs to an outer graph layer, then data
are forwarded to the corresponding Exchange, and finally forwarded by following
a binding rule and assuring data flow. Each graph node, upon becoming part of
the system, can specify if it acts as a data publisher, capable of handling and forwarding data to its layer's Exchange, or if it acts as data consumer only. A data
flow continues until it reaches the last layer's Exchange, responsible to manage
the notification to the external entities that are interested in final processed data
(ex. Data Warehouse, browsers, smart entities, other cloud graph processes, ...).

3.3 Application Register Implementation

The overall architecture is managed by a Java process (*Application Register*),
that has the role to coordinates the interactions between graph nodes and external services, like the RabbitMQ queue server and the MySQL [18] database.
It maintains and updates all information and parameters related to processing

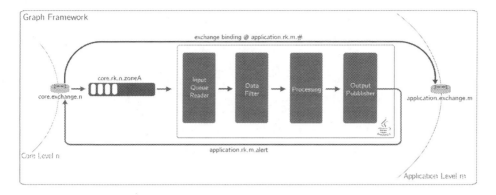

Fig. 6. Interaction between Core and Application layers with binding rule.

unit queues. As a first step, the Application Register starts up all the external connections, then it activates each layer's Exchange, binding them with their successors. At the end, it proceeds with the activation of a Jetty HTTP server, responsible for listening and handling all Core and Application nodes requests (as depicted in Fig. 7): (A) attach, (B) status request, (C) change publishing policy, (D) detach, and (E) reattach request, using a RESTful HTTP paradigm.

4 Performance Evaluation

The implemented architecture has been evaluated through the definition of a real use case, represented by a Smart Parking scenario. The data traces used for the

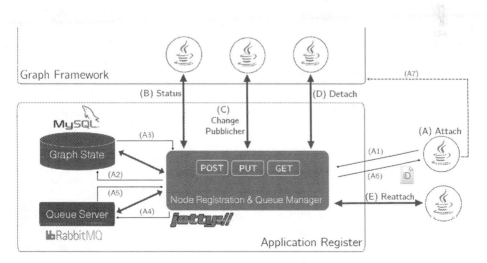

Fig. 7. Detail of Application Register module, with possibles actions required by graph nodes, deepening steps for ATTACH request.

evaluation of the proposed architecture have been provided by Worldsensing [19] from one of the company's deployments in a real-life scenario, used to control parking spots on streets. The traces are a subset of an entire deployment (more than 10,000 sensors) with information from 400 sensors over a 3-month period.

Experimental Setup. Each of 604k parking spots' data has been used in our cloud infrastructure using a Java-based data generator, which periodically selects an available protocol (HTTP, CoAP or MQTT) on a random basis and sends raw data to the corresponding acquisition node interface. Once the raw data has been received by the acquisition layer, they are forwarded to the dedicated normalization Exchange, where corresponding nodes enrich incoming data with parking zone's details, retrieved from an external database. Once the normalization module has completed its process, it sends the structured data to the Graph Framework, allowing the processing of the enriched data. This Graph Framework is composed by 7 Core Nodes and 7 Application Nodes. The processed data follows a path based on routing keys, until reaching the architecture's final external listener. Each Application node is interested in detecting changes of parking spot data, related to specific parking zones. Upon a change of the status, the Graph node generates a new aggregated descriptor, which is forwarded to the responsible layer's Exchange, which has the role to notify the change event to external entities interested in the update ($free \rightarrow busy$, $busy \rightarrow free$).

Results. The proposed architecture has been tested, using the testbed described above, by varying the inter-arrival time of each incoming raw data from 1 message per second, up to 100 messages per second. The evaluation consists in assessing the performance of (i) the acquisition stage and (ii) computation stage. First, performance evaluation has been made measuring the time period between points in time when data objects are sent from a data generator to the corresponding acquisition interface, and a point in time when the object is enriched by normalization nodes, thus becoming available for the first processing Core Node. The results are shown in Fig. 8(a). The acquisition time is slightly increasing but it is around 15 ms at all considered rates.

The second performance evaluation has been carried out by measuring the time (dimension: [ms]) between the instant in which enriched data become ready for processing activities, and the time when the message ends its Graph Framework routes, becoming available for external consumers/customers. The results, shown Fig. 8(b), have been calculated using the following expression:

$$T_{processing_{freq}} = \frac{T_{out} - T_{in} - \sum_{i=1}^{N} graph\_process_i}{N - 1}$$

Performance results were calculated by subtracting the processing time of all Core and Application Nodes, in order to consider only the effective overhead introduced by the architecture, and without considering implementation-specific times. Finally, these times have been normalized over the number of computational nodes, in order to obtain the per-node overhead introduced by

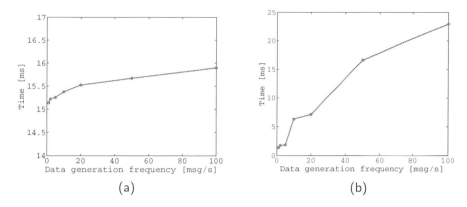

Fig. 8. (a) Average times (dimension: [ms]) related to the acquisition block. (b) Average times (dimension: [ms]) related to Graph Framework processing block.

the architecture, in a way that is independent of the specific routing that was implemented.

5   Related Work

The IoT paradigm brings to a worldwide "Network of Networks" scenario with billions of cooperating heterogeneous smart objects generating information from the environment. Information collected from this kind of data sources can be employed into several Smart-X applications. In order to simplify the integration of components and to provide interoperability with the traditional Internet, many standardization organizations and research projects are chartered to design mechanisms specifically intended to bring IP connectivity to things, that can implement standard IP-based communication protocols. In order to make the IoT a real and integral component of the Future Internet (FI), it is necessary to define mechanisms to deliver IoT services and applications to final consumers. Several research projects address their effort to provide a solution for the deployment and management of a pervasive IoT-Cloud infrastructure. The EU FP7 project OpenIoT (Open Source Cloud solution for the Internet of Things) [20] aims to provide a systematic and structured solution to the management of utilities based on IoT environments. OpenIoT can be considered as an extension of traditional Cloud computing implementations since it is specifically designed to allow access to different and heterogeneous IoT resources and capabilities. To summarize, the main objectives of OpenIoT framework are:

– to create an open source middleware for getting information from sensor clouds, without having to concern about what exact sensors are used;
– to explore efficient ways to use and manage cloud environments for IoT "entities" and resources (such as sensors, actuators and smart devices) and offering utility-based IoT services;

– to provide instantiations of cloud-based and utility-based sensing services enabling the concept of "Sensing-as-a-Service," via an adaptive middleware framework for deploying and providing services in cloud environments.

Another example of this approach is given by the FIware project [21], an open cloud-based infrastructure for cost-effective creation and delivery of Internet applications and services. FI-WARE API specifications are public, royalty-free, and OCCI (Open Cloud Computing Interface)-compliant [22], driven by the development of an open source reference implementation which allows developers, service providers, enterprises, and other organizations to develop innovative products based on FI-WARE technologies. The FI-WARE solution is based on the Openstack project [23], a global collaboration of developers producing an ubiquitous open-source cloud computing platform for public and private clouds. The project aims to deliver solutions for all types of clouds by being simple to implement, massively scalable, and feature-rich. The majority of research projects listed above addressing their work on Cloud and IoT architectures opt to use open source components for the implementation of their systems.

Other projects related to real-time and stream management are Apache Storm [24] and Apache S4 [25]. Storm is a free and open source distributed real-time computation system to reliably process unbounded streams of data. The system can be integrated with different queueing and database technologies and provides mechanisms to define topologies in which nodes consume streams of data and process those streams in arbitrarily complex ways. S4 is a general-purpose, near real-time, distributed, decentralized, scalable, event-driven, and modular platform that allows programmers to implement applications for processing streams of data. Multiple applications nodes can be deployed and interconnected on S4 clusters to create more sophisticated systems. Although there are several similarities between these systems and the proposed architecture, such as modularity, scalability, latency minimization and the graph topology, there are same notable differences. The most relevant use cases for Storm and S4 are stream processing and continuous computations related to data stored in databases (e.g., message processing for database update). The proposed architecture, on the other hand, is specifically designed to work in dynamic IoT scenarios comprising heterogeneous data sources and making no assumption on the repositories (if needed) where data can be retrieved or stored. Another major difference is related to the nature of the topology of the processing units. While Storm stream management is based on an operator-defined and static topology of the graph, the proposed architecture is extremely dynamic, as the number of nodes and edges in the Graph Framework can change according to the workload and listener requirements.

6   Conclusions

In this paper, we presented a novel Cloud architecture for the management of Big Stream applications in IoT scenarios. After describing the selected scenario requirements in terms of decreasing the latency between a point in time when a data object is created and point in time when the processed object can be delivered to a consumer, we have detailed the designed listener-based architecture and its components: Acquisition Module, Normalization Module, Graph Framework, and Application Register. The implementation of the overall system and its evaluation on a real-world Smart Parking dataset has been presented. The listener-oriented approach can lead to several benefits, such as (i) decreased latency: the push-based approach guarantees that no delays due to polling and batch processing are introduced; (ii) fine-grained self-configuration: listeners can dynamically "plug" to those that output data of interest; (iii) optimal resource allocation: processing units that have no listeners can be switched off, while those with many listeners can be replicated, thus leading to cost-effectiveness from the Cloud service perspective.

Acknowledgments. The work of Simone Cirani is funded by the European Community's Seventh Framework Programme, area "Internetconnected Objects", under Grant no. 288879, CAL*IP*SO project - Connect All *IP*-based Smart Objects! The work reflects only the authors views; the European Community is not liable for any use that may be made of the information contained herein.The work of Marco Picone is funded by Guglielmo srl, Reggio Emilia (RE), Italy. The work of Laura Belli is funded by Multitraccia S.C., Reggio Emilia (RE), Italy.

References

1. Postel, J.: Internet protocol. RFC 791 (INTERNET STANDARD) Updated by RFCs 1349, 2474, 6864 (September 1981)
2. Deering, S., Hinden, R.: Internet protocol, version 6 (ipv6) specification. RFC 2460 (Draft Standard) Updated by RFCs 5095, 5722, 5871, 6437, 6564, 6935, 6946, 7045, 7112 (December 1998)
3. IETF: The Internet Engineering Task Force. http://www.ietf.org/
4. European Community's 7th Framework Programme: CALIPSO - Connect All IP-based Smart Objects. http://www.ict-calipso.eu/
5. Hohpe, G., Woolf, B.: Enterprise Integration Patterns: Designing, Building, and Deploying Messaging Solutions. Addison-Wesley Longman Publishing Co Inc., Boston (2003)
6. Isaacson, C.: Software Pipelines and SOA: Releasing the Power of Multi-Core Processing, 1st edn. Addison-Wesley Professional, Upper Saddle River (2009)
7. Belli, L., Cirani, S., Ferrari, G., Melegari, L., Picone, M.: A graph-based cloud architecture for big stream real-time applications in the internet of things. In: Advances in Service-Oriented and Cloud Computing - Workshops of ESOCC 2014, Manchester, United Kingdom, 2–4 September (2014)
8. RabbitMQ. http://www.rabbitmq.com/
9. Vinoski, S.: Advanced message queuing protocol. IEEE Internet Comput. **10**(6), 87–89 (2006)
10. Fielding, R., Gettys, J., Mogul, J., Frystyk, H., Masinter, L., Leach, P., Berners-Lee, T.: Hypertext transfer protocol -HTTP/1.1 (1999)
11. Shelby, Z., Hartke, K., Bormann, C.: The constrained application protocol (CoAP). RFC 7252 (Proposed Standard) (June 2014)

12. MQTT: Message Queue Telemetry Transport. http://mqtt.org/
13. NGINX: The High-performance Web Server and Reverse Proxy. http://wiki.nginx.org/Main
14. Apache Software Foundation: Apache. https://httpd.apache.org/
15. Cirani, S., Picone, M., Veltri, L.: mjCoAP: an open-source lightweight Java CoAP library for internet of things applications. In: Žarko, P., et al. (eds.) FP7 OpenIoT Project Workshop 2014. LNCS, vol. 9001, pp. 118–133. Springer, Heidelberg (2015)
16. Apache ActiveMQ. http://activemq.apache.org/
17. Mosquitto: An Open Source MQTT Broker. http://mosquitto.org/
18. MySQL. http://www.mysql.com/
19. Worldsensing. http://www.worldsensing.com/
20. European Union's Seventh Framework Programme : OpenIoT - Open Source cloud solution for the Internet of Things (2007). http://openiot.eu/
21. European Community's 7th Framework : FI-Ware Project (2011). http://www.fi-ware.org/
22. OGF - Open Grid Forum: OCCI - Open Cloud Computing Interface. http://occi-wg.org/
23. Rackspace: OpenStack Cloud Software. https://www.openstack.org/
24. Apache: Storm. https://storm.incubator.apache.org/
25. Apache: S4. http://incubator.apache.org/s4/doc/0.6.0/overview/

Autonomic Frameworks Deployment Using Configuration and Service Delivery Models for the Internet of Things

Mahmudur Rahman Saniat[1], Hoan Nguyen Mau Quoc[2],
Huy Le Van[2], Danh Le Phuoc[2], Martin Serrano[2(✉)],
and Manfred Hauswirth[3]

[1] Tilburg University, Tilburg City, The Netherlands
sanmulty@gmail.com
[2] Insight Center for Data Analytics,
National University of Ireland Galway, Galway City, Ireland
{hoan.quoc, huy.levan, danh.lephuoc,
martin.serrano}@deri.org
[3] Fraunhofer – FOKUS, Kaiserin-Augusta 31, 10589 Berlin, Germany
manfred.hauswirth@fokus.fraunhofer.de

Abstract. Internet of Things systems rely on the principles for service deployment and configuration based on delivery models. The predominant service delivery model for the Internet of Things architecture is a novel approach to create a global IoT system for Internet Connected Objects. While the service control loop has already been proposed (autonomics), the dynamic deployment of the different modules of an IoT system is still due. In this paper an approach for IoT service delivery model using autonomic management principles, which can deploy and configure IoT services is presented. The use of an implemented framework that helps administrator/user to deploy IoT platform(s) with autonomic methods has been developed. Particularly and as proof of concept example an open source platform (www.superstreamcollider.org) is used to demonstrate service instantiation. The agent-based framework analyses the requirements, dependencies and resolves them following autonomic design principles and also, by design, it deploys the IoT service delivery model into desired platform(s) running in the cloud or into a local machine.

Keywords: Internet of Things · Service control loop · Service delivery · Cloud infrastructure · Management · Autonomics utility-driven models · Linked data · Cloud computing · Cloud services · Open source

1 Introduction

The predominant service delivery model for the Internet of Things architecture is a novel approach to create a global IoT system for Internet Connected Objects. The emergent introduction of this model has brought a new challenge, not only deploy, install, govern and manage the full service lifecycle efficiently but each and every device should be able to communicate with the systems and in some cases with each

© Springer International Publishing Switzerland 2015
I. Podnar Žarko et al. (Eds.): FP7 OpenIoT Project Workshop 2014, LNCS 9001, pp. 89–102, 2015.
DOI: 10.1007/978-3-319-16546-2_8

other enabling interoperability. Emerging technologies and systems development of the IT sector work for this interoperability challenge, additionally in this complex scenario, it is highly desirable and necessary endow the IoT system(s) with self-monitoring and self-managing capacity.

The deployment and management of IoT platform(s) in the large scalable, using cloud platforms, has brought even a bigger challenge. Starting from the initial deployment, the IoT system or service has to go through the learning phase of different scenarios, while serving its end users with maximum output with minimum cost possible. Currently available cloud architecture can itself be self-managing, but the complexity and dynamically changing requirements of the implementation of IoT system in the same form is much more complex and challenging than that of any general software application.

In the Internet of Things area, it is becoming a common practice using agent(s) for configuring and monitoring operations. IoT systems rely on the principles for deployment and configuration based on autonomic service delivery models. In autonomic systems, agents analyse the requirements, dependencies and resolves them following self-organizing principles and also, by design, it deploys the IoT service delivery model into the desired platforms. While the service control loop for distributed platforms has already been proposed, by means of autonomics [1], the dynamic deployment of the different modules of an IoT system is still due. At this moment the deployment of IoT service delivery models is manual, thus, much complex to handle for a non-technical user, as well as time consuming and error prone.

In the area of Internet of Things, autonomic agents can dynamically evaluate the system requirements and deploy dependencies of an IoT service delivery model. Autonomic agent(s) can also extensively be used on cloud optimization, for example using event data distribution or event splitting mechanism to control service infrastructures on demand. Autonomic in cloud services have been already proposed within the framework of the OpenIoT project (www.openiot.eu), where the self-tuning or self-configuration facility of the IoT service delivery model is a novel approach, this approach is explained.

In this paper a generic approach or framework to support the administrator/user deploying IoT platform(s) with an autonomic guideline [1] taking care of all the underlying details of the existing framework is intruded and explained. The framework functionality analyses the requirements, dependencies and resolve them "autonomically" and as main objective deploy the IoT service delivery model into the desired platform by means of cloud or local machine. As example an open source platform (www.superstreamcollider.org) to demonstrate cloud or local machine instantiation is used. Some experiments are performed under the SSC-Fed4FIRE experiments project to demonstrate the use of autonomic agents in IoT environments.

As a second part in this paper, an autonomic framework for continuously monitoring and optimizing the IoT test-bed, regardless the infrastructure on which the platform is hosted is discussed. Although many cloud monitoring services (e.g. monitis, nagios) are available in the market, the IoT platform(s) needs to extract the information and map those information into customized requirements that can serve into the tuning of the platform itself. Moreover, the proposed autonomic agent not only extracts and maps the information, but also it is able to tune-up the underlying IoT framework.

The structure of the paper is as follows: Sect. 2 presents the service delivery model for the Internet of Things including the service lifecycle modules. Section 3 analyses the required autonomic deployment operations based to identify autonomic requirements and desired functionality for IoT systems. Section 4 introduces the approach for an autonomic agent for services deployment with focus in the Internet of Things. Section 5 explains initial experiments conducted with he autonomic agent in the framework of running experiments in large-scale distributed platforms with a particular scenario on cloud infrastructures management for IoT cloud Data. Section 6 concludes the paper and define some next steps and finally some references are included.

2 Service Delivery Model for IoT

The current state-of-the-art about service delivery model for the Internet of Things consists of interdependent modules and their interactions [1] to support application(s) demands.

The details for the service lifecycle can be found at [2], It is relevant to highlight the event-driven nature and the self-x coordination aspects. The autonomic aspects affect not only the organizational view of the service lifecycle but also its operational behaviour. E.g. it enables semantic control to achieve interoperability and exploits the information necessary to control and manage IoT services.

The OpenIoT platform from a design conception includes reusability capabilities and autonomics. OpenIoT follows a service lifecycle or control loop that introduces autonomic principles for service management solutions. The OpenIoT lifecycle is presented in Fig. 1. From physical domain (sensor and actuators) to application (monitoring, billing, visualisation for example) OpenIoT pursues the objective of annotating information, describes them in/through services and use data models to enable end user services in a more autonomous form. OpenIoT can be seen as an extensible, reusable common manageability platform, which provides for the IoT space autonomic functionality for better managing resources, networks, systems and services [3].

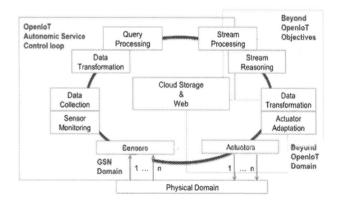

Fig. 1. Internet of Things service control loop

3   Autonomic Deployment Operations

By studying the state-of-the-art on IoT solutions, it is seen that generally IoT platforms consists of different modules developed to support a business model approach (vertical approach) [4, 5]. A vertical approach seeks for a single stack organisation in order to simplify operations and generate sort of abstraction that eventually can fit into a business model. At IoT verticals isolated and almost cero-exchange of information can get from them however a more controlled environment(s) can be offered as guarantee for better management and system stability. As consequence of this trade-off between control and stability system developers has adopted vertical designs instead of horizontal, building in this form IoT silos.

In the other hand, as part of the main features in IoT systems, it is required operations and services are inter-connected and inter-dependent. The service modules have dependencies in both functional and non-functional level. Particularly the proposed architecture has been developed keeping in mind the service computing paradigm, and the reusability and self-configuration of the platform itself (autonomics). The deployment platform might change, the requirements of the test-bed might change, and the dependencies might be different than the initial set-up. An autonomic design will support these and other self-x features. In practical terms an autonomic deployment will create a virtualization image in front of the actual IoT test-bed and provide and estimate, before hand, with the details that are necessary to deploy the system. Although lots of work has been done in the area of autonomics in IoT test-bed [6, 7] and distributed systems [8–11], Sensor Network Management [12], Dynamic Deployment of Software Component [13–15]. The Autonomic Deployment Agent for IoT test-bed has been designed following the IoT Autonomic lifecycle. The following identified autonomic operations for IoT Service Delivery model are parts of the requirements for designing the Autonomic architecture explained in the Sect. 4.

3.1   Data Collection and Sensor Monitoring

During the data collection and monitoring phase, the agent analyses the system and find out what resources are available, and also the requirements (e.g.: dependencies) of the IoT platform for deployment. It will map these two variables and will hold a *deployment_pair* in store to match the best combination with future pairs.

3.2   Analysis and Transformations

During this phase, the agent defines ways to resolve the dependencies. Some dependencies might be internal, for example one module depends on the deployment of another, and some will be external where the required resource has to be extracted from an external source. A dependency map is created in this phase and the system creates the list of dependencies (linked data) that needs to be resolved "somehow" during the Execution phase. In the Dependency map, the agent analyses and determine whether the dependencies can be resolved internally or it has to be dealt and solved with external changes such as increment of cluster memory or adding a new processor.

3.3   Plan and Processing

During the plan phase, the agent communicates with either the IoT platform or the underlying infrastructure and ask/do necessary changes. What changes need to be done is decided in this phase. The decision can vary from simply deploying the platform to increasing the initial resource allocation, and might result in negative feedback from the agent about the deployment. As an example, the defined algorithm to do this processing can be described as follow:

check system_resource
check IoT_rec_resource
map system_resource -> IoT_rec_resource
check performance_parameter
do PLAN

3.4   Adaptation and Execution

As the Plan phase decides what to do, the Adaptation and Execution phase follows the decision, and executes the decision taken by the Plan and Processing phase. The analysis phase has already resolved the dependency sources, the plan phase has set the platform to be best suited for the IoT platform, now the Execution phase will deploy the IoT test-bed into the infrastructure that has been prepared. Although the dependency map has been created in the Analysis phase, the resolving of those defined dependencies are done in the Execution phase.

4   Autonomic Configuration Agent

The self-tuning or self-configuration facility of the IoT service delivery model is a novel approach and is presented in this section. An autonomic framework for continuously monitoring and optimizing the IoT test-bed regardless the infrastructure on which the platform is hosted is described. The optimization can be done via several parts, but in this work the cloud optimization [3] segment is the main focus. The autonomic-configuration and adopted autonomic life cycle is the one described in the previous section of this paper. Figure 2 depicts the functional architecture of the autonomic agent and the designed features that it performs, the cycle start by monitoring the conditions or parameters of the resources to be offered, then the next step perform an analysis of the information and the operations defines the way the autonomic agent will work. The third phase defines the best performance based on conditions and finally the execution of the changes into the system is performed.

4.1   Adaptation for the Internet of Things

For the life-cycle design, the generic autonomic agent life cycle proposed by Horn [1] has been used as reference. In the very first stage of the deployment of the autonomic

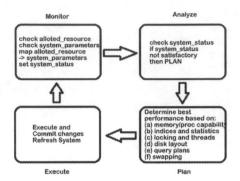

Fig. 2. Autonomic agent architecture diagram

agent, it monitors the IoT system. Monitoring involves multi-side monitoring: (a) IoT monitoring: the agent will monitor IoT requirements and keep record of the performance of the same under different scenarios monitored on the other phase. (b) Infrastructure monitoring: the agent keeps observations on the infrastructure and help to keep the performance parameters up to date. In this stage of the autonomic cycle the agent will monitor the resource parameters, and relevant performance parameters. For example, with a defined memory capacity, the system (IoT framework) can respond to any local request within a period of time. This performance record will be stored in the agent memory.

The learning phase of the autonomic agent might be approached in two different ways. The agent can be deployed empty, meaning the database keeping track of the performance parameter against different configuration parameter can be empty at the beginning of the deployment and it periodically learn from the system as time goes. In this case, at the beginning of the deployment, the agent only has an initial information for the IoT, for example what are the minimal resource requirements for the deployment of the platform, and it is assumed that the owner of the IoT system knows best on the issue that "what configuration ensures the best performance of the deployed IoT test-bed". But the system resource and requirements will change over time. So the Autonomic Agent have to maintain a performance log and keep track the relationship under which condition the system can perform the best. This is called the 'learning' phase of the Autonomic Agent, and can vary from minutes to weeks depending on the configuration. It also depends on the changes that the IoT system is facing. Customized change can be imposed to the IoT platform to 'teach' the system about different scenarios and help him to define algorithm to look for best performance parameters. On the other hand, it is also possible that the designer of the agent will pre-configure the 'best cases' and load them in a pre-deployment scenario. The 'best case' will depend on the designer of the agent, and the preference given by the user or IoT administrator/owner. The balance between two approaches is recommended.

During the analysis phase, the Autonomic Agent will develop a specific mapping of performance algorithm. How the 'best performance' will be evaluated, totally depends on the specific provider or designer. In the current experimentation, a fastest response to an IoT data access request has been considered as main goal. But it can range from the resource performance to query complexity. The analysed phase will sort out, according to the requirements of the IoT user/admin or Agent designer - "how the system is doing", and put this status in its "record book".

The analysis phase has been separated in two different segments. After analysing the IoT system health, the agent will be able to determine what changes are required to put the IoT in a best condition. This can be maximizing resource, or can be minimizing some other parameters that are consuming more resource than necessary. In case of dealing with other elements of the IoT services, the agent needs to communicate with other agents of the system. Agents will communicate with other agents, they will have a common goal, they will exchange information, and decide based on exchanged information the actions to take. The approach has been focused on the performance maximization parameters of the agent based on local Analysis. Note that the communication with other agents have not been implemented because the design of autonomic agent is still under-way and the communication between different agents and learning from each other and deciding on a common goal with the help of complex algorithm is out of focus of this research at this current stage. The planning phase should be able to determine what are the changes that might have an effect on the performance improvement of the IoT system. During the planning phase, the autonomic agent will inform the hosting infrastructure, or the owner of the system to change the environment according to its analysis done in the previous cycle.

The agent will inform the platform or the owner to increase the memory. This communication can be reverted as well. It is also possible that the owner configure the total infrastructure in such a way that the IoT system has to tune it up according to the limited resources available. For example, in case the owner does not want to increase the underlying platform, or set an upper limit of upgrade, and the IoT system has already reached that limit of resource usage. At this moment, the only option to make the system perform better is to add more indexes, or to reduce the maximum buffer size. In this scenario, the IoT Autonomic Agent will do the communication with the IoT service itself and in the execution phase, it will do the tuning accordingly and make sure that the system is performing the best with the resource available. The following logic has been implemented to set the status of the autonomic agent. This algorithm checks if the pair of allocated_resource and system_parameters supposed to perform in the best form. The agent checks the condition and set the system_status by following the algorithm as follow:

while true
  do
  check allocated_resource
  check system_parameters
  map allocated_resource -> system_parameters
  set system_status

The later part of the logic will check the system_status for the IoT platform. If the system_status is Ok, then the IoT system has already been tuned up for the best performance with available resource. If not, then the PLAN will happen.

check system_status
if system_status not satisfactory
then PLAN

The PLAN phase recommends necessary changes required either in the system or in the infrastructure hosting the system. The PLAN is designed in such a way that it will look for nearby 'best performance pair'. By 'performance pair' it refers to the (allocated_resource, system_parameters) pair and as described earlier, the user or the administrator defines 'best'. PLAN is not executed if the system status is in a good enough situations. Executing any of the phases takes resources, on the other hand system should learn from its steps and different situations as well. The system has been designed to learn only from the steps that it takes or the situations that it was in, but not from the scenario that it has not faced so far.

During the execution phase, the autonomic agent tune-up the system according to the data-store tuning parameters [16]. In this implementation work, the cloud database [17] is the main objective where this work has been concentrated on. The performance of cloud LSM database that the OpenIoT is using has several parameters that needs to be tuned up to get the best performance from it [18]: (a) memory and processing capability (b) indices and statistics (c) locking and threads (d) disk layout (e) query plans (f) swapping. In the implementation, have been considered the memory and processing capacity and demonstrated the outcome. The reason behind this narrow consideration is because the deployment of autonomic framework for IoT test-bed in general is limited to specific technology rather than broader technologies. The data store underlying the IoT platform is platform dependent and those parameters can vary from data store to data store. Regarding what parameter will determine the performance of the specific data store in what dimension and magnitude, it is a separate research area and it is out of the scope of this paper. The evaluation of parameters via autonomic configuration is also possible and this work defines a roadmap for those particular requirements.

5 Experiments

A use case has been created, to explain the functionality of SSC. Figure 3 represents the use case where data from sensors (left-hand side) needs to be offered as stream data mashup that is used by web services and to distribute multiple users (right-hand side). By means of this use case, data from Smart Santander is collected and transformed into universal open format (RDF) data streams. Then distributed in SSC distributed data servers hosted by Planet. The cloud-based distributed processing is performed in BonFIRE and as response of the service request in the form of multiple queries over the streamed data generated. Finally the SSC visual interface provide access to all the Smart Santander sensor data distributed in the world by using Virtual Wall API.

The experiment design, depicted in Fig. 4 follows the service lifecycle for IoT, in this particular experiments the open source open source platform super stream collider, a mash up builder (www.superstreamcollider.org), is used to demonstrate service instantiation. The agent-based framework analyses the requirements, dependencies and resolves them

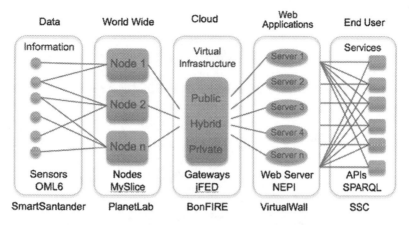

Fig. 3. SSC-designed experiments using Fed4FIRE platforms.

following autonomic design principles and also, by design, it deploys the IoT service delivery model into desired platform(s) running in the cloud or into a local machine.

In the executed experiments, collected data from the smart Santander experiment through Planet Lab is used and by means of the LSM data collector (left hand side) acts as an autonomic agent that collect, transform and process data. In a second stage of the experiment the BonFIRE platform was used to deploy autonomic services instantiation by means of IoT Servers distribution in wide-Europe locations via BonFIRE platform (right hand side). The distribution in Planet Lab and BonFIRE follows an autonomic configuration process. There are other processes related to cloud processing and clustering mechanism that are out of the focus of this paper, but the autonomic experiments details are described hereafter.

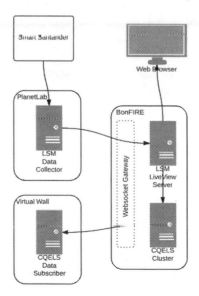

Fig. 4. Architecture for SSC-experiments using Fed4FIRE platforms.

5.1 Autonomic IoT Data Collection

LSM-Light module plays the role of central component of OpenIoT platform [16] and an instance was used in Super Stream Collider. It is used to collect data from different sensor sources, annotate and transform data into linked data. In SSC-Fed4FIRE experiments, an LSM-Light client module was distributed in a cluster of 10 nodes. The architecture of the deployment is shown in Fig. 5.

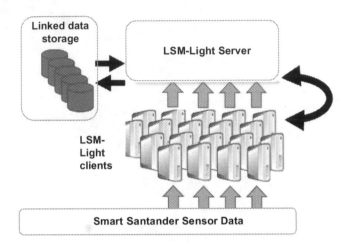

Fig. 5. LSM-Light architecture for SSC-Fed4FIRE experiment.

In SSC-Fed4FIRE experiment, a Hadoop cluster for fetching IoT data was used. Fetching tasks for over 2,000 Smart Santander sensor data sources including: humidity, air quality, noise pollution, parking status, temperature information was scheduled. The main reason of using Hadoop is to enable the autonomic feature by minimizing the fetching cycles, which cannot be processed manually or in a single machine.

The majority of the data sources in the deployment are published through HTTP as Web services or RESTful APIs, which are pull-based mechanisms. For these sources, the LSM-Light clients periodically fetch each data source to collect raw sensor data and transform it into triples. The fetching operations are built as asynchronous tasks, scheduled in the fetching cluster. The fetching algorithm can be described as follow:

*if sensor **haven't** be registered in the system*
*   Register sensor*
while true
*   do*
*   Collect raw data from sensor*
*   Transform raw sensor data into RDF*
*   Send RDF data to LSM-Light server*
*   Set system sleep for specific scheduled time*

In this experiment, a *sensor data exploration interface, is provided which* uses a map overlay to display the sensor information based on geographical location as shown in Fig. 6. Besides the map overlay, the public endpoint is deployed for users to query the IoT data (sensors in this case).

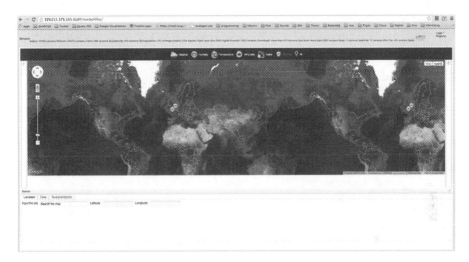

Fig. 6. Sensor data exploration interface

5.2   Autonomic IoT Data Processing

In the framework of the SSC-Fed4FIRE experiments LSM-Light can be used as a local instance or it can also work in the cloud. The modules that support LSM-light and their functionalities are described as follow:

- LSM-Light Data Collector Module
  - collect raw data from Smart Santander
  - convert data to RDF format
  - push data to LSM LiveView Server through Web Socket Gateway.
- LSM-Light LiveView Server
  - Receives data from Collectors
  - Displays raw data on Webserver, which can be accessed from browser (HTTP)
  - Also acts as a data forwarder, which forwards data to CQELS cluster.
- CQELS Cluster Module
  - Receives data in RDF format
  - Processes queries on request
  - Returns query results through Web Socket Gateway.
- CQELS Data Subscribers Module
  - Send query requests to CQELS cluster through Web Socket Gateway
  - Wait for answers to be returned.

5.3   Experiment Setup

LSM-Light modules can be deployed under different platform and the minimum requirement used in the performed experiment in Fed4FIRE are indicated at the Table 1 as follow:

Table 1. SSC-Fed4FIRE experimental setup

Fed4FIRE Platform	BonFIRE	PlanetLab	Virtual Wall
Number of servers	1 LSM Live View Server 5 nodes CQELS cluster (1 master, 4 slaves),	10 servers across different sites in Europe, Tomcat Webserver	10 servers × 10 (CQELS clients each)
CPU	4 cores	10 cores	10 cores
Memory	8 GB	8 GB	8 GB
Storage	10 GB internal + 80 GB Data block	10 GB internal + 50 GB Data block	10 GB internal + 50 GB Data block
Network	IPv4 + IPv6	IPv4	IPv6
OS	Debian	Fedora	Ubuntu
Imaging support	Yes	No	No
Tools used	Web Portal, CLI tools	jFed	jFed

The autonomic agent proposed deployment was partially tested in the Fed4FIRE platform. The Project Fed4FIRE is an effort to deliver a common federation framework for Future Internet Research and Experimentation facilities. It enables experimenters from different communities to easily access existing testbeds while federated tools support powerful experiment lifecycle management. During the course of this experiment, the use of three testbeds: BonFIRE, PlanetLab Europe and Virtual Wall to deploy IoT services, each of which has different capability and technical aspects, were required.

6   Conclusions and Future Work

The architecture design and development of competent autonomic elements for IoT requires an effective marriage of technology with the functionality and capacity of the Internet of Things systems.

An assortment of perfectly self-managing autonomic elements will not yield an autonomic computing system unless the elements share a set of common behaviours, interfaces and interaction patterns that are demonstrably capable of engendering system-level self management.

Initial experiments to test self-configuration and self-deployment capacity have been tested in the framework of SSC-Fed4FIRE experiments. It has been demonstrated the proposed architecture design with the autonomic functionality implemented can be used to support a full range of self-management capabilities for autonomic environments.

The described framework for the self-deployment and self-configuration individually introduce autonomic computing to the state-of-the-art IoT platforms as an approach for the IoT service lifecycle control loop implementation.

Future work might consist of developing frameworks/implement components for other parts of the service cycle and the development of other agents (autonomic self-healing and self-protection) and as well as integration of the agents.

Acknowledgments. Part of this work has been carried out in the scope of the project ICT OpenIoT Project, Open Source blueprint for large scale self-organising cloud environments for Internet of Things applications which is co-funded by the European Commission under seventh framework program, contract number FP7-ICT-2011-7-287305-OpenIoT and the project Fed4-FIRE, Federation for FIRE with contract number FP7-ICT-2011-8-318389.

References

1. Horn, P.: Autonomic computing: IBM's perspective on the state of information technology, IBM Corporation (2001)
2. Serrano, M., Hauswirth, M., Kefalakis, N., Soldatos, J.: A self-organizing architecture for cloud by means of infrastructure performance and event data. In: IEEE Cloudcom, Bristol, UK, 2–5 December 2013, ISBN: 978-0-7695-5095-4
3. Serrano, J.M.: Management and Context Integration Based on Ontologies for Pervasive Service Operations in Autonomic Communication Systems. Ph.D. thesis, UPC (2008)
4. Xu, X., Bessis, N., Cao, J.: An autonomic agent trust model for IoT systems. Comput. Sci. **21**, 107–113 (2013)
5. Rajan, M.A., Balamuralidhar, P., Chethan, K.P., Swarnahpriyaah, M.: A self-reconfigurable sensor network management system for internet of things paradigm. In: 2011 International Conference on Devices and Communications (ICDeCom), pp. 1–5. IEEE, February 2011
6. Ramakrishnan, A., Naqvi, S.N.Z., Bhatti, Z.W., Preuveneers, D., Berbers, Y.: Learning deployment trade-offs for self-optimization of Internet of Things applications. In: Proceedings of the 10th International Conference on Autonomic Computing, ICAC 2013, pp. 213–224, June 2013
7. Ghezzi, C., Pacifici, F.: Evolution of software composition mechanisms: a survey. In: Lucia, D., Ferrucci, F., Tortora, G., Tucci, M. (eds.) Emerging Methods, Technologies, and Process Management in Software Engineering, pp. 3–19. Wiley, New York (2008)
8. Ayala, I., Pinilla, M.A., Fuentes, L.: Exploiting dynamic weaving for self-managed agents in the IoT. In: Timm, I.J., Guttmann, C. (eds.) MATES 2012. LNCS, vol. 7598, pp. 5–14. Springer, Heidelberg (2012)
9. Deb, D., Fuad, M.M., Oudshoorn, M.J.: Achieving self-managed deployment in a distributed environment. J. Comput. Methods Sci. Eng. **11**, 115–125 (2011)
10. Gosling, J. (ed.): The Java Language Specification. Addison-Wesley Professional, Boston (2000)
11. Grimm, R., Anderson, T., Bershad, B., Wetherall, D.: A system architecture for pervasive computing. In: Proceedings of the 9th workshop on ACM SIGOPS European Workshop: Beyond the PC: New Challenges for the Operating System, pp. 177–182. ACM, September 2000

12. Schilit, B.N., Theimer, M.M.: Disseminating active map information to mobile hosts. IEEE Netw. **8**(5), 22–32 (1994)
13. Brumitt, B., Shafer, S.: Topological world modeling using semantic spaces. In: Proceedings of the Workshop on Location Modeling for Ubiquitous Computing, UbiComp, vol. 2001, pp. 55–62, September 2001
14. Tolle, G., Culler, D.E.: Design of an application-cooperative management system for wireless sensor networks. In: EWSN, vol. 5, pp. 121–132, January 2005
15. Bandyopadhyay, D., Sen, J.: Internet of things: applications and challenges in technology and standardization. Wirel. Pers. Commun. **58**(1), 49–69 (2011)
16. OpenLink Software: RDF Performance Tuning (2009). http://virtuoso.openlinksw.com/dataspace/doc/dav/wiki/Main/VirtRDFPerformanceTuning
17. OpenLink Software: Database Server Administration (2009). http://docs.openlinksw.com/virtuoso/databaseadmsrv.html
18. Soldatos, J., Kefalakis, N., Serrano, M., Hauswirth, M.: Design principles for utility-driven services and cloud-based computing modelling for the Internet of Things. Int. J. Web Grid Serv. **10**(2/3), 139–167 (2014). doi:10.1504/IJWGS.2014.060254

Interoperability Between Machine-to-Machine Communication System and IP Multimedia Subsystem

Vanesa Čačković[1](✉), Iva Bojić[2], and Mario Kušek[2]

[1] Ericsson Nikola Tesla, Krapinska 45, Zagreb, Croatia
vanesa.cackovic@ericsson.com
[2] Faculty of Electrical Engineering and Computing, University of Zagreb,
Unska 3, Zagreb, Croatia
{iva.bojic,mario.kusek}@fer.hr

Abstract. Machine-to-Machine (M2M) communication is communication between two or more M2M devices, with no need for a direct human intervention. The IP Multimedia Subsystem (IMS) is a standardized architecture for IP-based multimedia services that enables audio/video communication, instant messaging, and presence services in telecommunication network. These services are well-controlled by the IMS operators, in terms of, for example, Quality of Service (QoS), security, and accounting, which can be used for M2M application. In this paper, a focus is set on interworking between M2M communication system and an IP Multimedia Subsystem (IMS) network. The paper analyzes current standards and proposes interworking possibilities. In one case, regarding home security, the proposed solution, was applied.

Keywords: IP multimedia subsystem · Machine-to-Machine communication · Interworking · Standards

1 Introduction

Machine-to-Machine (M2M) communication is established between two or more M2M devices, with no need for a direct human intervention [9]. The main characteristic of an M2M system is its heterogeneity, both in sense of different device capabilities and different communication technologies, used for exchanging information among M2M devices. In this paper we focus on one possible way of connecting M2M devices by using an IP Multimedia Subsystem (IMS) network. IMS is the next generation service platform for IP-based multimedia services that enables audio/visual communications, instant messaging, and presence services among users [10]. These services are well-controlled by the IMS operators, in terms of, for example, Quality of Service (QoS), security, and accounting. Since IMS is access technology-agnostic, it can be applied not only to cellular networks, but also to fixed broadband networks, which implies that in the near future, it will be possible to benefit from IMS almost everywhere (e.g. from peoples' homes, offices, streets, cafes, stations).

© Springer International Publishing Switzerland 2015
I. Podnar Žarko et al. (Eds.): FP7 OpenIoT Project Workshop 2014, LNCS 9001, pp. 103–117, 2015.
DOI: 10.1007/978-3-319-16546-2_9

At first glance, it is hard to make connections between IMS networks and M2M systems, since M2M systems are not conceived as multimedia communication systems, but are simply seen as systems where only different numerical sensor data, sensor event information, and remote control commands can be exchanged. However, the IMS architecture defines several components that are capable of providing functionalities needed for an M2M type of communication. Functionalities provided by IMS, like authentication and authorization mechanisms, charging support, interworking with legacy network, QoS assurance, presence and user data management, already exist in the IMS architecture. Therefore, these IMS components can be reused for the M2M type of communication, if the operators have already deployed an IMS network. With reusing the existing standard IMS components, the operators can reduce their costs of service deployments, as well as reduce the time to market for new services. On the other hand, an IMS service can benefit by using data from M2M system and IMS can customize service based on that data.

Section 2 describes Machine-to-Machine communication standards and system architecture. ETSI M2M is used as the base standard in this paper. In Sect. 3, IP multimedia subsystem (IMS) is introduced and Sect. 4 explains the interworking between IMS and M2M. The proposed solution is compared with the related work in Sect. 5; and Sect. 6 explains the use case in the home security area, that uses interworking between IMS and M2M. Finally, Sect. 7 concludes the paper.

2   Machine-to-Machine Communication Standards and System Architecture

The European Telecommunication Standards Institute (ETSI) has a Technical Committee (TC M2M), which goal was to set the standard of the application layer that is independent of the underlying communication network. The result was published as a set of technical reports and standards that specify functional architecture, and interfaces. The interfaces follow RESTful approach and HTTP and Constrained Application Protocol (CoAP), standardized by the IETF, were chosen as an application protocol. ETSI collaborates with other standardization bodies (e.g. 3GPP, OMA, Broadband Forum, ZigBee Alliance, KNX, Z-Wave) and is involved in their standardization activities, in order to minimize the number of standards. The next step was to avoid the creation of competing M2M standards. Thus, ETSI started a global initiative oneM2M (similar to 3GPP) to develop one global M2M specification. Currently, oneM2M is working on the first draft and ETSI M2M is the only available standard. This is the reason that this paper is based on interoperability between IMS and ETSI M2M.

ETSI M2M architecture is shown in Fig. 1. ETSI proposes a high-level architecture of M2M system that consists of a *device and gateway domain*, and a *network domain* [11].

The device and the gateway domain consist of M2M devices, M2M gateways and an M2M area network. Every M2M device runs its own M2M Device

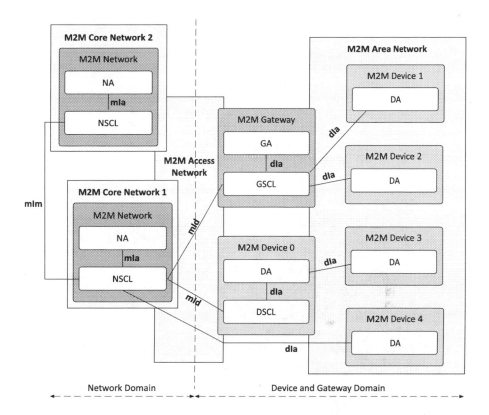

Fig. 1. High-level architecture of M2M system (adapted from [11])

Applications (DA), using M2M Device Service Capabilities Layer (DSCL), while every M2M gateway runs M2M Gateway Applications (GA) using M2M Gateway Service Capabilities Layer (GSCL). Finally, M2M area network provides connectivity based on personal or local area network technologies (e.g. Zigbee, Bluetooth, WI-FI) between M2M devices and M2M gateways.

The network domain consists of M2M access network, M2M Network Applications (NA), M2M network management functions and M2M management functions.M2M access network allows M2M devices and gateways to communicate with the core network that enables interconnection with other networks, provides IP connectivity or other connectivity options, service and control functions, and roaming. M2M Network Service Capabilities Layer (NSCL) provides M2M functions that are shared by different M2M NA that run the service logic and use the M2M available service capabilities via open interfaces. M2M network management functions encompass all the functions (e.g. provisioning, supervision, and fault management) required to manage access and core networks, while M2M management functions encompass all the functions (e.g. M2M service bootstrap function), used to facilitate the bootstrapping of permanent M2M service layer security credentials), required to manage M2M service capabilities in the network domain.

Each M2M domain has its own service capability layers: Network SCL, Gateway SCL, and Device SCL providing functions exposed on the mIa, dIa, mId, and mIm reference points [12].

- The mIa reference point enables an NA access to the M2M service capabilities in the network domain. It supports an option for NA to register to the NSCL, to subscribe for notifications for specific events, with a proper authorization to read or write information in N/G/DSCLs, and to conduct device management actions.
- The dIa reference point enables a DA, residing in an M2M device, the access to different M2M service capabilities in the same M2M device or in an M2M gateway. Moreover, this reference point enables a GA residing in an M2M gateway to access the different M2M service capabilities in the same M2M gateway, and supports the ability of DA/GA to register to the GSCL or DA to register to the DSCL. Through this reference point, DA and GA should also be able, with a proper authorization, to read or write information in N/G/DSCLs.
- The mId reference point enables an M2M SCL residing in an M2M device or an M2M gateway to communicate with the M2M SCL in the network domain and vice versa. It supports the ability of G/DSCLs to register to the NSCL. It should also give support for information exchange between N/G/DSCLs, subscription to specific events, device management, and provide security related features.
- Finally, the mIm reference point extends the reachability of services offered over mId reference point. It is an inter-domain reference point, used for communication between NSCLs of different M2M service providers, which relies on the public core network connectivity functions.

3   IP Multimedia Subsystem

IP Multimedia Subsystem, IMS is a standardized architecture, originally designed to enable the creation of value added services like HD voice, VoLTE, video communication, HD video conferencing, PSTN transformation and multimedia communication. As shown in Fig. 2 IMS has a layered architecture, which separates functionality into three layers – an application layer, a control layer and a connectivity layer [2].

The application layer consists of: applications, content servers with the purpose to execute value added services to the end user. The control layer consists of network control servers, which are in charge of call or session setup, modification and release. The control servers may also handle functions like security, charging and inter-working towards external networks on a control plane level. The connectivity layer consists of routers, switches, media gateways and other user plane elements. The routers and switches provide transport capabilities for both control plane and user plane traffic. The media gateways provide different kinds of inter-working on a user plane level, including inter-working between

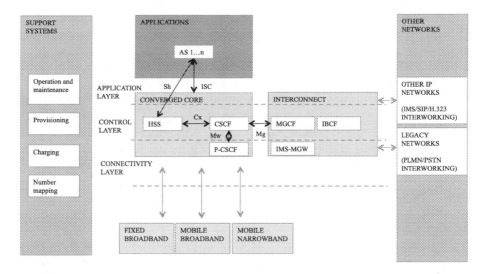

Fig. 2. IMS layered architecture with main interfaces

different transmission technologies and inter-working between different media formats [5]. The supporting functions encompasses functions for: operation and management, network and self-provisioning, Domain Name System/Telephone Number Mapping functionality, etc. A brief description of main functionalities used in our use case that are included in IMS is given below.

The Call Session Control Function (CSCF) is an essential node in IMS for processing signaling, using SIP as the signaling protocol [3]. It also provides support for Internet protocols. The CSCF handles session establishment, modification and release of IP multimedia sessions using the SIP/SDP protocol suite. The CSCF can act as Proxy CSCF (P-CSCF), Serving CSCF (S-CSCF) or Interrogating CSCF (I-CSCF).

I-CSCF is the contact point inside an operator's network for all SIP requests destined to a user of that network operator. It locates the S-CSCF that was assigned to the user at registration through interaction with HSS.

S-CSCF performs session control services for the endpoint. This includes routing of originating requests to the terminating network and routing of terminating requests to the P-CSCF. The S-CSCF supports establishment, modification and release of IP multimedia sessions using the SIP/SDP protocol suite. The S-CSCF also decides whether an application server is required to receive information related to an incoming SIP request outside a dialog to ensure appropriate service handling. The decision at the S-CSCF is based on trigger information received from the HSS, as an initial filter criteria. The trigger information includes identifiers of the application server(s). The trigger information can then provide indirect service invocation through an ISC interface towards the Applications layer.

P-CSCF handles User-to-Network Interface (UNI) interactions and is the first point of contact within the IMS network for the User Equipment (UE). The P-CSCF address is discovered by the UE using a P-CSCF discovery mechanism. The P-CSCF forwards the SIP messages received from the UE to an I-CSCF or S-CSCF (and vice versa). P-CSCF keeps track of UE registration information (like UE contact information and S-CSCF address) and active call sessions. The Session Boarder Gateway in the P-CSCF role performs correlation and tunneling of signaling and media sessions across the interface between the IMS core network and the access network towards SIP clients.

The Home Subscriber Server (HSS), is a master user database that supports the IMS network entities that actually handle calls. It contains the subscription-related information (subscriber profiles), performs authentication and authorization of the user, and can provide information about the subscriber's location and IP information.

Application Server (AS) is a Session Initiation Protocol (SIP) application server that provides real time peer-to-peer communication services. IMS enables M2M servers to be realized as specific ASs and M2M devices, which host an IMS client, that can be controlled by and participate in IMS dialogs.

4   Interworking Between M2M and IMS

IMS system and M2M system can co-exist without any direct connection, or they can interwork on different levels when they can benefit one from another with reusing functionalities (e.g. M2M authentication, authorization uses mechanisms in IMS) that enhance a service or help achieve a complex service (IMS service uses data from M2M devices). One example is when the IMS service uses data from an M2M system in order to provide better service, e.g. getting the context from M2M [14] and from that context service adapt its' behaviour. Another example, that is given in this paper, is when M2M application triggers IMS service and uses IMS as mobility layer for M2M device. The two ways of IMS and M2M system interworking are shown as in Figs. 3 and 4.

As already described in Sect. 2, M2M device connects directly or via M2M gateway to an M2M network. Both figures show that M2M application is a part of an M2M network (NA). SIP application is integrated in NA, and in that way IMS and M2M are interworking in the network layer. In the IMS system, in order to access to IP Multimedia services, the IMS user agent (IMS UA) must first register in IMS. After the IMS UA registers and authenticates in IMS network, multimedia sessions can be routed to some other IMS UA. Interworking between IMS and M2M in the M2M area network can be achieved by collocating M2M application and IMS user agent while connecting both to M2M network and IMS core network.

In Fig. 3, the device application (DA) in the device contains the IMS UA and the device is a part of IMS and M2M system. However, in Fig. 4 M2M gateway contains the gateway application (GA) that contains IMS UA, and in this case M2M gateway is a part of IMS and M2M. M2M device capabilities determine

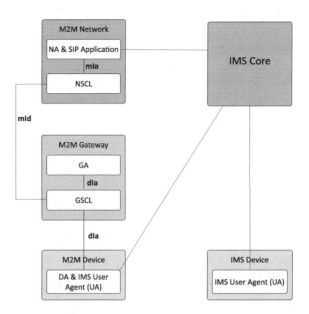

Fig. 3. IMS system and M2M system device interworking

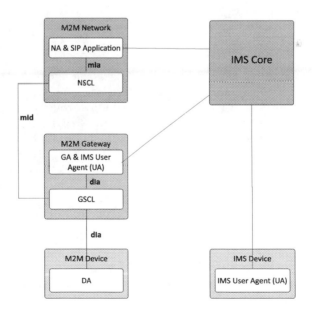

Fig. 4. IMS system and M2M system gateway interworking

which case is used. If M2M device is not capable of running software with IMS UA then the M2M gateway needs to do that.

An example shows the advantage of IMS and M2M interworking is when M2M service re-uses mechanisms from an IMS system to achieve the desired quality of M2M service, as opposed to the solutions based on best effort connectivity. When to trigger the IMS service is based on some criteria. For a certain service, it may be enough to stay within the M2M domain, while for some other service, after the specific criteria is met, the service is routed via IMS network. The triggering criteria we researched in this paper is for streaming (multimedia) services. In M2M system there is no support defined for streaming services, thus IMS is ideal for achieving the complex M2M service where multimedia communication is needed.

5   Related Work

In [8] the authors introduced a new Universal Communications Framework (UCF), which is a generic middleware solution that intermediates between underlying network infrastructure and various application functions, such as mobile Machine-to-Machine (M2M) communication. In this case, UFC is between M2M application and IMS core. Their generic M2M communication platform that is based on IMS technology is OpenMTC [7]. An OpenMTC platform is a prototype implementation of an M2M middleware, aiming to provide a standard-compliant platform for M2M services. It has been designed to act as a horizontal convergence layer supporting multiple vertical application domains, which may be deployed independently, or as a part of a common platform. They designed a reference use case for smart home application, where the user gets the possibility to configure the system for various purposes, such as home automation, security and energy consumption control. In their energy consumption control scenario, the user will get notifications about the devices that are still switched on, as soon as the user exits in certain user-defined radius from home, and the user client application presents a list of supported actions (e.g. switch off one or more devices).

Our enhancement of previously described scenario is (i) that our approach does not need generic middleware and (ii) that IMS is triggered only when certain criteria is met. In this case, IMS resources are optimized since the traffic is routed through IMS network in only some cases, while for the other cases it stays in M2M domain.

In [13] the authors use IMS as a basic network infrastructure for exchanging M2M data. They introduced M2M gateway in the M2M domain and that gateway is communicating with IMS core. All communication is directed over IMS core. On the other side (application domain) there is an M2M AS (application server) which communicates over IMS core with an M2M gateway. This approach is similar to the proposed approach in this paper and the difference is that in the proposed approach herein, the communication goes over M2M and IMS network, depending whether the QoS is needed or not.

In [15], the authors researched similar concept to the one described in this paper. They also considered IMS as possible solution for establishing a cost-efficient and inter-active video connections between the dorbell and a user's mobile terminal. The paper focuses mainly on different IMS standardized mechanisms like presence, supplementary subscriber services or policy control to realize the service that works in dependence to various conditions. For example, mixture of three different IMS subscriber services: call forwarding conditional, presence and call notification, were used to route incoming video calls to different users (house residents) on different locations (home or abroad) under different conditions (busy on meeting or free). In their case, IMS is triggered every time and IMS supplementary services were used to make the services more flexible. In our paper, we researched one scenario when users are at home and when there is no need to trigger IMS and no need to consume IMS resources while second scenario when the user are not at home M2M system used IMS to establish a video call which is not possible with the research in [15].

6   Use Case

A use case for interworking between M2M and IMS would be smart home application for home security: User has an intercom camera/speaker/mic with bell button installed at the front door, intercom terminal and alarm inside the home indicating when user is at home or not. When user is at home (alarm is off) and somebody is at the door, the user at home on the intercom terminal sees via the intercom camera who is the person at the door and can talk to the person and/or open the door. This part is achieved as pure M2M service - video service (see Fig. 5). The nodes in M2M system are communicating with HTTP protocol. The M2M device, terminal at the door, sends a messsage to M2M gateway that the door bell button is pushed. The M2M application in M2M gateway is responsible for logic and it communicates with M2M intercom terminal inside the home. The M2M device inside the home plays a sound. If a user at home pushes the answer button on M2M device (intercom terminal) inside the home, the video session starts between M2M devices (dotted arrow in Fig. 5). That session is executed in the local network and does not need to use IMS.

When the user is out of home, complex M2M service using the IMS system is triggered with SIP protocol (see Fig. 6). When the IMS User Agent application (UAA) at home indicates that there is nobody at home (alarm is off), it triggers registering IMS user agent (UA) in M2M gateway. The IMS UA, inside UAA, gets registered and authenticated in IMS system. The whole process is described as follows (Fig. 7) [2]:

1 Alarm application updates (UPDATE) GSCL data that alarm is turned on.
2 GSCL accepts update and respond with STATUS-OK.
3 GSCL notifies IMS User Agent Application (UAA), which is subscribed to alarm status data, that alarm is on.

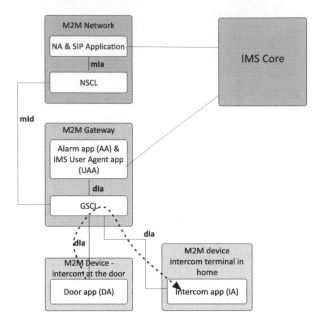

Fig. 5. M2M service – video service

4 UAA accepts data.
5 UAA (UE-A – user equipment A) initiates registration and sends a SIP
  REGISTER towards the user's home network domain (Request URI pre-
  configured in the UE). The REGISTER includes the user's public address
  to be registered as well as their private address and the IP address of
  the UE. The REGISTER is routed to a P-CSCF using a proxy address
  that is pre-configured in the UE.
6 The P-CSCF stores the UE-A contact (IP) address, before it adds a Path
  header to the REGISTER and proxies it to an I-CSCF by inserting a
  Route header. The Route-header is composed using the received Request
  URI of the REGISTER and a locally configured prefix. The Path header
  contains a P-CSCF-URI to inform the S-CSCF where to route future
  terminating requests for the user.
7 The I-CSCF sends a Cx USER AUTHORISATION REQUEST (Diameter) containing the user's private and public address to the HSS (address
  determined using locally configured data).
8 The HSS returns the required S-CSCF capabilities to the I-CSCF.
9 Based on the received information (and locally configured data), the
  I-CSCF selects the S-CSCF and forwards the REGISTER to the selected
  S-CSCF by inserting the S-CSCF URI in a Route-header. The S-CSCF
  stores the contents of the REGISTER Path header (the P CSCF address;
  to be used for routing terminated requests towards this public address)
  and the UE-A IP address (received in REGISTER Contact header).

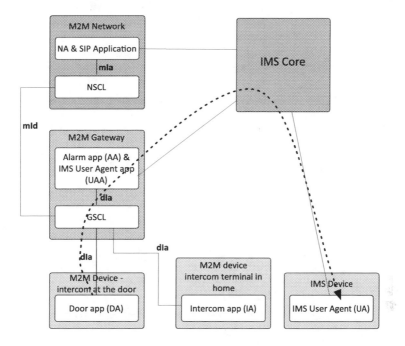

Fig. 6. M2M to IMS video service

10 The S-CSCF requests an Authentication Vector (AV) from the HSS to be used to challenge the user as part of the authentication procedure. The Cx MULTIMEDIA AUTHENTICATION REQUEST (MAR) contains the public and private user address, as well as the selected S-CSCF address.

11 The HSS stores the S-CSCF address and returns an AV (including nonce value) in the Cx MULTIMEDIA AUTHENTICATION ANSWER (MAA).

12–14 The S-CSCF invokes an Authentication Challenge by returning 401 UNAUHORISED towards the UE-A. The WWW-Authenticate header of the message includes the nonce.

15 Based on the received information, the UE computes the response and returns this value as well as the nonce in a new REGISTER request sent to the P-CSCF.

16 The P-CSCF proxies the REGISTER to the selected I-CSCF.

17 The I-CSCF sends a Cx USER AUTHORISATION REQUEST (UAR) (Diameter) containing the user's private and public address to HSS.

18 The HSS returns (UAA) the S-CSCF URI that was previously received from the S-CSCF (6).

19 The REGISTER request is forwarded from the I-CSCF to the S-CSCF.

20 The S-CSCF Sends the Server Assignment Request to HSS to notify that it is serving the user and to request user data.

21 The HSS sends the Server Assignment Answer to S-CSCF. HSS stores the name of the S-CSCF and provides the user data to the S-CSCF.

114   V. Cackovic et al.

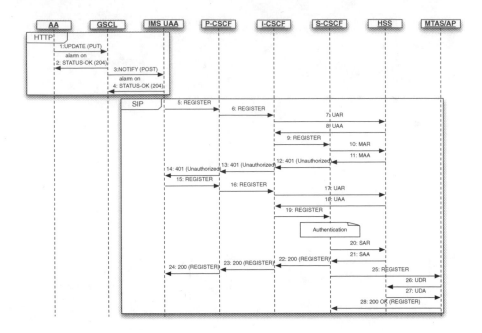

Fig. 7. Triggering IMS UA registration

22–24 The S-CSCF sends a 200 OK response to the UE indicating that the registration was successful.
25 Register request is sent from S-CSCF towards Application Server (MTAS/ AP) for third party registration.
26 Application Server (MTAS/AP) further sends a User data request to the HSS for retrieving the subscriber related data for telephony and supplementary services.
27 HSS sends a User Data Answer towards Application Server (MTAS/AP) containing user data details for supplementary and telephony services.
28 Application Server sends the 200 OK towards S-CSCF after successful 3rd Party Registration.

When somebody is at the door and rings the bell, door application (DA) sends message to M2M gateway (GSCL) which starts the multimedia session from intercom application (IA) to the user's mobile phone or any other IMS UA that is defined in the application (see Fig. 8). The user is alerted that somebody is at the door by an incoming call. The user can pick up the multimedia call on the mobile phone that is running IMS client and talk to the person at the door like he or she is at home (see Fig. 6). The multimedia session establishment is comprised by the following steps [1]:

1 Door application updates (UPDATE) GSCL data that door bell is ringing.

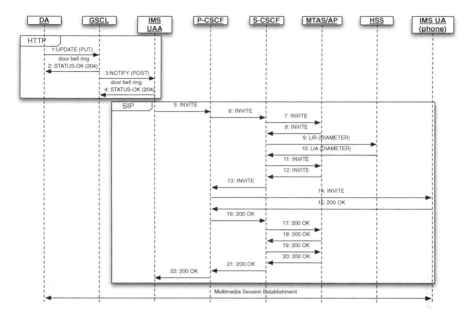

Fig. 8. Multimedia session establishment

2 GSCL accepts update and respond with STATUS-OK.

3 GSCL notifies IMS User Agent Application (UAA), which is subscribed to door bell status data, that door bell is ringing.

4 UAA accepts data.

5–6 The UAA on gateway initiates a SIP-INIVITE request with SDP Offer [4,6] towards S-CSCF (A) via P-CSCF keeping UE-B IP Address in Request URI to establish the session.

7–8 Based on initial filter criteria (IFC) configured in S-CSCF (A) for the originating services of UE-A, the S-CSCF (A) sends the INVITE request towards the application server (MTAS) to invoke telephony services. MTAS initiates a new INVITE request with a CALL-ID towards S-CSCF (A).

9–10 Based on the UE-B IP in Request URI within INVITE message, S-CSCF sends the Location Information Request towards HSS requesting the S-CSCF details for UE-B. HSS acknowledges the request by providing the IP address of the S-CSCF serving UE-B.

11–12 Based on IFC's configured in S-CSCF (B) for the terminating services of UE-B, the S-CSCF (B) sends the INVITE request towards MTAS to invoke telephony services. MTAS initiates a new INVITE request with a CALL-ID towards S-CSCF (B).

13–14 S-CSCF sends the INVITE request towards UE-B via P-SCSF to establish the session.

15–16 UE-B acknowledges the request by sending 200 OK towards S-CSCF (B) via P-CSCF including the SDP Answer.

17–20 S-CSCF (B) sends 200 OK towards MTAS (B) and S-CSCF (A) towards MTAS (A).

21–22 S-CSCF (A) sends 200 OK towards UE-A (UAA) with acknowledgement after which the session is established over RTP between UE(A)-BGF(A)-BGF(B)-UE(B).

This is example of complex M2M service that uses IMS infrastructure for providing M2M service.

7   Conclusion

This paper analizes the current state of the standards in the area of M2M and IMS. Interworking betweeen M2M system and IMS is introduced and compared with the related work. Currently, only few papers consider interworking between the two and all of them introduce new nodes in the network. The proposed solution from this paper does not include new nodes, but the existing nodes need to extend their functionality. The proposed solution is better because if M2M communication does not benefit from IMS, it will not use it. However, if IMS can provide some extra functionality that is not in the M2M system, then it can use IMS. The paper shows this in the case of home security area.

The future work will include implementation of different cases (including this one) and further research on interworking and using IMS and its quality of service for streaming other media (not audio and video) such as continuous critical measurements (e.g. M2M applications in medicine).

References

1. 3GPP TS 23.218 - IP Multimedia (IM) session handling. http://www.3gpp.org/DynaReport/23218.htm. Accessed July 2014
2. 3GPP TS 23.228 - IP Multimedia Subsystem (IMS). http://www.3gpp.org/DynaReport/23228.htm. Accessed July 2014
3. IEFT, RFC 3261 - SIP: Session Initiation Protocol. http://www.ietf.org/rfc/rfc3261.txt. Accessed July 2014
4. IEFT, RFC 3264 - An Offer/Answer Model with Session Description Protocol (SDP). http://www.ietf.org/rfc/rfc3264.txt. Accessed July 2014
5. IEFT, RFC 4240 - Basic Network Media Services with SIP. http://tools.ietf.org/html/rfc4240. Accessed July 2014
6. IEFT, RFC 4566 - SDP: Session Description Protocol. http://www.ietf.org/rfc/rfc4566.txt. Accessed July 2014
7. OpenMTC. http://www.open-mtc.org/index.html. Accessed May 2014
8. Blum, N., Fiedler, J., Lange, L., Magedanz, T.: Application-driven quality of service for M2M communications. In: 2011 15th International Conference on Intelligence in Next Generation Networks (ICIN), pp. 41–45, October 2011
9. Boswarthick, D., Hersent, O., Elloumi, O.: M2M Communications: A Systems Approach. Wiley-Blackwell, Oxford (2012)
10. Camarillo, G., Garcia-Martin, M.A.: The 3G IP Multimedia Subsystem (IMS): Merging the Internet and the Cellular Worlds. Wiley, Chichester (2007)

11. ETSI: TS 102 690 M2M Functional Architecture (2011)
12. ETSI: TS 102 921 mIa, dIa and mId Interfaces (2012)
13. Padilla, J.E.V., Lee, J.O., Kim, J.H.: A M2M horizontal services platform implementation over IP multimedia subsystem (IMS). In: 2013 15th Asia-Pacific Network Operations and Management Symposium (APNOMS), pp. 1–3 (2013)
14. Pinto, F.C., Videira, A., Dinis, M.D.: Context as an IMS service. In: International Conference on Mobile Services, Resources, and Users (MOBILITY 2011), pp. 58–62, October 2011
15. Taleb, T., Kunz, A., Schmid, S., Bottazzi, D.: Call-handling by an IMS-HNB based interactive edoorbell. In: Wireless Communications and Networking Conference (WCNC), 2010 IEEE, pp. 1–6, April 2010

mjCoAP: An Open-Source Lightweight Java CoAP Library for Internet of Things Applications

Simone Cirani[✉], Marco Picone, and Luca Veltri

Department of Information Engineering, University of Parma,
Viale G.P. Usberti, 181/A, 43124 Parma, Italy
{simone.cirani,marco.picone,luca.veltri}@unipr.it

Abstract. The Internet of Things (IoT) is expected to pervasively interconnect more than 50 billion devices, denoted as *"smart objects"*, by 2020 in an Internet-like structure, which will extend the current Internet, enabling new forms of interaction between physical objects and people. The IoT will be made up of heterogeneous devices, featuring extremely diverse capabilities, in terms of computational power, connectivity, availability, and mobility. In such a scenario, characterized by the heterogeneity and large number of involved devices, in order to effectively allow and foster the growth of new applications and services, it is necessary to provide appropriate standards that can guarantee full interoperability among existing hosts and IoT nodes. Standardization organizations, such as the Internet Engineering Task Force (IETF), and research projects are chartered to bring IP to smart objects and to define suitable application-layer and security protocols for IoT scenarios. In order to cope with the limitations of smart objects, the IETF CoRE Working Group has defined the Constrained Application Protocol (CoAP), a standard application-layer protocol for use with constrained nodes and constrained networks. In this work, we present *mjCoAP*, an open source lightweight Java-based implementation of CoAP, which aims at simplifying the development of CoAP-based IoT applications. The mjCoAP library is fully RFC-compliant and integrates several IETF CoRE WG specifications, such as blockwise transfers, resource observing, and HTTP/CoAP mapping. We also present some application scenarios and we describe how they can be easily implemented based on mjCoAP.

Keywords: Internet of Things · CoAP · Application-layer protocols · Interoperability · Standardization

1   Introduction

The Internet of Things (IoT) refers to a global network of networks comprising billions of heterogeneous devices, denoted as *"smart objects"* or *"things."* Smart objects are constrained devices, characterized by limited computational power and available memory, typically battery-powered and equipped with a radio

© Springer International Publishing Switzerland 2015
I. Podnar Žarko et al. (Eds.): FP7 OpenIoT Project Workshop 2014, LNCS 9001, pp. 118–133, 2015.
DOI: 10.1007/978-3-319-16546-2_10

interface and sensors/actuators. The limitations of smart objects are not just hardware-related. In order to achieve energy efficiency, communication protocols and operating systems/software must be properly designed and implemented in order to minimize energy consumption. Smart objects operate in low-power and lossy networks (LLNs), which make use of wireless communication protocols, such as IEEE 802.15.4.

The Internet Protocol (IP) has been envisaged to be the true enabler for a global IoT. An IP-based IoT would seamlessly integrate and interact with the traditional Internet, forming the so-called *"extended Internet."* As billions of smart objects are expected to be deployed and due to IPv4 address depletion, IPv6 has been identified as the perfect candidate to be the *lingua franca* of the IoT.

Due to the diverse nature of devices, in order to guarantee true and effective interoperability, standard communication protocols must be adopted, based on the IP stack. Bringing IP to smart objects has been and still is the focus of many standardization organizations, such as the Internet Engineering Task Force (IETF) and the International Telecommunication Union Telecommunication Standardization Bureau (ITU-T), and research projects, such as the FP7 EU project CALIPSO [1].

The IETF Constrained RESTful Environments (CoRE) [2] Working Group is chartered to provide a framework for resource-oriented applications running on constrained IP networks. The Constrained Application Protocol (CoAP) [3] has been designed to be standard application-layer protocol for bringing the REpresentational State Transfer (REST) [4] paradigm, originally conceived for HTTP-based applications [5], to constrained IoT applications. CoAP is an UDP-based lightweight binary protocol based on a request/response communication model, which maps to HTTP for integration with the Web. CoAP meets constrained application requirements, such as very low overhead and supports multicast communications. Depending on the specific scenario, other application-layer protocols may be considered for IoT applications. Indeed, there are two paradigms that can be adopted for communication between application: (i) request/response (polling) and (ii) publish/subscribe (push-based). In the former, a client node explicitly requests some information to a server node, which replies with the requested information. In the latter, a node publishes content, which is subsequently delivered to one or more subscribers, through a broker or directly. CoAP and HTTP implement a polling model, while other protocols such as MQTT [6] and AMQP [7] implement a push-based communication model. CoAP also supports resource observation, through a specifically designed option, which allows a client node to request a resource and receive notifications upon resource state changes in subsequent responses. The FP7 EU project IoT6 [8] aims at overcoming the fragmentation of IoT by exploiting standard communication protocols (6LoWPAN, CoAP).

Other interoperability efforts are being currently investigated, such as the possibility to provide application frameworks for the management of IoT data. The FP7 EU project OpenIoT [9] is chartered to provide an open source middleware for getting information from sensor clouds, i.e., a platform for "Sensing-as-a-Service."

As the IoT is characterized by an enormous-scale interconnection of heterogeneous devices operating in highly dynamic environments, the adoption of standard communication protocols and open-source development platforms and tools (e.g., operating systems and software libraries) can foster the widespread adoption of IoT-based Smart-X applications. For these reasons, in this work we present *mjCoAP*, an open-source lightweight Java implementation of CoAP. With respect to other state-of-the-art implementations, the mjCoAP library features a small footprint and is compatible with any Java-enabled devices running either J2SE, J2EE, J2ME/Embedded Java platforms, thus making it suited to being used on a wide range of devices.

The rest of this work is organized as follows. Section 2 discusses the details of the CoAP protocol and some of its extensions. In Sect. 3, an overview of CoAP implementations is presented. In Sect. 4, we present the architecture and details of the mjCoAP library. Section 5 presents some application scenarios based on mjCoAP. Finally, in Sect. 7, we draw our conclusions.

2   Constrained Application Protocol

In order to deal with packet loss and subsequent retransmissions, applications running in constrained environments, such as LLNs, should send the fewest amount of data and application-layer protocols should introduce as little overhead as possible. Application-layer protocols should be designed by taking into account the requirements of low overhead deriving from lower layers. CoAP is a standard application-level protocol for bringing the RESTful paradigm into constrained applications. CoAP is a lightweight binary protocol that can be mapped easily to HTTP and therefore it can integrate with the Web. Moreover, CoAP meets several constrained application requirements, enhancing the capabilities of HTTP, by supporting multicast communications, resource observing, and service discovery. CoAP uses binary messages, which are used to embed mandatory fields (Version, Type, Token, Code, Message-ID) and optional fields (CoAP Options and Payload), designed to keep their size as small as possible. The semantics of CoAP requests and responses are carried in the messages. Similarly to HTTP headers, a CoAP message can contain additional information embedded in specific "*options*," which can be used to better instruct the endpoint of the communication of how to process the message.

2.1   CoAP Messaging

CoAP implements a request/response (client/server) communication model on top of UDP. The use of UDP instead of TCP has several reasons: (i) it is a small-overhead transport protocol introducing only an 8-byte header; (ii) it does not require a connection to be setup between the endpoints of communication;

and (iii) it is compatible with duty-cycled devices, which sleep for consistent periods of time and, therefore, might not keep a connection alive.

UDP provides a low-overhead transport for CoAP messages, making it more suited to communication between constrained devices. However, the lightweight nature of UDP introduces some limitations (which are intrinsically managed by TCP instead) that must be addressed at the application layer, such as reliability (retransmission) and request/response matching. CoAP messages (either requests or responses) can be marked as Confirmable (CON) or Non-confirmable (NON). Reliable communication is achieved by using CON messages. When a CON request is sent, the client expects to receive an Acknowledgement (ACK) message from the server (prior to a retransmission timeout with exponential back-off) to confirm the successful delivery of the request. If this does not happen, the client retransmits the request to server. Similarly, when the server sends a response in reply of a CON request, it includes it in a CON message: it expects to receive an ACK message (prior to a retransmission timeout with exponential back-off) to confirm the successful delivery of the response. Should not this happen, the server retransmits the response to server. A reliable transaction is therefore achieved by a three-message transaction, consisting of an initial CON request, a server ACK, and a client ACK. NON messages are used for unreliable transmissions, that is, for requests and responses that must not have guaranteed delivery. The response to a NON request is returned in a NON message.

When a CON request is sent, the server can respond with two different responses.

– **piggy-backed response**, if the server can respond immediately, the server includes the response in the ACK message that acknowledges the request;
– **separate response**, if the server is unable to response immediately, the server sends the ACK message that acknowledges the request immediately and sends the response later in a CON message.

CoAP communications are secured using DTLS [10], similarly to HTTP with TLS [11].

2.2   Proxying

CoAP has been designed to easily map to HTTP in order to provide a transparent integration with the Web. A *"cross-proxy"* is a network element that provides protocol translation functionalities, in order to allow the integration between HTTP and CoAP endpoints. Cross-proxies are crucial elements to guarantee maximum interoperability between the Internet and the Internet of Things and represent the contact point between them. The use of proxies can also have other advantages, such as the possibility to hide the details of the constrained network to external clients and to shield constrained nodes from being directly accessible by Internet hosts (for instance, by providing caching), in order to achieve better security (e.g., from DoS attacks) and minimize energy consumption (by preventing too many requests from being sent to constrained nodes). HTTP clients can interact with CoAP servers through the mediation of "*HTTP-to-CoAP proxies*", which map HTTP requests to CoAP requests and CoAP responses to HTTP responses. Rules for HTTP-to-CoAP mapping are being defined in a specialized draft [12].

2.3 CoAP Extensions

Besides the CoAP specification, the IETF CoRE WG is also defining additional drafts in order to address some issues that CoAP does not take into account.

The Block Option [13] is introduced to allow the transmission of payloads of arbitrary size. In fact, the use of UDP introduces a restriction on the maximum size of the payload that can be sent within a CoAP message. Moreover, since CoAP is intended to be used by constrained devices, it might happen that the endpoints of communication do not have enough resources to handle payloads of certain sizes. This option is therefore used to split payloads into chunks, which are going to be sent in sequence of messages, each carrying a single chunk. The Block Option draft provides mechanisms so that a client and a server are able to negotiate the chunk size, according to their capabilities.

The Observe Option [14] has been designed to allow resources to be observed. Observing resources introduces a new communication model, which differs from the traditional request/response (polling). When a client is willing to observe a resource, it sends a GET request for a given resource and includes an Observe option. The server sends a response with the requested resource and registers the client as subscribed to receive notifications upon changes of the resource state. When the state of the observed resource changes, the server sends a new response with the updated resource. Therefore, a single request can result in more than one response being received by the client, thus implementing a publish/subscribe communication model.

The Resource Directory (RD) [15] hosts descriptions of resources held on other servers, allowing lookups to be performed for those resources. The draft describes the interfaces to register, maintain, lookup and remove resources descriptions. A RD can used by applications as a means to discover services and resources in a standardized way, based on Web Linking [16,17], allowing applications to discover resources dynamically. The RD is reachable in a standard and uniform way by accessing the `/.well-known/core` URI.

3 Related Work

The RESTful architectural style has been conceived to web (HTTP-based) applications, in order to provide a set of rules intended to promote software longevity and independent evolution, by minimizing interdependence between client and server applications. RESTful applications are therefore intrinsically resilient to changes that might occur over time. Such an approach is particularly suitable for IoT and Machine-to-Machine (M2M) applications, since these kinds of systems comprise nodes that might be deployed to unattended locations and require long-term operation (e.g., Smart Parking applications require smart objects to be deployed inside the asphalt and stay active for many years). CoAP has been designed specifically to meet constrained application requirements, such as low overhead and multicast support, while preserving a RESTful approach to application development. Service discovery mechanisms, based on Web Linking, have also been defined to be used with CoAP. Through service discovery, resources can be dynamically discovered and accessed, thus enabling application to be self-configuring and self-managing, so that they can operate already at start-up.

Some CoAP implementations, both open-source and commercial, already exist in literature supporting different programming languages and operating systems and versions/features of the protocol. Table 1 shows a list of available CoAP implementations, with their corresponding programming language, supported protocol version, and supported features.

Table 1. List of available CoAP implementations and comparison with mjCoAP.

Library	Programming language	CoAP version	Resource observing	Blockwise transfer
libcoap	C	RFC 7252	✓	✓
Californium	Java	RFC 7252	✓	✓
Erbium	C	RFC 7252	✓	✓
nCoAP	Java	RFC 7252	✓	×
mjCoAP	Java	RFC 7252	✓	✓

Californium (Cf) [18] is an open-source implementation of the Constrained Application Protocol. Californium is a full-featured library composed by several sub libraries dedicated to the implementation of all details of the protocol and its extensions, as well as support for secure CoAP, through DTLS, in the Scandium (Sc) project. It has been selected as part of the Eclipse IoT project, aiming at enabling the creation of extensible services and frameworks for developing IoT applications on top of open APIs. Californium is a rich resource-oriented library: it comprises a great amount of APIs for interacting with CoAP resources in a standardized and uniform way.

nCoAP[1] is a Java implementation of the CoAP protocol using the netty non-blocking I/O framework[2]. nCoAP is a more lightweight implementation than Californium, yet it has several dependencies on external libraries to accomplish its tasks.

Constrained operating systems, such as Contiki OS [19] and TinyOS [20], have been designed in order to provide standardized way to interact with the hardware of smart objects, through abstractions such as sockets and threads. The Contiki OS includes a CoAP implementation, named Erbium. Erbium (Er) [21]

---

[1] https://github.com/okleine/nCoAP.
[2] http://netty.io/.

is a low-power REST Engine for Contiki. libCoAP[3] is a C implementation of CoAP that can be used both on constrained devices (running operating systems such as Contiki) and on a larger POSIX system.

On the client-side, CoAP application testing can be performed by using the Copper (Cu) [22] browser extension. Copper can be used to perform custom CoAP requests through a web browser interface, by intercepting requests with the *coap:* scheme.

The use of Java for IoT applications has received much attention lately after the release of the Oracle Java Embedded platform [23]. In fact, Java features several advantages from a programming perspective, such as flexibility, Object-oriented approach, and cross-platform portability. Moreover, Java has an established developer base, which can develop IoT applications while reusing previous experience.

4   The mjCoAP Library

In this section, we describe the CoAP implementation provided by mjCoAP [24]. mjCoAP is a development project that provides a completely open-source Java-based implementation of the standard CoAP protocol as defined by RFC 7252.

The main objective of the mjCoAP project is to provide a powerful and easy to use CoAP library for developing both server-side and client-side CoAP-based IoT applications. For such a reason, the library is at the same time as lightweight as possible, in order to be included and executed in tiny devices, and as rich as possible, in order to provide to the programmer suitable APIs for easily developing powerful server applications (possibly including various CoAP extensions as defined by other RFCs and Internet-Drafts). Hereafter, the list of requirements that the mjCoAP was based on is reported:

1. standard compliant - the mjCoAP should provide a CoAP implementation completely compliant to the current IETF standard RFC and extensions;
2. easy to use - the library should provide a set of APIs that should be as much intuitive as possible, in order to let the programmer to immediately develop CoAP based applications without requiring a particular training phase;
3. lightness - the resulting library should be as simple and compact as possible in order to be easily used and integrated in constrained devices with limited processing and memory resources; the library should feature a very small footprint;
4. Java compatibility - it should be compatible with any Java-enabled devices running either J2SE, J2EE, J2ME/Embedded Java platforms, thus making it suited to being used on a wide range of devices;
5. rich set of functions - the library should at the same time include a rich set of APIs in order to allow the programmer to access both high-level and low-level CoAP functionalities; the idea was to develop a single library that can be used for developing both very small and simple CoAP applications and rich and powerful server-side applications;

---

[3] http://libcoap.sourceforge.net.

6. up-to-date - one of the main intents of the project was to provide a library that could be constantly updated to the current standards, including the various CoAP extensions that will be proposed and defined during the time; the structure of the library was designed in order to enable and to simplify future extensions;
7. re-usability - the same library should be re-usable for the development of other protocols that could be defined in future, and that will share with CoAP the same message structure, syntax, and protocol architecture; an example of such a protocol is the CoSIP (Constrained Session Initiation Protocol), a SIP-like signaling protocol, proposed and used in [25,26] for session setup and session tear-down in constrained IoT scenarios.

In order to satisfy some of the above requirements, we chose Java as programming language for the mjCoAP project, to take advantage of the simplicity and portability of Java-based developments. A porting in C language of the core of the mjCoAP library is also under development in order to fulfill also the requirements of specific devices (for example Arduino boards) that do not support Java programming. In particular a first C porting of mjCoAP has been already provided and tested with Arduino devices.

4.1   mjCoAP Architecture

In order to run within constrained networks (and onto constrained devices), UDP as been chosen as standard transport protocol for CoAP. For such a reason, CoAP must support mechanisms for reliable message transmission over the unreliable transport offered by the UDP. This results in a "layered" architecture of CoAP. This is emphasized in mjCoAP where a layered architecture is explicitly considered and implemented as depicted in Fig. 1. The mjCoAP core is formed by the following three sub-layers:

– *Transaction* - In mjCoAP, a *Transaction* is defined as the request-response basic interaction, which corresponds to exchange of a CoAP request (a *GET*, *POST*, *PUT*, or *DELETE* method) and the corresponding CoAP response (of type 2.xx, 4.xx, or 5.xx). At CoAP client side, the *transaction* layer offers a RESTful service to the user by taking charge of sending a method request and receiving the corresponding response; similarly, at the server side, it provides functions for receiving and processing a method request and for creating and sending the selected response. Possible retransmissions of the same request and/or response are dealt by the transaction layer (through the use of the underlying *Reliable transmission* layer).
– *Reliable transmission* - It is the sublayer that is responsible for dealing with the reliable transmissions of CoAP messages (both requests and responses); when a message is marked as *CON* (i.e., its reception has to be confirmed by the sending of an *ACK* message), the *CON* message can be passed to the *Reliable transmission* layer, which will take care of the transmission, and possibly the retransmission, of the message until a corresponding *ACK* message is received,

or a number of *MAX_RETRANSMIT* retransmissions is reached, according to
the CoAP standard; in both cases the user of the *Reliable transmission* layer
is informed of the result of the transmission, that is whether the message has
been received by the remote entity (confirmed by the *ACK*), or a transmission
failure (transmission timeout) has occurred. Similarly, at the server side, the
Reliable transmission is responsible of receiving and processing *CON* messages
and automatically sending the corresponding *ACK* messages; according to
RFC 7252, both separate and "piggybacked" responses are supported; in the
latter case, the *Reliable transmission* layer is also responsible of sending the
piggybacked responses.
– *Messaging* - It is the sublayer that is responsible for sending and receiving
single CoAP messages, regardless they are requests or responses, *CON*, or
NON, *ACK*, or *RST* messages.

Under the *Messaging* sublayer, there is the standard transport protocol (UDP
or DTLS).

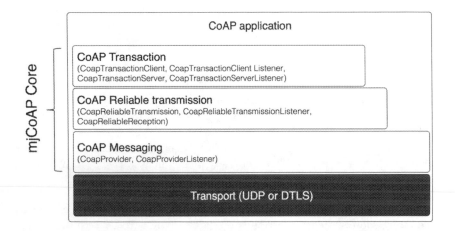

Fig. 1. mjCoAP stack architecture.

The *Transaction* layer is implemented by the mjCoAP classes *CoapTransactionClient* and *CoapTransactionServer*, and the corresponding listening interfaces *CoapTransactionClientListener* and *CoapTransactionServerListener*, used
for intercepting transaction events (e.g. at the client-side, the reception of a
response within a CoAP transaction). The *Reliable transmission* layer is implemented by the classes *CoapReliableTransmission* and *CoapReliableReception*,
and the listener interface *CoapReliableTransmissionListener*. Finally, the *Messaging* layer is implemented by the class *CoapProvider* and the listening interface *CoapProviderListener*. Within the *Messaging* layer, the following classes has
been also defined: (i) *CoapMethodId*; (ii) *CoapTransactionId* and *CoapReliableTransmissionId*, which extend the abstract class *CoapId*, and that are used for

specifying the type of messages that a user of the *Messaging* layer is interested to listen to.

Note that the mjCoAP user is usually expected to interact only with the *Transaction* layer, which is therefore responsible for interacting with all underlying functions and corresponding sub-layers.

In addition to the previously described classes implementing the various CoAP sub-layers, the core mjCoAP also includes classes for dealing with CoAP messages. These classes are: *BasicCoapMessage*, *BasicCoapMessageFactory*, and *CoapOption*.

The listed classes form the core of the mjCoAP stack in a very compact and easy-to-use manner. Note that this core part of mjCoAP implements only the basic CoAP protocol including the message syntax, transmission, reception and request-response interactions, regardless the specific meaning of a request method, a response, and regardless the various possible CoAP header fields (CoAP Options) that form a CoAP message. This part (formed by all previously listed classes an interfaces) forms the core mjCoAP package *org.zoolu.coap.core*.

All other CoAP specific functions, such as header fields, and protocol behavior, are implemented within the additional packages *org.zoolu.coap.message* and *org.zoolu.coap.option*.

The separation between the core of the CoAP protocol and all other specifications has the advantage that possible future CoAP-like protocols (i.e., protocols that might reuse the CoAP message format and the basic protocol architecture) can be easily implemented based on the same mjCoAP core. In [26], we proposed a Constrained Session Initiation Protocol (CoSIP), based on CoAP, that has been also (easily) implemented through the mjCoAP stack, and used to build a P2P overlay [27].

In order to validate mjCoAP, extensive compatibility tests has been carried on interacting with other CoAP implementations. In particular, interoperability tests have been successfully done with Californium [18], Erbium [21], and with Copper [22] libraries.

4.2   Using mjCoAP

In order to provide an efficient and non-blocking behavior (which can be preferable, for instance, in mobile applications), mjCoAP is designed to follow an asynchronous style: methods that imply communication terminate immediately and the result is then notified to the application through *callback* methods. There are two main typical ways to use mjCoAP into a Java application: (i) at the *Transaction* layer and (ii) at the *Messaging* layer. The choice between them depends on the degree of abstraction that best fits the needs of the developer. For instance, the low-level functionalities provided by the *Messaging* layer are best suited to applications that might require simple communication between endpoints. Regardless of the layer that is going to be used for development, the fundamental class that always needs to be present in any mjCoAP application is the *CoapProvider*. The *CoapProvider* is the basic communication enabler that is responsible for sending and receiving CoAP messages over a datagram socket bound to a specific UDP port. An instance of *CoapProvider* can be created by specifying which UDP port to use. This can be made by providing one or no argument: in the former case the provided UDP port number is used (this is the best choice for server-side applications), while in the latter a random available port is used (this is the best choice for client-side applications). An instance of *CoapProvider* can then be bound to one or more instances of *CoapProviderListeners* through the *setListener()* method. The *CoapProviderListener* interface defines just one method (*onReceivedMessage()*), which is called any time the *CoapProvider* receives a message that matches the filtering options that the listener has specified. For instance, a specific listener might be interested in processing only *GET* requests, while another only *POST* requests. In order to send a CoAP message, the *CoapProvider*'s *send()* method can be used.

The simplest and most common way to integrate mjCoAP is to use the high-level APIs provided by the *Transaction* layer, since, at this layer, the library takes care of matching requests with their corresponding response, while also providing reliable transmissions in case of *CON* messages. The *Transaction* layer provides server-side and client-side APIs for managing request-response pairs. In order to create a client-side transaction, a new instance of *CoapTransactionClient* must be created by providing two arguments: the *CoapProvider* object (which will handle the messaging over a datagram socket) and an instance of a *CoapTransactionClientListener* (which is the object which will be notified when the corresponding response will be received). Requests can then be sent with the *request()* method. The listener's *onReceivedResponse()* method will be executed when the corresponding response is received. If the sent request is *CON* and the client does not receive a response, the *onTransactionFailure()* method is called. On the server side, an incoming CoAP message dispatched to a *CoapProviderListener* can be handled by a *CoapTransactionServer*. In order to do so, a new instance of *CoapTransactionServer* must be created by providing three arguments: the *CoapProvider* object (which will handle the messaging over a datagram socket), the received *CoapMessage*, and an instance of a *CoapTransactionServerListener* (which is the object which will be notified in case the response delivery fails – for *CON* messages only). Responses can then be sent with the *respond()* method.

5   CoAP Application Scenarios

The mjCoAP library has been used extensively to build a IoT application for real-time environmental monitoring involving highly heterogeneous devices and connectivity. An illustrative representation of the reference application scenario is shown in Fig. 2. The environmental monitoring application, which was used to sense noise, light, temperature, and humidity, has been setup in order to assess the interoperability of the mjCoAP library and other CoAP implementations, as well as the integration of different networks through the use of IP.

The experimental setup consists in the following hardware: Raspberry Pi, Arduino Yún, Intel Galileo, Zolertia Z1, and Android smartphones. Table 2 shows the list of hardware and software used for the demonstrative IoT application.

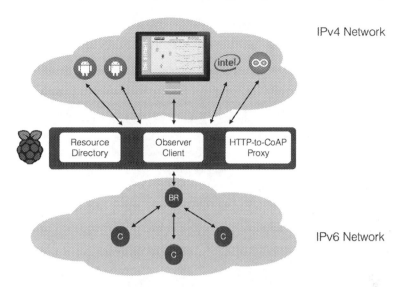

IPv4 Network

IPv6 Network

Fig. 2. A complex IoT application scenario for real-time environmental monitoring based on the mjCoAP library.

The Raspberry Pi is connected to an IPv4 network via IEEE 802.3 and to an IPv6 (6LoWPAN) constrained network using IEEE 802.15.4, acting as 6LoWPAN border router (6LBR), by means of a Zolertia Z1 node connected via USB and running Contiki OS in order to provide a network interface to the 6LoWPAN network.

Table 2. List of hardware and software used for the real-time environmental monitoring IoT application with corresponding connectivity.

Device	Connectivity	Operating system	CoAP implementation
Raspberry Pi	IPv4/IEEE 802.3	Raspbian	mjCoAP
	IPv6/IEEE 802.15.4	Raspbian	Erbium
Arduino Yún	IPv4/IEEE 802.11	OpenWrt-Yún	mjCoAP
Intel Galileo	IPv4/IEEE 802.3	Linux	mjCoAP
Zolertia Z1	IPv6/IEEE 802.15.4	Contiki OS	Erbium

The central element of the architecture is the Raspberry Pi, which is also denoted as *"IoT Gateway"*, as it provides several features that are needed to enable full operativity by all network nodes. The mjCoAP library has been used to develop an HTTP-to-CoAP Cross-Proxy, following the set of rules specified in the HTTP-to-CoAP mapping draft [12]. A RD has also been implemented using mjCoAP. The IoT Gateway runs an HTTP-to-CoAP proxy and a RD, as well as an *observer process* (OBS), which is used to keep track of all the resources that are in the network. The Arduino Yún and Intel Galileo run CoAP servers, also implemented using the mjCoAP library, which provide some observable resources, such as temperature and light sensors. The Zolertia Z1 nodes also run CoAP observable resources (temperature and free-fall detection), implemented using the Erbium library. Finally, one Android application, based on mjCoAP, provides a noise detection service, using the smartphone's microphone.

The OBS registers to the RD's services list resource. When a resource enters the network, the CoAP server sends a POST message to the RD, which in turn notifies the OBS of the change in the network's state. The OBS then registers for updates related to the newly available resource. When a resource changes its state, the OBS receives a notification and uses this information to update the content shown by a Smart Display (SD), which shows the value of the resources being monitered in real-time. The available resources can be also accessed by Android applications, based on mjCoAP. The app can request the list of available resources to the RD and then send requests to the constrained resource either directly, using CoAP, or through the proxy, using HTTP.

The experimentation that we have conducted has shown the absolute interoperability and compatibility among the used CoAP implementations, and proved the easy development of mjCoAP-based applications. Even more importantly, the evaluation that has been setup has highlighted how an IP-based IoT can, in fact, integrate seamlessly with traditional Internet technologies and devices, thanks to the use of standard communication protocols.

6   Performance Evaluation

An experimental benchmark evaluation has been conducted in order to assess the performance of the mjCoAP library. The experimentation involved the evaluation of (i) the response time and (ii) maximum number of processed requests by a mjCoAP-based server. The server runs on a Raspberry Pi device and receives CoAP requests sent by a test client application, implemented for the purpose of stress testing, which can send requests to a target endpoint at a given rate. A comparison with the performance of Californium with the same operational conditions has also been carried out. The results of the experimentation are shown in Fig. 3.

Figure 3(a) shows the number of received responses per second (for a limited arbitrary observation time interval) at different request rates, ranging from 1 request/s to 1000 requests/s. Each experiment consists in a running time of 10 s at a fixed request rate. The graph reports the number of responses received within such a running interval: responses received outside the observation interval are not counted. Both servers are able to handle all incoming requests until they reach a saturation point ($\sim$220 requests/s for mjCoAP and $\sim$240 requests/s for Californium). If the rate of incoming requests surpasses the saturation point, the requests are partly lost and partly delayed of an amount of time which depends on the size of the receiver buffer. Californium's null rate is likely due to

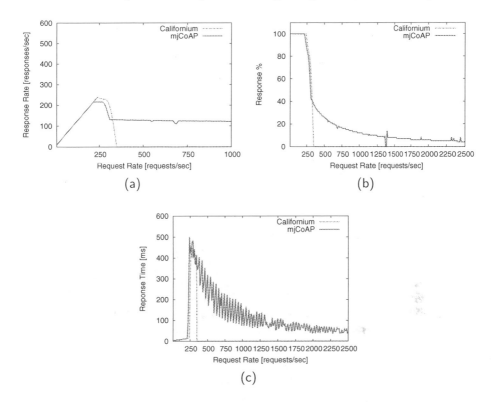

Fig. 3. Performance evaluation results with comparison between mjCoAP and Californium. (a) Number of received responses per second at different request rates. (b) Percentage of responded requests at different request rates. (c) Response time at different request rates.

the size of its internal buffer (which makes it possible to postpone the moment of request serving), which causes the request to be served after the end of the observation time. This does not mean that requests are not served, but that responses are received after the observation timeout and are therefore not counted.

Figure 3(b) shows percentage of responded requests at different request rates, ranging from 1 request/s to 2500 requests/s, and allows to highlight the saturation point. Finally, Fig. 3(c) shows the delay measured by the client between the time of transmission of a request and the time of reception of the corresponding response. In both cases, the delays are low (below ∼14 ms) until reaching the saturation point.

7 Conclusions

In this paper, we have introduced and described a novel lightweight and open-source implementation of the Constrained Application Protocol, called *mjCoAP*. mjCoAP is a standard-compliant Java-based library supporting several IETF

CoRE WG draft-based CoAP extensions, such as blockwise transfer, resource observing, and HTTP/CoAP mapping. The library supports the J2SE, J2EE, J2ME/Embedded Java platforms, thus making it suited to being used on a wide range of devices. mjCoAP is characterized by a layered architecture with the following layers (in ascending abstraction order): Messaging, Reliable transmission, and Transaction. The proposed library is extremely lightweight and can be used for fast development of CoAP-based applications. In order to assess the design goals of interoperability, development simplicity, and code reusability, we have presented a long-running CoAP-based application scenario for real-time environmental monitoring, comprising heterogeneous devices and different CoAP implementations. A performance evaluation of the mjCoAP library has also been presented. The results show that mjCoAP's performance is comparable to that of Californium in terms of average response time and maximum number of concurrent requests that can be handled. In conclusion, mjCoAP provides several interesting and useful features that can make it suited for the development of CoAP-based applications, by achieving the design goals of extreme simplicity and small footprint. Moreover, due to its compatibility with J2ME/Embedded Java platforms and its performance, the design principles and implementation of mjCoAP make it a perfect fit for Java-enabled limited devices (such as smartphones), while Californium is designed for unconstrained devices to be used for developing scalable and high-performance IoT Cloud services.

Acknowledgments. The work of Simone Cirani and Luca Veltri is funded by the European Community's Seventh Framework Programme, area "Internetconnected Objects", under Grant no. 288879, CAL*IP*SO project - Connect All *IP*-based Smart Objects! The work reflects only the authors views; the European Community is not liable for any use that may be made of the information contained herein. The work of Marco Picone is funded by Guglielmo srl, Reggio Emilia (RE), Italy.

References

1. European Community's 7th Framework Programme: CALIPSO - Connect All IP-based Smart Objects. URL http://www.ict-calipso.eu/
2. IETF Constrained RESTful Environments Working Group. http://tools.ietf.org/wg/core/
3. Shelby, Z., Hartke, K., Bormann, C.: The Constrained Application Protocol (CoAP). RFC 7252 (Proposed Standard), June 2014
4. Fielding, R.T.: Architectural styles and the design of network-based software architectures. Ph.D. thesis, University of California, Irvine, AAI9980887 (2000)
5. Fielding, R., Gettys, J., Mogul, J., Frystyk, H., Masinter, L., Leach, P., Berners-Lee, T.: Hypertext Transfer Protocol. HTTP 1.1. RFC 2616 (Draft Standard), June 1999. Obsoleted by RFCs 7230, 7231, 7232, 7233, 7234, 7235, updated by RFCs 2817, 5785, 6266, 6585
6. MQTT: Message Queue Telemetry Transport. http://mqtt.org/
7. Vinoski, S.: Advanced message queuing protocol. IEEE Internet Comput. **10**(6), 87–89 (2006)

8. European Community's 7th Framework Programme: Universal Integration of Internet of Things Through an IPv6-Based Service Oriented Architecture Enabling Heterogeneous Components Interoperability (2011). http://www.iot6.eu/
9. European Community's 7th Framework Programme: OpenIoT: Open Source Cloud Solution for the Internet of Things (2012). http://openiot.eu/
10. Rescorla, E., Modadugu, N.: Datagram Transport Layer Security. RFC 4347 (Proposed Standard), April 2006. Obsoleted by RFC 6347, updated by RFC 5746
11. Dierks, T., Rescorla, E.: The Transport Layer Security (TLS) protocol version 1.1. RFC 4346 (Proposed Standard), April 2006. Obsoleted by RFC 5246, updated by RFCs 4366, 4680, 4681, 5746, 6176
12. Castellani, A., Loreto, S., Rahman, A., Fossati, T.: Guidelines for HTTP-CoAP Mapping Implementations. Internet-Draft draft-ietf-core-http-mapping-04, Internet Engineering Task Force, July 2014
13. Shelby, Z., Bormann, C.: Blockwise transfers in CoAP. Internet-Draft draft-ietf-core-block-15, Internet Engineering Task Force, July 2014, Work in progress
14. Hartke, K.: Observing Resources in CoAP. Internet-Draft draft-ietf-core-observe-14, Internet Engineering Task Force, June 2014
15. Shelby, Z., Bormann, C., Krco, S.: CoRE Resource Directory. Internet-Draft draft-ietf-core-resource-directory-01, Internet Engineering Task Force (Proposed standard), December 2013
16. Nottingham, M.: Web Linking. RFC 5988 (Proposed Standard), October 2010
17. Shelby, Z.: Constrained RESTful Environments (CoRE) Link Format. RFC 6690 (Proposed Standard), August 2012
18. Kovatsch, M., Lanter, M., Shelby, Z.: Californium: Scalable cloud services for the Internet of things with CoAP. In: Proceedings of the 4th International Conference on the Internet of Things (IoT 2014), Cambridge, MA, USA, October 2014
19. The Contiki Operating System. http://www.contiki-os.org
20. TinyOS. http://www.tinyos.net/g
21. Kovatsch, M., Duquennoy, S., Dunkels, A.: A low-power CoAP for Contiki. In: 2011 IEEE 8th International Conference on Mobile Adhoc and Sensor Systems (MASS), pp. 855–860, October 2011
22. Kovatsch, M.: Demo abstract: human CoAP interaction with copper. In: Proceedings of the 7th IEEE International Conference on Distributed Computing in Sensor Systems (DCOSS 2011), Barcelona, Spain, June 2011
23. Oracle: Java Embedded. http://www.oracle.com/technetwork/java/embedded/overview/index.html
24. mjCoAP (2014). http://www.mjcoap.org/
25. Cirani, S., Picone, M., Veltri, L.: CoSIP: a constrained session initiation protocol for the Internet of things. In: Canal, C., Villari, M. (eds.) Advances in Service-Oriented and Cloud Computing. CCIS, vol. 393, pp. 13–24. Springer, Heidelberg (2013)
26. Cirani, S., Picone, M., Veltri, L.: A session initiation protocol for the Internet of things. Scalable Comput. Pract. Exp. **14**(4), 249–263 (2014)
27. Cirani, S., Davoli, L., Picone, M., Veltri, L.: Performance evaluation of a SIP-based constrained peer-to-peer overlay. In: 2014 International Conference on High Performance Computing Simulation (HPCS), pp. 432–435 (2014)

IoT Applications

Addressing Information Processing Needs of Digital Agriculture with OpenIoT Platform

Prem Prakash Jayaraman[1]([✉]), Doug Palmer[1], Arkady Zaslavsky[1], Ali Salehi[1],
and Dimitrios Georgakopoulos[2]

[1] CSIRO Digital Productivity, Canberra 2601, Australia
{prem.jayaraman,doug.palmer,arkady.zaslavsky}@csiro.au
[2] School of Computer Science and Information Technology, RMIT University,
GPO Box 2476, Melbourne 3001, Australia
dimitrios.georgakopoulos@rmit.edu.au

Abstract. Food security is a global challenge and agriculture can address this challenge through radical improvements in productivity, efficiency and effectiveness. Internet of Things (IoT) is a major enabler of such improvements. This paper discusses challenges that agricultural industry is facing and proposes a solution based on IoT technology and a specific platform called OpenIoT developed jointly by the EU FP7 OpenIoT consortium. Phenonet is an OpenIoT use case developed by CSIRO, Australia and demonstrates how digital agriculture benefits from deploying the IoT. Experience and lessons from using OpenIoT middleware for Phenonet development are also presented and analysed.

1 Introduction

Agricultural industry faces many challenges, such as climate change, water shortages, labour shortages due to an ageing urbanized population, and increased societal concern about issues such as animal welfare, food safety, and environmental impact [11]. Quoting from a recent article by IBM [5]. "Agriculture is ultimately driven by the mathematics of science; balancing the pH levels of soil, the rate of Nitrogen depletion and many other factors for optimum growth of grains and produce". The goal is to use information technology to harness the vast amount of data available from the field, equipment sensors and other third-party sources, to provide fact- and math-based decision support to augment farmers experience.

Pervasive and ubiquitous computing have addressed agriculture in different precision agriculture projects. One such example is the use of sensor networks for viticulture [4]. Modern agriculture is a knowledge-intensive industry that thrives on multiple facets of information such as climate, farm/field management, supply chain, consumer demand, environmental impact, livestock management and health etc. According to the United Nations Food and Agriculture Organization

---

Prof. Zaslavsky is a visiting Professor at St. Petersburg National Research University of IT, Mechanics and Optics, Russia.

I. Podnar Žarko et al. (Eds.): FP7 OpenIoT Project Workshop 2014, LNCS 9001, pp. 137–152, 2015.
DOI: 10.1007/978-3-319-16546-2_11

(http://www.fao.org/home/en/), food production must increase by 60 % to be able to feed the growing population expected to hit 9 billion in 2050. The use of technology to advance agricultural in particular precision agriculture approaches are no longer regarded "new" [3]. However, within the Australian context, a number of precision agriculture standards e.g. grid based approaches are not suitable [2]. E.g. the sampling grid size standard in precision agriculture methods is 75 m while for vineyards, the suggested sampling size is 20 m to obtain high resolution crop information.

The recent advancements in technologies more specifically the Internet of Things (IoT) paradigm has paved way to high resolution crop analysis at lesser costs allowing farmers, biologist and plant scientists to capture real-time data from the field which in the past was difficult and expensive [3]. IoT promotes the vision of a globally interconnected continuum of devices, objects and thing. The data produced from IoT devices can greatly aid in making informed real-time decisions that can significantly impact the yield and quality of the produce. For example, good pasture growth is the basis of productivity in gazing operations. It is important to understand the key factors affecting pasture growth when seeking to maximize productivity. Technologies like IoT, broadband connectivity, cloud-computing and smart personal mobile devices can greatly help in understanding the factors that affect pasture growth (e.g. pH levels of soils, rate of Nitrogen depletion) in real-time and share it to the benefit of the community. These emerging technologies have the capacity to transform/digitalise our agricultural practices, markets and the way we produce products. Moreover, by leveraging upon the increasingly important area of Big Data analytic [12] and mobile sensing [6,7,9] further meaningful insights to data can be discovered.

The IoT paradigm has further fuelled the Big Data revolution more specifically in agriculture domain requiring new methods and approaches to process, store, discover and retrieve data. Organisations such as John Deere [1] are currently exploring vendor-based precision farming tools and techniques to meet big data challenges in digital agricultural. A vendor specific approach towards IoT adoption leads to the development of IoT information architecture silos that have very little interoperable capabilities. The key is to develop an open architectures that facilitates open sharing of data securely, promotes data discovery both within and across domains, provides utility-based metrics for usage of data and service-oriented. One of the fundamental challenges faced by an average farmer is the ability to cope with explosion of data. Addressing this challenge requires the development of tools, techniques and interfaces that will allow farmers and other plant biologist and scientist to access relevant data (e.g. outcomes of plant experiments) by discovering, fusing and analysing data from heterogeneous sources such as precision farming equipments and IoT devices using do-it-yourself tools. E.g. an intuitive mobile notification service can be configured and deployed by discovering relevant data required to make a decision on when to irrigate depending on soil condition, nitrogen in the soil, crop growth and climatic condition. In this paper, we present Open Internet of Things (OpenIoT), a open source IoT middleware. We discuss a digital agriculture usecase namely

Phenonet and present our experience in implementing Phenonet on OpenIoT architecture. This paper makes the following contributions:

– A detailed description of a digital agriculture usecase namely Phenonet (enabling high resolution precision agriculture driven by IoT) currently being trialled at CSIRO Australia
– An ontology developed to semantically annotate phenonet sensor data streams
– An architectural description of a middleware for internet of things namely Open Internet of Things (OpenIoT)
– Outcomes of Phenonet usecase implementation on OpenIoT platform

2 Phenonet Usecase

Phenonet describes the network of wireless sensor nodes (IoT devices) collecting information over a field of experimental crops. The term Phenomics describes the study of how the genetic makeup of an organism determines its appearance, function, growth and performance. Plant phenomics is a cross-disciplinary approach, studying the connection from cell to leaf to whole plant and from crop to canopy[1]. The goal of the Phenonet is to provide scientists and farmers with a platform for high resolution crop analysis in real world growing conditions. Analysing the size, growth and performance of plants in a greenhouse or field site can be time-consuming and laborious. More specifically, when a field site is located in a remote area, it becomes quite expensive to send people out to the field. The ability to collect this information from remote locations and send it back to the laboratory in real time is an invaluable tool for plant scientists and farmers. Figure 1 presents a sample Phenonet in-field deployment.

The Phenonet system is currently supported by a proprietary software developed at CSIRO that provides a RESTful interface for data upload and analysis. Based on the in-field deployments, the Phenonet system follows a data model that best captures the needs of scientists and biologist performing experiments.

Fig. 1. Sample phenonet deployment

[1] http://www.csiro.au/en/Outcomes/ICT-and-Services/National-Challenges/
Wireless-sensors-in-agriculture.aspx.

2.1 Data Model

The Phenonet logical data model is depicted in Fig. 2. In Phenonet, a user is a logical entity (e.g. a project or a research group), which owns a group of experiments. An experiment has only one owner. Each experiment is a group of nodes and each node belongs to a single experiment. A node can also have its location associated with it, represented using latitude and longitude. A node itself is a group of streams and a stream is a series of timestamps and real number pairs with a unit of measurement. Phenonet allows metadata to be attached at every hierarchical layer of the data model. The data model conforms to the following policies.

- Any user can have zero or more experiments
- Any experiment can have zero or more nodes
- Any node can have zero or more streams. Each node can also have latitude, longitude and altitude values.
- Any stream is a set of (timestamp, value) pairs. Each stream has one unit of measurement.

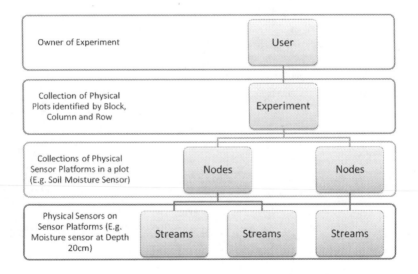

Fig. 2. Phenonet data model - logical

The mapping of a typical field experiment to the logical data model is illustrated in Fig. 3. In this example, the experiment is an ordered arrangement of 2 m wide by 6 m length plots with each plot identified by a combination of physical Block, Row and Column number. The plots are subdivided into experimental units and are mapped to the node level in Phenonet. The nodes are a collection of physical sensor platforms assigned a specific location in using latitude and longitude or plot location. E.g. a node is a soil moisture monitoring platform with a base station as depicted in Fig. 3. On some of these experiments, measurements of soil moisture are made at multiple depths. A measurement of soil

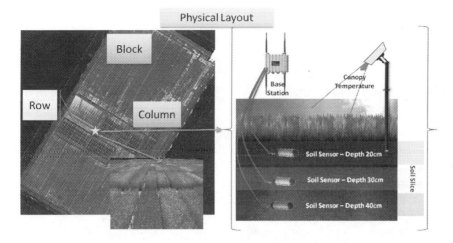

Fig. 3. Phenonet data model - physical

moisture at a particular depth is mapped to the stream, associated to a node. In summary, the stream maps to the physical sensor that monitors a phenomenon while nodes and experiments are used for logical grouping at different levels.

The metadata associated at each level is critical for providing contextual information. In the above example, for the experiment level, metadata could include information such as the year when the experiment was run; the block identification, the date the experiment was sown; description about the objectives of the experiment and even descriptions about the experimental site like e.g. soil type. At the node level the most relevant metadata fields are the crop genotype, treatments applied to individual experimental units and the relative location of the experimental unit within the experimental plot (in most cases for this application a row/column notation is used). At the stream level, in this example the depth, the sensor type and the sensor serial number are the most relevant metadata fields, while sensor information like the date of calibration or settings of the sensor can also be important depending on experiment.

3   Cloud-Based Open Source Middleware for Internet of Things (OpenIoT)

The EU FP7 OpenIoT project (http://openiot.eu/) is to provide an open source blueprint infra-structure for on-demand utility-based IoT applications, i.e., applications that promote and realise the convergence of cloud-computing with the Internet-of-Things. The heart of this infrastructure comprises a middleware framework, which facilitates service providers to deploy and monitor IoT applications in the cloud, while also enables service integrators and end-users to access and orchestrate internet-connected objects (ICOs) and their data.

3.1   OpenIoT Architecture Overview

OpenIoT Architecture is comprised by six main elements as depicted in Fig. 4. The Sensor Middleware, the Cloud Data Storage, the Scheduler in conjunction with Discovery Services functionality, the Service Delivery and Utility Manager, the Request Definition, the Request Presentation and the Configuration and Monitoring.

Sensor Middleware collects filters and combines data streams from virtual sensors or physical devices. It acts as a hub between the OpenIoT platform and the physical world. The sensor middleware uses an extension of the Global Sensor Networks (GSN-http://sourceforge.net/apps/trac/gsn/) middleware namely x-GSN.

Cloud Data Storage (Linked Sensor Middleware Light [8], LSM-Light) enables the storage of data streams stemming from the sensor middleware thereby acting as a cloud database. The cloud infrastructure stores also the metadata required for the operation of the OpenIoT platforms (functional data).

Scheduler processes all the requests for on-demand deployment of services and ensures their proper access to the resources (e.g. data streams) that they require. This component undertakes the following tasks: it incorporates semantic discovery of sensors and the associated data streams that can contribute to service setup; it manages a service and selects/enables the resources involved in service provision.

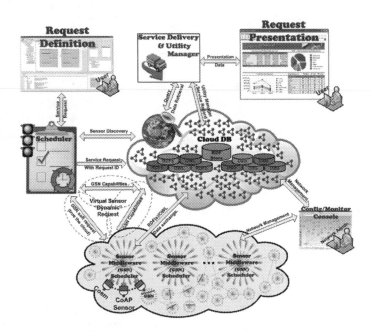

Fig. 4. OpenIoT middleware architecture

Service Delivery & Utility Manager (SDUM) performs a dual role. On one hand, it combines the data streams as indicated by service work flows in order to deliver the requested service. On the other hand, this component performs service metering to keep track of individual service usage.

Request Definition and Request Presentation components enable on-the-fly specification and visualisation of service requests to the OpenIoT platform. The component selects mashups from an appropriate library in order to facilitate service definition and presentation.

3.2 OpenIoT Service Oriented Approach

Service formulation and delivery in OpenIoT is designed according to the following properties:

On-demand: Service formulation and delivery in OpenIoT should be performed on-demand. Therefore, service formulation should provide the means to dynamically select sensors in order to meet the service request demand.

Semantic Discovery: The openness of OpenIoT enables data from multitude of heterogeneous source to be shared across domain. To search across data streams, a semantic discovery mechanism is implemented to meet the requirements of dynamic service composition.

Cloud-based: OpenIoT services are provided in a cloud environment. Its central component is a scalable sensor cloud infrastructure, which provides sensor data access services.

Service-Oriented: OpenIoT is service-oriented and requests result in the deployment of services. This may require the composition of other services, such as services for accessing data streams in the cloud.

4 Phenonet-OpenIoT Architecture and Implementation

4.1 Phenonet-OpenIoT

The integration of OpenIoT within the Phenonet project is a starting point for several interesting activities that are beneficial to both projects. OpenIoT aim at breaking application silos in the Phenonet project allowing a community of users at CSIRO to discover and reuse the data collected via various experiments. In particular, Phenonet benefits from OpenIoT middleware platform that facilitates the integration of new sensor types and do-it-yourself data analysis tools through exploiting the richness of semantically annotated sensor data and dynamic discovery capabilities. On the other hand, the availability of phenonet data in the OpenIoT cloud benefits OpenIoT in showcasing a practical smart farming use case. The successful deployment and use of OpenIoT in the scope of Phenonet experiments is an ideal showcase for the several capabilities of the OpenIoT platform, such as easy integration of any type of sensors, support for data collection and unification at a large scale, as well as flexible application development based on the OpenIoT do-it-yourself tools.

4.2   Scenario Description

A sample experiment, Kirkegaard and Danish was chosen to demonstrate Phenonet on OpenIoT middleware system. This experiment evaluates the effect of sheep grazing on crop re-growth by looking at root activity, water use, crop growth rate and crop yield. In this experiment soil moisture sensors namely GBHeavy (hardware name of the sensor) have been installed at multiple depths from 10 cm to 2 m below the soil surface. This enables the end-user to track the extraction of water from the soil by the roots throughout the crop growing season. This information can then be used to obtain an indirect measurement of root activity. Such an experiment also encourages dual-purpose cropping systems i.e. enriching live stock growth by allowing them to feed on healthy crops and control crop growth to increase yield and reduce fertiliser and water usage.

4.3   Phenonet Ontology

The Phenonet ontology is one of the key contributions of this paper and is presented in Fig. 5. The Phenonet ontology describes the structure of a Phenonet experiment and links the experiment to the sensors that gather data. Crops with a specific *genotype* are sown into *plots*, the crops are then subjected to a specific *treatment* (e.g. irrigation). The processes and regions described by the Phenonet ontology use the DOLCE Ultra-Light upper ontology[2]. The sensors themselves

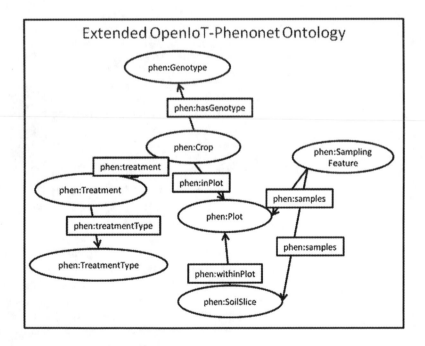

Fig. 5. Phenonet ontology

---

[2] http://www.loa.istc.cnr.it/old/DOLCE.html.

are described using the Semantic Sensor Network Incubator Group (SSN-XG) ontology [10], which is used to describe the physical and technical nature of the installed sensor network (e.g. what phenomenon a sensor observes or what platform the sensor is on and, therefore, where it is located).

Once deployed, the sensors observe a sampling feature that samples either the plot as a whole, the experimental site or some sub-feature of the plot (e.g. a layer of soil within plot). The sampling feature allows sensors to be linked to plots and from the plot to the combination of genotype, treatments and events such as sowing dates that define the crop. Features can be related, so that a soil layer can be built from the individual plot/layer segments or plots linked into an experimental site. The ability to relate features means that measurements of larger systems, such as the site weather, can be seen to apply to sub-parts such as individual plots. The ontology allows mapping of the Phenonet data model to the OpenIoT system enabling on-the-fly annotation of sensor data streams.

The ontology allows queries expressed in the domain of the experiment to navigate to sensors that measure appropriate information. For example, selecting the sensors that observe plots sown with a specific genotype; selecting the sensors that observe plots in a specific block; or selecting the sensors that sample a specific depth of soil. Sensors can also be queried using sensor-specific information, such as location. Conversely, the ontology can be used to navigate from a sensor property to experiment-specific information. For example: the types of treatments that have canopy temperature data available.

4.4   Architecture

Figure 6 presents a detailed architecture of Phenonet application using OpenIoT middleware. The sensed data captured from the field via the OpenIoT X-GSN component is pushed to the cloud storage via LSM. The X-GSN component performs basic error checking such as identifying outliers. Once the annotated data is available in the cloud store, the OpenIoT Request Definition, Request Presentation, Scheduler and SDUM services are employed to discover relevant data streams based on the ontology, compose a service with operators like *min, max, avg* and deploy the composed service for reuse.

Phenonet Ontology Integration with X-GSN and LSM-Light. The OpenIoT X-GSN component is responsible to interface with the sensors in the field, collect data, semantically annotate the data based on the extended OpenIoT-Phenonet ontology and push the data into the cloud RDF store via LSM-Light. The X-GSN wrapper connects to the sensors in the field. We implemented Phenonet specific X-GSN wrapper to interfaces with the sensor data streams. The wrapper is also responsible to generate RDF's descriptions of sensors by encoding domain specific information based on the Phenonet ontology. A sample RDF description of a sensor and a plot is listed in Listings 1.1 and 1.2.

In Listing 1.1, we define a sensor of type */ontology/phenonet#ArduCrop* with identifier *sensor/arducrop/20140611-1962-0012*, which is deployed in a

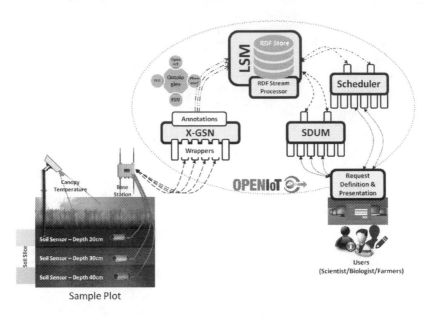

Sample Plot

Fig. 6. Phenonet application implementation - architecture

deployment site identified by the resource *deployment/site/ges-creek-range/ 20140611-1962-0000* and samples data in a plot identified by the plots sampling feature *experiment/kirkegaard-and-danish/plot/4001/sf*. The properties observed by this sensor is defined by the sensor type *ArduCrop*. The Listing 1.2 defines the plot in which the experiment is conducted as identified by the plot iden- tifier *phenonet/experiment/kirkegaard-and-danish/plot/7002*, its *plotBlock, plot- Column* and *plotRow* as defined in Sect. 2.1.

Listing 1.1. Phenonet sensor description in RDF

```
<rdf:Description  rdf:about="http://sensordb.csiro.au/
    phenonet/sensor/arducrop/20140611-1962-0012">
    <ssn:onPlatform rdf:resource="http://sensordb.csiro.
        au/phenonet/experiment/kirkegaard-and-danish/plot
        /4001/platform/phen077"/>
    <ssn:inDeployment rdf:resource="http://sensordb.
        csiro.au/phenonet/deployment/site/ges-creek-range
        /20140611-1962-0000"/>
    <ssn:ofFeature rdf:resource="http://sensordb.csiro.
        au/phenonet/experiment/kirkegaard-and-danish/plot
        /4001/sf"/>
    <dcterms:modified rdf:datatype="http://www.w3.org
        /2001/XMLSchema#string">2014-05-23</dcterms:
        modified>
```

```
<dcterms:created rdf:datatype="http://www.w3.org
   /2001/XMLSchema#string">2014−05−23</dcterms:
   created>
<dcterms:identifier rdf:datatype="http://www.w3.org
   /2001/XMLSchema#string">537f54a084ae3ab43a06dc78</
   dcterms:identifier>
<rdfs:label rdf:datatype="http://www.w3.org/2001/
   XMLSchema#string">Canopy Temp</rdfs:label>
<rdf:type rdf:resource="http://sensordb.csiro.au/
   ontology/phenonet#ArduCrop"/>
</rdf:Description>
```

Listing 1.2. Phenonet plot description in RDF

```
<rdf:Description rdf:about="http://sensordb.csiro.au/
   phenonet/experiment/kirkegaard−and−danish/plot/7002">
      <phenonet:plotBlock rdf:datatype="http://www.w3.org
         /2001/XMLSchema#string">3</phenonet:plotBlock>
      <phenonet:plotColumn rdf:datatype="http://www.w3.org
         /2001/XMLSchema#string">7</phenonet:plotColumn>
      <phenonet:plotRow rdf:datatype="http://www.w3.org
         /2001/XMLSchema#string">2</phenonet:plotRow>
      <dcterms:modified rdf:datatype="http://www.w3.org
         /2001/XMLSchema#string">2014−05−23</dcterms:
         modified>
      <phenonet:withinSite rdf:resource="http://sensordb.
         csiro.au/id/site/ges−creek−range"/>
      <dcterms:created rdf:datatype="http://www.w3.org
         /2001/XMLSchema#string">2014−05−23</dcterms:
         created>
      <dcterms:identifier rdf:datatype="http://www.w3.org
         /2001/XMLSchema#string">537f549984ae3ab43a06dc67</
         dcterms:identifier>
      <phenonet:plotID rdf:datatype="http://www.w3.org
         /2001/XMLSchema#string">7002</phenonet:plotID>
      <rdfs:label rdf:datatype="http://www.w3.org/2001/
         XMLSchema#string">Revenue_C07R02</rdfs:label>
      <rdf:type rdf:resource="http://sensordb.csiro.au/
         ontology/phenonet#Plot"/>
      <rdfs:comment rdf:datatype="http://www.w3.org/2001/
         XMLSchema#string">imidacloprid + impact</rdfs:
         comment>
</rdf:Description>
```

4.5   Prototype Implementation

In this section, we present the Phenonet proof-of-concept implementation on the previously proposed Phenonet-OpenIoT architecture. Figure 7 presents the sensor metadata used to annotate incoming data stream and the discovery interface for semantic sensor discovery. The discovery mechanism allows a user to discover sensors of specified characteristics within a given area of interest (e.g. location) using the OpenIoT Request Definition tool. The discovered sensors are later used to compose customised services by applying operators such as *max, min, avg* etc. This function enables efficiently filtering of sensors and sensor data based on user requirements.

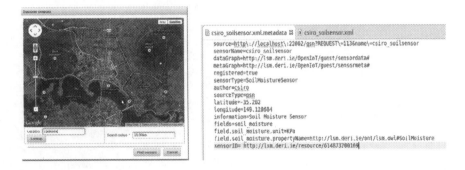

Fig. 7. Sensor discovery using request definition

For proof-of-concept, we have implemented the following queries that are commonly used by scientists and plant biologist in the scenario described in Sect. 4.2. We use the term "faceted search" to define these queries. The facets search automatically derives annotations such as *crop bar code, genotype, plot, treatment type, bounding box* from the OpenIoT-Phenonet ontology. Some sample SPARQL queries uses to perform the faceted search is presented in Listings 1.3 and 1.4.

Listing 1.3 shows how crops, plots, sampling features and sensors are linked together. A crop is in a specific plot. A sensor samples a sampling feature. To get from crop to sensor, the SPARQL query works out what plot it is in and then builds a union of sampling features that are connected to the plot. This will result in a set of sensors that sample the interested features.

Listing 1.4 shows how a treatment is filtered. A crop has a treatment, which is an event with dates and treatment type. This SPARQL query find out the treatment type that applies to the crop and then filters the result based on treatment type. This is an example of domain-side filtering, where we limit the crops based on domain specific definition e.g. treatment, genotype etc.

Listing 1.3. SPARQL query for crop to sensor

```
{ {    { ?samples  phenonet:samples  ?plot }
       UNION
         { ?samples  phenonet:samples  ?slice  .
           ?slice  phenonet:withinPlot  ?plot  .
           ?slice  <http://www.w3.org/1999/02/22-rdf-
             syntax-ns#type> phenonet:SoilSlice
           OPTIONAL
             { ?slice  phenonet:hasDepth  ?depth  .
               ?depth  rdfs:label  ?depthName
             }
         }
  }
  ?crop  <http://www.w3.org/1999/02/22-rdf-syntax-ns#
    type> phenonet:Crop  .
  ?crop  phenonet:inPlot  ?plot  .
  ?plot  rdfs:label  ?plotName  .
  ?sensor  ssn:ofFeature  ?samples  .
  ?sensor  rdfs:label  ?sensorName
```

Listing 1.4. SPARQL query for treatment type

```
{ ?crop  phenonet:treated/phenonet:treatmentType  ?
  treatment
    FILTER ( bound(?treatment) && ( ?treatment = <http
      ://sensordb.csiro.au/id/treatment-type/grazed-
      high-n> ) )
}
```

Figure 8 presents the Phenonet experiment composition interface and the corresponding SPARQL query generated by the OpenIoT middleware to support the requested Phenonet experiment service. As depicted, the interface is very intuitive and allows the farmer/user/biologist to configure experiment based on their needs. In the example depicted, the user configures an experiment to compute the average soil moisture from a soil moisture sensor in Acton, Canberra (the location specified during discovery). Once the Phenonet experiment is configured, OpenIoT middleware is responsible to deploy and manage the service. The output of the deployed experiment is visualised in a Line Chart as depicted in Fig. 9 via the request presentation interface.

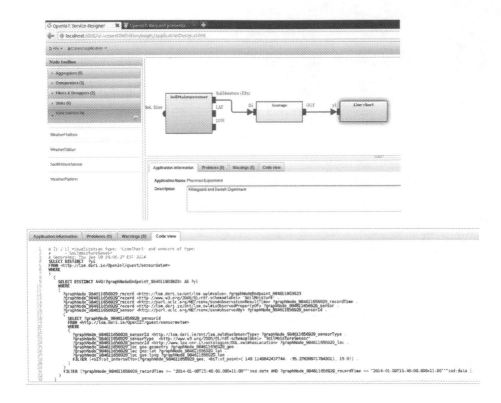

Fig. 8. OpenIoT Phenonet experiment composition and SPARQL query

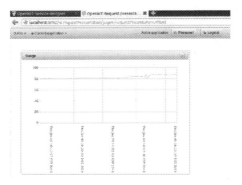

Fig. 9. Phenonet application - request presentation output of deployed service

5   Conclusion

Food security is a global challenge and agriculture can address this challenge through radical improvements in productivity, efficiency and effectiveness. Internet of Things (IoT) is a major enabler of such improvements through sensing, actuation, use of analytics and visualisation. This paper discussed challenges that agricultural industry is facing and has proposed a solution developed as part of the EU FP7 OpenIoT project. Phenonet is an OpenIoT use case developed by CSIRO, Australia and demonstrated how digital agriculture can and should benefit from deploying the IoT and commercialising sensing-as-a-service and cloud-based solutions. Phenonet development included development of a phenonet ontology, extensive experimentation with various sensors deployed in the field, semantic transformation of acquired data, analytical processing and user-driven visualisation of the results. Experience and lessons from using OpenIoT middleware for Phenonet development have also been presented and analysed.

Acknowledgement. Part of this work has been carried out in the scope of the ICT OpenIoT Project which is co-funded by the European Commission under seventh framework program, contract number FP7-ICT-2011-7-287305-OpenIoT. The authors acknowledge help and support from CSIRO Sensors and Sensor Networks Transformational Capability Platform (SSN TCP).

References

1. BigData-Startup: John deere revolutionizing farming big data (2013)
2. Bramley, R.G.V., Janik, L.J.: Precision agriculture demands a new approach to soil and plant sampling and analysis – examples from Australia. Commun. Soil Sci. Plant Anal. **36**(1–3), 9–22 (2005)
3. Bramley, R., Trengove, S.: Precision agriculture in Australia: present status and recent developments. Engenharia AgrÃcola **33**, 575–588 (2013)
4. Burrell, J., Brooke, T., Beckwith, R.: Vineyard computing: sensor networks in agricultural production. IEEE Pervasive Comput. **3**(1), 38–45 (2004)
5. IBM: Analytics in agriculture: Driving efficiencies and insight to create "smarter agribusiness", March 2013. http://public.dhe.ibm.com/common/ssi/ecm/en/gbw03201usen/GBW03201USEN.PDF
6. Jayaraman, P., Perera, C., Georgakopoulos, D., Zaslavsky, A.: Efficient opportunistic sensing using mobile collaborative platform mosden. In: 2013 9th International Conference Conference on Collaborative Computing: Networking, Applications and Worksharing (Collaboratecom), pp. 77–86, Oct 2013
7. Jayaraman, P.P., Zaslavsky, A., Delsing, J.: Sensor data collection using heterogeneous mobile devices. In: IEEE International Conference on Pervasive Services, pp. 161–164, July 2007
8. Le-Phuoc, D., Quoc, H.N.M., Parreira, J.X., Hauswirth, M.: The linked sensor middleware-connecting the real world and the semantic web. In: Proceedings of the Semantic Web Challenge (2011)

9. Sherchan, W., Jayaraman, P., Krishnaswamy, S., Zaslavsky, A., Loke, S., Sinha, A.: Using on-the-move mining for mobile crowdsensing. In: 2012 IEEE 13th International Conference on Mobile Data Management (MDM), pp. 115–124 (2012)
10. W3C Semantic Sensor Network Incubator Group: Semantic sensor network ontology (2005)
11. Wark, T., Corke, P., Sikka, P., Klingbeil, L., Ying, G., Crossman, C., Valencia, P., Swain, D., Bishop-Hurley, G.: Transforming agriculture through pervasive wireless sensor networks. IEEE Pervasive Comput. **6**(2), 50–57 (2007)
12. Zaslavsky, A., Jayaraman, P.P., Krishnaswamy, S.: Sharelikescrowd: mobile analytics for participatory sensing and crowd-sourcing applications. In: 2013 IEEE 29th International Conference on Data Engineering Workshops (ICDEW), vol. 0, pp. 128–135 (2013)

Autonomic Aspects of IoT Based Systems: A Logistics Domain Scheduling Example

Septimiu Nechifor[1], Dan Puiu[1]([✉]), Bogdan Târnaucă[1],
and Florin Moldoveanu[2]

[1] Siemens Corporate Technology Romania, Braşov, Romania
dan.puiu@siemens.com
[2] Transilvania University of Braşov, Braşov, Romania

Abstract. A logistics domain application based on IoT paradigm and autonomic computing is presented in this paper. We have considered a logistics scenario, where at the outskirts of a city several depots are located, which provide construction materials and equipment for different construction sites located inside the city. The transport company minivans are responsible for delivering the construction materials. The application dynamically reconfigures the routes of the minivans based on the traffic conditions. In order to generate data for the smart city IoT environment, we have used the CoReMo (Constraints Responsive Mobility) emulator. The dynamic reconfiguration system is based on the MAPE-K (Monitor, Analyse, Plan, Execute - Knowledge) autonomic loop. For the analysis phase we have used the Esper complex event processing engine and the planing phase is ensured by the CHOCO constraints solver.

1 Introduction

Even if the last decade had a constant increase for the price of fuels, the transportation of persons and goods has increased [1]. The national and local authorities face complicated problems, because of the big number of vehicles present on roads. The authorities are forced to constantly maintain, adapt and extend the traffic infrastructure, very often under severe spatial, temporal and financial constraints. Also the inhabitants' comfort, productivity and health are affected by road based terrestrial transportation conditions [2]. In addition to that, the increasing traffic directly affects the environment because of the resulting CO_2 and other harmful gases and particle emissions [2].

Because the number of vehicles present on roads cannot be reduced, the authorities and city planners are highly interested for implementing solutions that can optimise the existing resources and infrastructure. These optimizations should decrease the number of traffic jams, reduce the transportation cost and fuel consumption and increase the comfort of travellers, drivers or inhabitants of traffic rich communities [2]. In technical literature there are several papers which present solutions for traffic optimisations, such as [3–5].

Fortunately, the technological advances in the Information and Communications Technology (ICT) domain, such as wireless communications, sensor networks, mobile devices, Global Positioning Systems (GPS) devices can be used to

© Springer International Publishing Switzerland 2015
I. Podnar Žarko et al. (Eds.): FP7 OpenIoT Project Workshop 2014, LNCS 9001, pp. 153–168, 2015.
DOI: 10.1007/978-3-319-16546-2_12

develop applications that can optimize the use of existing traffic resources and infrastructure. More and more traffic monitoring and control devices (such as loop detectors, radars, traffic surveillance cameras, smart traffic lights, dynamic signs, weather sensors, etc.) are connected to the Internet and in this way they form a rich Internet of Things (IoT) environment. But such a vast amount of devices (sensors and actuators) doing real-time data reporting pose a new range of problems regarding:

- data collecting, filtering and processing, in other words transforming data into useful information;
- decision making about the actions that must be performed using the derived information;
- actions execution.

The overall paradigm that is able to cover the needs of such environment is inspired by the research area of Autonomic Computing, which has greatly increased over the course of the last ten years the common understanding on how to realize systems with self-managing capabilities. The main steps of such feature pack are inspired in its high-level design by the MAPE-K (Monitor, Analyse, Plan, Execute - Knowledge) loop, which is one key conceptual aspect of the Autonomic Computing field [6].

A logistics domain application based on IoT paradigm and autonomic computing is presented in this paper. We have considered a logistics scenario, where at the outskirts of a city several depots are located which provide construction materials and equipments for several construction sites located inside the city. The transport company minivans are responsible for delivering the construction materials. The application dynamically reconfigures the routes of the minivans based on the traffic conditions. In order to generate data from the smart city IoT environment, we have used CoReMo (Constraints Responsive Mobility) software, which is based on Repast Symphony multi-agent system [7]. The dynamic reconfiguration system is based on the MAPE-K autonomic loop. For the analysis phase we have used Esper complex event processing engine [8] and the planing phase is ensured by CHOCO constraints solver [9].

Presented experimental work is based entirely on open source platforms. There is no dependency regarding any particular technological option and each individual step in the autonomic loop can be easily made interoperable with equivalent implementation.

In the following part of this section are briefly presented the main concepts and paradigms used in this paper, as follows: autonomic computing, complex event processing and constrains satisfaction problem. The Chap. 2 presents the scenario used to test the proposed solution. The architecture description and the implementation details are included in Chap. 3. The paper conclusions are documented in Sect. 5.

2   Autonomic Computing Concepts

The logistic domain application was designed to respect self-* capabilities related to healing, configuration optimization and protection. Such approach is of interest on at least two levels: one related to things (or their virtualization as agents) and services overlay responsible for large scale business systems behaviour orchestration.

The overall paradigm able to cover the needs of such environment is inspired by the research area of Autonomic Computing, which has greatly evolved over the course of the last ten years the with thecommon understanding on how to realize systems with self-managing (covering all previous self-* phases) capabilities. The main steps of such feature pack are inspired in its high-level design by the MAPE-K loop, which is one key conceptual aspect of the Autonomic Computing field. The MAPE-K autonomic loop (Monitor, Analyze, Plan, Execute and Knowledge) represents a blueprint for the design of autonomic systems where a managed element is coordinated by a loop structured in 4 phases and a common knowledge [6,10]. The common known image depicting the concept is presented in Fig. 1.

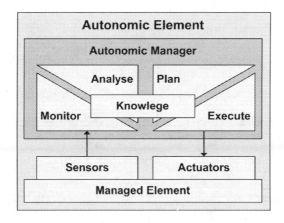

Fig. 1. Autonomic systems base architecture [6,10].

The MAPE-K loop is structured in 4 correlated phases [6,10]:

– *Monitoring:* The monitoring component is in charge to observe and manage the different sources of relevant data (named sensors here) that provide information regarding the way how system performs. In the current context, sensors can capture the current consumption of critical resources but also other performance metrics (such as the number of processed requests in a time window and the request process latency). The monitoring granularity is usually specified by rules. Sensors can also generate notifications when changes to the system configuration happen and a reaction is expected.

- *Analysis:* The analysis function is responsible for processing the information captured by the monitoring component and for generating high level events. For instance, it may combine the values of calls on a service and memory utilization to signal an overload condition in the platform.
- *Planning:* The planning component is responsible for selecting the actions that need to be applied in order to correct some deviation from the desired operational envelope. The planning component relies on a high level policy that describes an adaptation plan for the system. These policies may be described, for example, using Event Condition Action (ECA) rules that are defined by a high level language. An ECA rule describes for a specific event and a given condition what action should be executed. In the context of IoT, the actions may affect the usage of virtualized things and the bindings among these ones in terms of use.
- *Execution:* The execution component applies the actions selected by the planning component to the target components.

Additionally, the shared knowledge includes information to support the remaining components. In the context of logistics, it maintains information about managed elements both related to transport infrastructure and relevant goods.

2.1   Where and How Was Used

When systems are large, complex, and heterogeneous (the case of logistics fits in this category), a single MAPE loop may not be sufficient for managing adaptation. In such cases, multiple MAPE loops may be employed that manage parts of the system. In self-adaptive systems with multiple MAPE loops, the functions for monitoring, analyzing, planning and executing may be made by multiple components that coordinate with one another. Various patterns of interacting control loops have been used in practice by centralizing and decentralizing the functions of self-adaption in multiple ways. For example, in the Rainbow framework monitoring and execution are delegated to the various nodes of the controlled system, whereas analyzing and planning are centralized. The IBM architectural blueprint organizes MAPE loops hierarchically, where each level of the hierarchy contains instances of all four MAPE components. In this setting, higher level MAPE loops determine the set values for the subordinate MAPE loops. In fully decentralized settings, relatively independent MAPE components coordinate with one another and adapt the system when needed. The *On Patterns for Decentralized Control in Self-Adaptive Systems* paper presents a selection of MAPE patterns that model deferent types of interacting MAPE loops with multiple degrees of decentralization (like Coordinated Control Pattern, Information Sharing Pattern, Master/Slave Pattern, Regional Planning Pattern, and Hierarchical Control Pattern).

   The application of the centralized control loop pattern to a large-scale software system may suffer from scalability problems. There is a pressing need for decentralized, but still manageable, effective, and predictable techniques for constructing self-adaptive software systems. A major challenge is to accommodate a systematic engineering approach that integrates both control-loop approaches with decentralized agent inspired approaches.

Of course that MAPE-K loop only represents a vision that leaves lower level details of the architecture purposely unspecified (i.e., they do not impose constraints on the implementation). Each individual analysis of requirements should define a reference conceptual architecture for the runtime platform which we here describe and that follows the MAPE-K loop design approach. The details and implementation of this conceptual architecture might be deployment dependent at detail level. The only purpose of this section is to provide a high-level intuition of the systems that will compose the architecture, which is required in order to identify the actors that are involved in the requirement specification of the logistic application.

Our focus here is to provide an adequate toolset for monitoring part of the MAPE-K loop.

2.2   Application

Autonomic computing and its extensions in the area of autonomic networking find its most representative application area until now in telecommunication and networks management. One of the most representative problems addressed is the one of congestion control. Designing efficient congestion control scheme is, therefore, a very relevant issue to improve the control of network congestion and to fulfill data transmission effectively. The main difficulty in designing such scheme lies in the large propagation delay in transmission that usually leads to a mismatch between the network resources and the amount of admitted traffic. The crucial issue of the network control is that we should adapt the controllable flows to the changing network environment, so as to achieve the goal of data transfer and to alleviate network congestion. Congestion is the result of an issue between the network resources capacity and the amount of traffic for transmission. But congestion problems can easily be scaled to any other traffic capacity problems or even to economic value chains such as logistic ones.

Another use case, relevant for the Internet of Things area, known as virtualization as a service layer, is the one of service engineering, more specific the one of self-verifying service based systems [11]. Service systems are under the challenge of continuous service availability and quality risk and may benefit from the use of autonomic control where knowledge of probabilistic failure models supports the continuous adaptation during runtime.

Based on those examples, it is visible that an autonomic computing approach generates large benefits to IT governance systems. Foundational methodologies such as ITIL (IT Infrastructure Library) [12] may find a coherent technological mirror in self-management features.

Autonomic computing provides an architecture that enables systems, including networked software systems, to be flexible, dynamic, and adaptable. It provides technologies to offset the inherently increased complexity as grids expand the domain of computing. For example, self-managing autonomic systems can help optimize process performance and manage workloads across the whole landscape to ensure that resources are most efficiently utilized. Likewise, they can enable the provisioning of software and configuration specifications so that servers can be allocated or de-allocated on the fly. Conversely, cloud like technologies provide enhancements to facilitate distributed computing that can be leveraged to implement autonomic behavior across distributed, heterogeneous resources.

Looking at the Internet of Things domain we observe two critical areas to benefit from autonomic approach: service oriented exposure of things and large scale virtualization.

Through the use of standards-based interfaces and connections, SOA enables IT organizations to create application building blocks that can be *wired* together as needed. For example, an energy distribution services organization may create a smart provisioning and metering capability based on an SOA that can be easily coupled with its service subscriptions application (to approve subscriptions), its credit card application (to determine a customer's credit limit), and its customer service application (to determine the appropriate reputation and service provisioning for each customer). Autonomic computing leverages this same integration services model to facilitate communication among heterogeneous things exposed as services. At the same time, autonomic computing helps simplify the conceptualization, modeling, assembly, deployment, and management of the discrete processes that are composed together using an SOA to help organizations to perform more effectively and efficiently, create the required building blocks for service delivery.

Similarly, we should observe that virtualization technology and autonomic computing share an equally win-win relationship. Virtualization technology allows an IT infrastructure owner or manager to pool its computing resources - servers, networks, storage devices into a single environment with a common interface so that they can be allocated as needed and managed more efficiently, crossing the boundaries of administrative or technological limitation domains. However, within a virtualized environment, IT staffs awareness on continuous operations may sky rocketing with regard on available capacity provisioning. On such extended highly heterogeneous landscape of IOT environments they rapidly need to move workloads aiming to keep performance on green zone. Another relevant job to do in this perspective is to ensure that data from business-critical applications, infrastructures and devices is moved to storage devices with the highest quality of service. Through the virtualization of resources, autonomic computing can manage IT resources on a more granular level, dynamically provisioning software and managing workloads at multiple levels. At the same time, autonomic computing provides critical *sense and respond* capabilities to reduce the complexity of managing virtualized resources.

3   Scenario Description

In order to illustrate the way how autonomic control can work in the IOT space problem, a logistics use case was selected due to the fact that logistics problems family is heavily approached starting with RFID age. Our purpose here is to leverage the combination of different functional requirements under autonomic computing approach.

The solution proposed in this paper has been evaluated using the scenario of a route scheduler for logistics companies. It consists of several depots, located at the outskirts of a city, providing construction materials and equipment. Inside the city there are a number of construction sites, which have limited storing capacity. Several minivans agents are used to transport materials and equipment, from and to the construction sites, according to the dispatcher approvals. The minivans have to deliver the materials in the shortest time possible, so they have to reconfigure the route if a traffic jam occurs or other exceptional traffic condition occurs.

Computing the traffic load on the city streets has been done using the following approach. All the agents (transport company minivans and also the other vehicles participating to the traffic) transmit anonymously their location to a traffic information service provider. The raw location data is used to detect traffic jams and other unpredictable events which are broadcasted to the interested parties.

Figure 2 depicts the main entities that are considered in the material delivery scenario. The construction sites agents send the materials and equipment needs to the depot agent. The transport company has several minivans which are used for delivering the construction materials from the depot to the different construction sites. Because the storage capacity of each construction site is limited, the transport company has to deliver only those materials needed in the current construction stage.

In the presented scenario the following interactions between agents are needed (see Fig 2):

(1) each construction site dispatcher sends the material and equipment needs to the depot administrator;

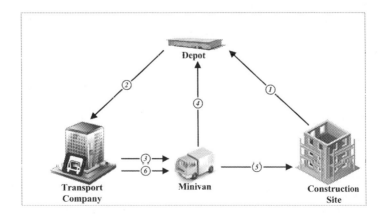

Fig. 2. The construction materials delivery system.

(2) the depot administrator sends the list of materials to be transported (for all the construction sites) to the transport company;

(3) the transport company sends the transport plans to the minivan drivers;

(4) the minivan drivers request the materials from the depot;

(5) the minivan drivers requests approval to unload the construction materials;

(6) the transport company monitors the state of the traffic; reconfigures the plans if an unexpected event (e.g. traffic jam) occurs and sends the new transportation plans to the minivan drivers.

4   System Architecture

4.1   Autonomic Route Scheduler

The complex environment required to evaluate the proposed autonomic aspects of the IoT system has been recreated using the Constrains Responsive Mobility (CoReMo) software platform, which is based on Repast Symphony multi-agent system [7].

CoReMo has been developed as an extensible emulator platform used for testing a variety of concepts and solutions. A dedicated extension of the platform is focused on autonomic systems involving mobile as well as fixed agents. While the former represent vehicles the latter are exposing fixed infrastructure elements such as traffic lights, loop detectors, crossings or road signs. Different traffic load conditions are simulated using a wide range of *dummy agents* whereas the weather conditions are replicated using the integrated environments simulator.

The version of the emulator deployed for this scenario, whose architecture of is depicted in Fig. 3, consists of *CoReMo Core* and an updated version of the *CoReMo Citadel* extension.

CoReMo Core represents the simulator kernel providing generic simulation functionality and is build on top of the RepastSymphony simulation framework. A set of *contexts* and *projections* are used to build the agent space. Contexts are used as containers for different agents, grouping them based on functionality or other user defined criteria. Projections are used to relate agents to the Cartesian or 3D space, or to a network structure supporting graph processing.

Complex agent behaviors are modeled using the Petri Nets formalism and the translation of these nets into executable code is achieved by using *PetriNetExec* [13]. *PetriNetExec* is Java library we have developed in order to allow embedding of Petri Nets into executable code. This functionality is critical especially when complex behavior is modeled using Petri Nets thus leading to a large number of places, transitions or inhibitor arcs whose translation into code without this dedicated library would be difficult and prone to errors. A set of callback functions are attached to events relevant for the network evolution at runtime and their description is documented in [14].

The *Simulation Control* component provides the simulation time keeping and advance mechanism whereas the *Event Messaging* provides support for the interconnection of different components of the simulator.

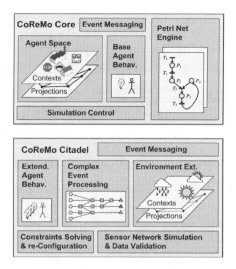

Fig. 3. CoReMo emulator architecture.

CoReMo Citadel complements *CoReMo Core* with urban traffic simulation and specialized components for autonomic behavior. It adds extensions to the agent behaviors and to the simulated environment and introduces dedicated processing components such as those for CEP or CS (*Constraints Solving*) techniques.

While the former two extensions are closely related to the *monitoring* step of the MAPE loop, the latter ones are related to the *analysis* and *planning* steps, respectively, which will be described later.

4.2 MAPE-K Loop Monitor Step

Figure 4 presents the interface of the CoReMo emulator, which was configured according to the considered scenario. The image shows the Repast Simphony framework running the emulation and displays the traffic network for the city of Brasov (the roads and the infrastructure elements), the simulated vehicles and the thermal map.

In addition to the minivan agents belonging to the transport company, the emulation environment has several car agents, which are used for generating the traffic load.

As mentioned in the previous section, the CoReMo emulator is able to simulate temperature, humidity and atmospheric pressure variation in the city (the emulator generates maps so that they mimic the dynamics of weather throughout the simulation).

The following IoT devices are deployed in the emulator:

- loop detection based on speed sensors that allows detection of a car's speed;
- loop detection sensors which are placed at the entry and at the exit of a road segment (used for counting the number of cars in that particular area);

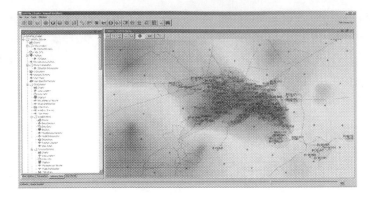

Fig. 4. CoReMo emulator.

- speed and position sensors mounted on each vehicle;
- temperature, humidity and atmospheric pressure sensors spread through the city;
- terminals for transport company drivers (used for sending the routes and notifications).

4.3   MAPE-K Loop Analyse Step

As presented in the previous sub section, the traffic emulation environment has a lot of interconnected arrays of traffic sensors (such as loop detectors and radars) and weather sensors. In order to be able to process the generated data and transform it into useful information, dedicated tools have to be used, witch have the ability to process in near real-time vast amounts of data with reduced latencies and also to include temporal, causal and structural relations between incoming process events. Such abilities are provided by CEP and in this case the Esper [15] CEP engine is used.

CEP was originally designed for system architecture prototyping with powerful event oriented semantics. Although near real-time event processing platforms and solutions exists for decades [16], CEP has consolidated itself as a separate topic rather recently. The temporal, causal and structural relations between the raw events are exploited with the goal of producing added value information represented as complex events. The usual event–oriented operations [17] implemented by a CEP engine are: filtering, translation, aggregation, composition, pattern detection. The Event Processing Language (EPL) is a crux characteristic for the CEP platform, and represents all the operators which can be used by the developer to express the logic which is executed by PNs (such as the operations presented above). Because the EPL of the CEP engines provides operators such as windows, aggregation, joining and analysis functions the developer can define Event Processing Networks (EPNs) that perform event stream analysis.

In the follow paragraphs of this section we will present an EPN used for detecting traffic jams the GPS data generated by the vehicles (see Fig. 5). The

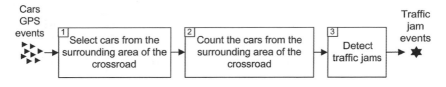

Fig. 5. The EPN used for detecting a traffic jam.

presented queries have been slightly modified for the sake of readability. Other traffic jams detection methods (using the loop detector sensors) are described in the following paper: [18].

It had been considered that a certain crossroad is prone to traffic jams. One method to detect if a traffic jam has occurred is to count the number of cars that have reported positions in the surrounding area of the crossroad. If the result of cont is bigger that a threshold ($TRAFFIC\_JAM\_THRESHOLD$) then a traffic jam event is generated for that crossroad.

The traffic jam area is considered to be a circle with the radius $TEST\_AREA\_RADIUS$, centred on the crossroad (which has the following GPS coordinates $CROSSROAD\_LAT$ and $CROSSROAD\_LONG$).

The statement from Listing 1 selects all the car GPS position events, that are reported in the surrounding area of the crossroad. The Euclidian distance had been used to determine if the car is located inside the circle with the radius $TEST\_AREA\_RADIUS$.

```
insert into CurrentCrossroadCars select * from CarPosition
    where ((( CarPosition . Latitude − CROSSROD_LAT) * (
    CarPosition . Latitude − CROSSROD_LAT) + ( CarPosition .
    Longitude − CROSSROD_LONG) * ( CarPosition . Longitude −
    CROSSROD_LONG)) < TEST_AREA_RADIUS * TEST_AREA_RADIUS)
```

Listing 1.1. Selects all the car GPS position events, that are reported in the surrounding area of the crossroad.

After that, at each $REPORTING\_PERIOD$ seconds a complex event is generated which contains the number of cars reported in the surrounding area of the crossroad from the last count reporting (see Listing 2).

```
insert into CrossroadCarsNumber select count(*) as
    numberOfCars from CurrentCrossroadCars : win . time (
    REPORTING_PERIOD seconds) output every REPORTING_PERIOD
    seconds
```

Listing 1.2. Counts the cars from the surronding area of the crossroad.

A traffic jam event is generated for the crossroad when the result of the count is bigger than $TRAFFIC\_JAM\_THRESHOLD$ (see Listing 3).

```
1 insert into CrossroadTrafficJams select * from
        CrossroadCarsNumber(numberOfCars > TRAFFIC_JAM_THRESHOLD
```

Listing 1.3. Detect traffic jams.

4.4   MAPE-K Loop Plan Step

The *planning* step in our solution relies on CS techniques, in fact the application of CS for scheduling problems. The decision of this approach is natural since scheduling represents the problem of fulfilling a set of soft and hard constraints involving the temporal dimension as well.

Constraints Satisfaction Problems (CSPs) are meant to identify a set of valid values for variables which satisfy the requirements defined as constraints [19]. A CSP is defined using a $\{V, D, C\}$ tuple where [20]:

$$V = \{v_1, v_2, ..., v_n\}, \tag{1}$$

$$D = \{D_1, D_2, ..., D_n\}, \tag{2}$$

$$C = \{c_1, c_2, ..., v_m\}. \tag{3}$$

V represents the set of variables, D defines contains the variable domains and C is the set of constraints. A constraint c_k is defined as a cartesian product of the variable domains $D_1 \times D_2 \times ... \times D_n$.

Different techniques and algorithms have been developed and implemented for CSP. The solution proposed in this paper is based on the Choco solver [9].

In our case, the planning step consists of scheduling the minivan agents' delivery plan based on the possible routes modeled as a graph an a set of hard an soft constraints. The hard constraints define the items which have to be delivered and their corresponding recipients, while the soft constraints define client time windows (when a delivery is possible) as well as minimization of the costs.

Based on the inputs obtained after the *analysis* step about the traffic conditions and the delivery requirements specific to each constructing site, the variables and the constraints of the problem are defined and fed to the solver. The expected outcome is a set of possible routes. The method is described in detail in [21].

4.5   MAPE-K Loop Execute Step

In order to close the loop, after the system has detected that a traffic jam has occurred (see Sect. 4.3) and the new routes have been generated (see Sect. 4.4), it sends the new routes to the minivan agents.

As mentioned above, the behaviour of the agents, from the CoReMo simulator platform, is described using PNs. In Fig. 6 is presented the the PN which

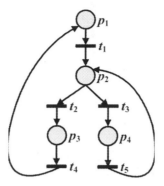

Fig. 6. Minivan agent PN.

describes the behavior of the minivan agent. The model contains 8 places and 5 transitions, which are described in Table 1. The PN contains only one token and depending on the sequence of events, the token travels from one place to another. The minivan agent has to execute the action specified by the active place (the place that contains the token).

Initially, the minivan agent is parked and is waiting for a task from the transport company agent. A task request contains the following information: the location where the minivan agent has to travel and the operation that has to be done at destination (load/unload materials and/or equipments).

Table 1. Notation of the PN which describes the minivan agent behavior (see Fig. 6)

Place	Description	Transition	Description
p_1	Stopped	t_1	New task (route) received
p_2	Travelling to destination	t_2	Arrived at destination
p_3	Executing operation at destination (loading/unloading)	t_3	Reconfiguration requested
p_4	Receiving the route	t_4	Load/unload finished at destination
		t_5	New route received

When the minivan agent receives a new task (the event associated to t_1 is produced) it gets in *traveling to destination state* (the token is in stare p_2), where it remains until one of the following events is generated: t_2 (arrived to the destination) or t_3 (reconfiguration requested by the transport company). If the minivan agent has arrived to the destination it starts to execute the operation specified by the task request (the token is located in p_3). When the operation is finished (the event t_4 is generated), the minivan gets in parking mode. In the other situation, when the minivan agent has received a request to reconfigure the route, it fetches the route and after that goes in the travel to destination mode (the token is placed in p_2).

5   Conclusions

This paper documents the work on the CoReMo core, which provides an event rich environment, and CoReMo citadel, which had been used for implementing the MAPE-K loop. We have considered the following scenario in order to test the application: at the outskirts of a city several depots are located which provide construction materials and equipments for several construction sites located inside the city. The transport company minivans are responsible for delivering the construction materials. The application dynamically reconfigures the routes of the minivans based on the traffic conditions.

The MAPE-K loop was used to implement the dynamic reconfiguration behaviour of the application. In the monitoring step, the application collects data from the following IoT resources: loop detectors, speed and position sensors mounted on each vehicle and weather sensors. The raw data was generated by the CoReMo emulator.

All the data generated by the CoReMo emulator is processed, in the MAPE-K loop analyse step, by the Esper CEP engine. The CEP engine deploys a set of event processing nodes which detect different abnormal situations such as: traffic jams, special weather conditions and delays in the delivery process.

The derived information, from the previous step, is used to determine if one or several routes of the minivans have to be updated, because it contains a traffic jam. In order to obtain the new route, in the MAPE-K planning step, the transportation requirements and city traffic conditions are described as hard, respective soft, constraints. Then the CHOCO constraints solver is used to obtain the optimal route.

In the last step of the the MAPE-K loop, the routes are transmitted to the minivan agents of the CoReMo emulator. The behaviour of the agents from the CoReMo platform was described using PNs and implemented using the *PetriNetExec* java library.

Acknowledgment. This paper is supported by: the CityPulse project, *Real-Time IoT Stream Processing and Large-scale Data Analytics for Smart City Applications (http://www.ict-citypulse.eu)* and by the iCore project, *Internet Connected Objects for Reconfigurable Ecosystems* (http://www.iot-icore.eu/). CityPulse is a Small or medium-scale focused research project (STREP) funded within the European 7th Framework Programme, contract number: CNECT-ICT-609035. iCore is an EU Integrated Project funded within the European 7th Framework Programme, contract number: 287708.

References

1. Campestrini, M., Mock, P.: European vehicle market statistics. Technical report, The International Conuncil on Clean Transportation (2011)
2. Campestrini, M., Mock, P.: White paper on transport. Technical report, European Commission, Directorate-General for Mobility and Transport (2011)
3. Byon, Y., Shalaby, A., Abdulhai, B.: Travel time collection and traffic monitoring via GPS technologies. In: Intelligent Transportation Systems Conference, ITSC 2006, pp. 677–682. IEEE (2006)
4. Setchell, C., Dagless, E.: Vision-based road-traffic monitoring sensor. IEE Proc. Vis. Image Signal Process. **148**(1), 78–84 (2001)
5. Guo, C., Mita, S., McAllester, D.: Robust road detection and tracking in challenging scenarios based on markov random fields with unsupervised learning. IEEE Trans. Intell. Transp. Syst. **13**(3), 1338–1354 (2012)
6. Mpitziopoulos, A., Gavalas, D., Konstantopoulos, C., Pantziou, G.: Mobile agent middleware for autonomic data fusion in wireless sensor networks. In: Zhang, Y., Yang, L.T., Denko, M.K. (eds.) Autonomic Computing and Networking, pp. 57–81. Springer, Heidelberg (2009)
7. Mpitziopoulos, A., Gavalas, D., Konstantopoulos, C., Pantziou, G.: Repast Simphony, University of Chicago (2013). http://repast.sourceforge.net/. Accessed June 2013
8. Mpitziopoulos, A., Gavalas, D., Konstantopoulos, C., Pantziou, G.: Esper Complex Event Processing Engine, EsperTech (2012). http://www.espertech.com/products/esper.php. Accessed June 2013
9. Mpitziopoulos, A., Gavalas, D., Konstantopoulos, C., Pantziou, G.: CHOCO - CSP and CP Solver, CHOCO (2014). http://www.emn.fr/z-info/choco-solver/. Accessed June 2014
10. Calinescu, R.: General-Purpose Autonomic Computing, pp. 3–29. Springer, Heidelberg (2009). http://web.comlab.ox.ac.uk/people/Radu.Calinescu/ACNchapter 2008.pdf
11. Calinescu, R.: Methodology for the model-driven development of self-managing systems. In: Proceedings of the 2008 ACM International Conference on Computing Frontiers, p. 115 (May 2008)
12. Ganek, A.: Overview of autonomic computing; origins, evolution, direction. In: Parashar, M., Harir, S. (eds.) Autonomic Computing: Concepts, Infrastructure, and Applications, pp. 4–17. CRC Press, Boca Raton (2007)
13. Tarnauca, B.: PetriNetExec: Java Embeddable Petri Nets (2013). http://tarnauca. net/petrinetexec. Accessed June 2013
14. Tarnauca, B., Puiu, D., Comnac, V., Suciu, C.: Modelling a flexible manufacturing system using reconfigurable finite capacity petri nets. In: 2012 13th International Conference on Optimization of Electrical and Electronic Equipment (OPTIM), pp. 1079–1084 (May 2012)
15. Tarnauca, B., Puiu, D., Comnac, V., Suciu, C.: Esper reference documentation version 4.3.0. Technical report, EsperTech (2011)
16. Leavitt, N.: Complex-event processing poised for growth. Computer **42**(4), 17–20 (2009)
17. Etzion, O., Niblett, P.: Event Processing in Action, 1st edn. Manning Publications Co., Greenwich (2010)
18. Tarnauca, B., Puiu, D., Damian, D., Comnac, V.: Traffic condition monitoring using complex event processing. In: International Conference on System Science and Engineering (ICSSE) 2013, pp. 123–128 (2013)

19. Rossi, F., van Beek, P., Walsh, T.: Handbook of Constraint Programming (Foundations of Artificial Intelligence). Elsevier Science Inc., New York (2006)
20. Policella, N., Cesta, A., Oddi, A., Smith, S.F.: From precedence constraint posting to partial order schedules: A csp approach to robust scheduling. AI Commun. **20**(3), 163–180 (2007). http://dl.acm.org/citation.cfm?id=1365527.1365531
21. Cobeanu, I., Tarnauca, B., Nechifor, S., Comnac, V.: Real-time scheduling of mobile agents using answer set programming. In: 2012 13th International Conference on Optimization of Electrical and Electronic Equipment (OPTIM), pp. 1505–1510 (2012)

Reporting Road Problems in Smart Cities Using OpenIoT Framework

Alexey Medvedev[1]([⊠]), Arkady Zaslavsky[2], Sergey Khoruzhnikov[1],
and Vladimir Grudinin[1]

[1] ITMO University, Kronverkskiy pr., 49, St. Petersburg, Russia
{alexey.medvedev,grudinin}@niuitmo.ru, xse@vuztc.ru
[2] CSIRO, Melbourne, Australia
arkady.zaslavsky@csiro.au

Abstract. Video streaming from cameras, closed-circuit television (CCTV), smartphones and Internet-connected objects (ICO) largely contributes to big data traffic on the Internet. Video streaming provides enormous amount of useful information for delivery of efficient and effective services in smart cities. Modern cities have large networks of surveillance cameras including CCTV, street crossings and the like. In this paper we discuss the challenges of annotating and retrieving video data streams from vehicle-mounted surveillance cameras. We also propose and evaluate the CityWatcher application – an Android application for recording video streams, annotating them with location, timestamp and additional context in order to make them discoverable and available to authorized Internet of Things applications. One of such applications is based on crowdsourced alerts to city authorities about road problems, like potholes, cracks, traffic accidents. These alerts are driver-initiated and are rewarded through an incentive mechanism. OpenIoT platform is used for infrastructure and development support.

Keywords: Smart city · Video streaming · Internet of Things (IoT) · Crowdsensing · Intelligent Transportation Systems · Vehicle-mounted surveillance camera (VMSC)

1 Introduction

Digital pervasive video cameras can be abundantly found everywhere these days and their numbers grow continuously. Sometimes we need a video-recording of some road accident (or of some other event) to understand what happened and identify a driver who may have been at fault. Many car owners, not only in Russia but elsewhere, use Vehicle-Mounted Surveillance Cameras (VMSC, or in other words, car black boxes, video registers or smartphones) for recording their driving and events of interest. These video recordings are potentially valuable sources of data. Drivers can use video recording from their devices as evidence in case of a road accident. However, video recordings from VMSC can't be retrieved by others and shared. Besides, using

Arkady Zaslavsky is an International Adjunct Professor at ITMO University since 2012.

I. Podnar Žarko et al. (Eds.): FP7 OpenIoT Project Workshop 2014, LNCS 9001, pp. 169–182, 2015.
DOI: 10.1007/978-3-319-16546-2_13

recorded video to report some problem or accident is a complicated task for the user, as he/she has to extract the needed part of the record manually and then write an annotation/description and then send it to authorities (an average citizen does not know where). Therefore, we highlight the challenge of retrieving such video fragments for evidence collection and the methods of annotating, discovering, retrieving and processing video data streams or their fragments. In particular, we argue that smartphones playing the role of VMSC can be used for evidence collection in case of a road accident. Besides, smartphone owners can use the proposed CityWatcher Android-based application for sending their automatically or manually annotated reports about road accidents, or any other city problems, e.g., road potholes and cracks, problems with streetlights, aggressive driving, and crime to relevant authorities. In this paper we propose, develop, discuss and evaluate a new scenario for the "CityWatcher" app that uses OpenIoT platform as a middleware.

Functioning of a modern city strongly depends not only on the city infrastructure, but also on the availability and quality of information for citizens and authorities about different aspects of city life. Various applications enhancing and making easier the city life lead to the concept of a 'smart city', which has received a lot of attention in last few years. The "Smart City" concept essentially implies efficiency, effectiveness and resource optimization. Efficiency is largely based on the intelligent management and integrated ICT (Information and Communication Technology) infrastructure, and active citizen participation. Therefore, citizens can and may choose to participate in implementing public policies in the form of crowdsourcing and crowdsensing [1–3].

Applications for smart cities are usually divided into six main areas: smart living, smart governance, smart economy, smart environment, smart people and smart mobility [4]. A very important feature for all these types of applications is the feasibility of data collection, which is primarily using sensors and sensor networks. Smart city applications need flexible access to open public data through the web for visualizing, transforming and making use of it. Active participation of all stakeholders is also very important for the smart city.

As the number of cars continues to grow, road problems become one of the main issues for city management. In smart cities, Intelligent Transportation Systems (ITS) [5] are used for solving transportation and congestion problems using Information and Communication Technology (ICT). ITSs help in problem detection, violations of traffic regulations, traffic analysis, evidence collection, safety provisioning, reducing costs and delays and much more. Therefore, ITSs appear to be one of the most important parts of a smart city. There's a recent development titled the Internet of Vehicles, as part of the Internet of Things.

Rapid problem solving is really important for the smart city. If a citizen encounters a problem, he/she should be able to draw city management attention to it without taking any complicated actions. On the other side, all city services must be ready to receive such requests and take measures to solve the problem. Besides, they must have instruments to ask for some help from citizens. This help is called crowdsourcing. If this help takes a form of getting any information from computers, smartphones or other devices that incorporate sensors, than we can speak about Urban Crowdsensing. Working in close contact with citizens is very important part of moving towards smart cities.

Every year road accidents cause loss of lives, loss of money and serious delays on city streets and freeways. Approximately 50 %–60 % of the delays on urban freeways are caused by road accidents [6]. Reducing delays by faster accident analysis is a challenging task. This task includes building an evidence collection system that can help the police and city authorities to make more accurate and faster decisions. The best way to achieve it is to provide video recordings from different angles and sources to the decision maker. If such videos are available, cars that participated in an accident can be faster moved out of the road and unblock traffic. A modern and efficient system for collecting reports about road (and other) problems from citizens in an important part too.

During last decade vehicle-mounted surveillance cameras (VMSC) gained significant popularity [7]. VMSC can also be referenced as cars video registers or black boxes or dash cams. They can help to prove innocence in case of a road accident or just make a video of something interesting and uncommon. By now, VMSCs already have a feature of annotating video with street name, as they have a GPS module onboard. The most modern VMSCs have Internet access. It can be predicted, that in future most of such smart cameras will have Internet access. VMSCs are produced by various manufacturers, for example, Garmin,[1] Prestigio,[2] HP.[3] A typical VMSC is shown in Fig. 1 (left). Millions of surveillance cameras are deployed, many of them are private. Also, many people just make recordings with their smartphones. As a smartphone has a camera, it can easily act as a VMSC if it is fixed on a front window. Many smartphone apps are available in Google Play and Apple AppStore. Examples of such applications include: DailyRoads Voyager,[4] Axel Voyager,[5] AVR,[6] AutoBoy BlackBox,[7] CaroO Pro[8] etc. their characteristics will be briefly discussed in the 'related work' section. A smartphone acting as a VMSC is shown in Fig. 1 (right).

Eventually, the cloud storage would keep videos of many events that can be of interest for city management, police, road services and other governmental organizations. The challenge is in retrieving relevant video streams when they are really needed. Owners of the surveillance camera may not be informed, that an accident happened just in his/her camera view. Owner of a VMSC could pass by without stopping, when an accident happens in front of their car. In such a situation, police has to understand what happened just by listening to stories of accident participants, that not always lead to correct analysis and respective decisions.

According to [8], surveillance video is now the biggest source of Big Data. It is predicted, that the percentage will increase by 65 percent by 2015. As we are adding video recordings from users Internet Connected Objects (ICO), using the Internet of

---

[1] https://buy.garmin.com/en-US/US/shop-by-accessories/other/garmin-dash-cam-20/prod146282.html.

[2] http://www.prestigio.com/catalogue/DVRs/Roadrunner_300.

[3] http://www.shopping.hp.com/en_US/home-office/-/products/Accessories/Camera_photo_video/H5R 80AA?HP f210 Car Camcorder.

[4] http://www.dailyroads.com/voyager.php.

[5] https://play.google.com/store/apps/details?id=net.powerandroid.axel.

[6] https://play.google.com/store/apps/details?id=com.at.autovideosregistrator&hl=uk.

[7] https://play.google.com/store/apps/details?id=com.jeon.blackbox&hl=ru.

[8] https://play.google.com/store/apps/details?id=com.pokevian.prime.

Fig. 1. VMSC (left) and smartphone acting as a VMSC (right)

Things terminology, the amount of data increases significantly. One of the most critical challenges is how to transmit and store all this video. First of all, it seems to be very hard to transmit and store all the video recordings from ICOs to some central storage, whether it's cloud or a video repository. Secondly, not many people might want to share their video recordings in some way, as there's no certainty what it will be used for. It is a serious privacy concern. The solution can be found in storing data in the device, where it was recorded. If we were able to make requests to all possible ICOs, the need to transfer and store the video data would be reduced or eliminated. So, as data stays in ICOs, we are to look at massively distributed Internet of Things system with challenging indexing, search and processing requirements. The challenge is also to communicate with millions of ICOs, make requests and process user reports to get annotated videos of events that we are interested in. As these ICOs are heterogeneous, opportunistically available and spread all over the region (however big), building such a system becomes a global IoT challenge. One of the key concepts of the system is crowdsourcing [9].

For implementing and deploying such a system we need a flexible, powerful, extensible, easy-to-use and open middleware platform that will simplify the process of ICOs discovery and orchestration. Besides, the platform must provide services enabling the concept of "Sensing-as-a-Service". Other important features of the middleware platform include support for working with ontologies and semantic reasoning. For these reasons OpenIoT platform has been selected as it combines the identified features in favorable comparison with similar IoT middleware platforms.

In Sect. 2 of the paper we discuss related work in this field and highlight several applications for smartphones that have similar functionality. Section 3 of the paper gives information about CityWatcher concepts and "reporting problems" use case. Architecture, implementation and coupling with OpenIoT middleware is discussed in Sect. 4 and future work and directions are presented in Sect. 5.

2   Related Work

Getting video streams and fragments from surveillance cameras is already well investigated [10]. Our research focus is not on existing road or traffic intersection cameras, as is the case with most current applications, but mainly, on opportunistically available mobile data sources, e.g., smartphones owned by users. The problem of crowdsourcing with smartphones is discussed in [11]. A prototype of a crowdsourced evidence collection system is presented in [7]. Though, some principles are similar with the proposed CityWatcher system, their prototype is developed for laptops, which is not as ubiquitous and convenient as using smartphones and besides, as a major drawback, does not incorporate annotating and discovering relevant video recordings. The number of possible use cases is limited only to requesting the video and the research challenge of how to deal with the heterogeneous world of IoT is not discussed. The problem of crowdsourced video annotation is widely discussed in [12].

As was mentioned above, there are a number of applications, which allow using an Android smartphone as a VMSC. We will discuss their characteristics and main features, typical for applications of this class. Main characteristics of a typical VMSC emulating application include but aren't limited to: (a) Free or not?; (b) Video format, possibility to choose the format; (c) Cycle video recording; (d) Possibility of making photos; (e) Annotation with timestamp; (f) Annotation with GPS coordinates; (g) Annotation with location information (street name); (h) Map, navigation; (i) Acting as a car's computer (measuring maximum and average speed, etc.); (j) Possibility of loading video to the Internet via wireless networks; (k) Indexing significant moments manually or by a sensor; (l) Resource consumption; (m) Possibility of working in background. Some of the mentioned apps are briefly discussed below:

- DailyRoads Voyager – free, easy to use application. Axel Voyager – complicated full featured application, supports navigation functionality and can make indexes of significant moments.
- AVR – usual video recording features, image stabilization function, navigation, can send video to the Internet.
- AutoBoy BlackBox – full featured video player, displays additional information (speed, compass), very big choice of settings.
- CaroO Pro - additional functionality includes features, usual for cars computer.

Any of these apps can be used as a VMSC, but none of them support answering requests to share video recordings and make their video recordings discoverable. In the proposed CityWatcher application we focus on request processing and answering, so that interested parties could make use of locally stored and annotated video recordings. A number of recent interesting projects like ImproveMyCity [13, 14], BuitenBeter (Netherlands) [15] and Fix My Street (UK) [16, 17] discuss "reporting problems" use case. These projects gather citizens' reports about city problems via a web site form or smartphone application for further processing. The user can make a picture of a problem with a smartphone, select problem type, select a location or use automatic GPS annotation and send the information to the city council, helping to identify potholes, stray garbage, broken street lamps and other problems. Some projects like RosYama (Russia) [18] and RosZKH (Russia) [19] gather reports and generate papers of a special form for sending them by post to municipal or road services. This can be an effective approach as official services can't ignore official letters, but on the other hand it produces a lot of unneeded and time consuming manual paper work.

The novelty of CityWatcher approach is that we make not only a text or photo report, but also produce a video fragment that has been recorded while driving as a main source. Secondly, voice recognition with later automatic ontological processing for filtering, aggregating and redirecting reports is also a step ahead. Thirdly, City-Watcher is designed to be maintained and administered by city management services to become an effective instrument of gathering important information about the life in a smart city.

3   CityWatcher Concepts

As it was already mentioned, in this paper we propose, develop, discuss and evaluate a new scenario for the "CityWatcher" Android-based app. The application of CityWat-cher for searching video clips with road accidents on smartphones and is discussed in [20]. This paper focuses on driver-initiated alerts which are communicated to city authorities along with relevant video clips and uploaded to the OpenIoT middleware platform which is hosted by the cloud. The cloud could be managed and run by city administration on any private or public cloud, e.g. Amazon EC2 [21].

ICOs owner can be not only passive carriers of a camera. If a VMSC is a smart-phone application, it is possible to add a special feature, which allows the user to push information to a specialized center, when the user notices something important. Let's consider one more scenario as illustrated in Fig. 2. The user is driving a car, when he/

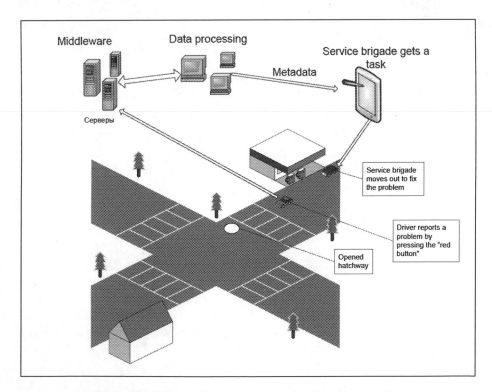

Fig. 2. The "driver-initiated alert" scenario (Color figure online)

she sees an opened hatchway on the road. As the user is driving a car, he/she has no possibility to search for a proper phone, dial it to report a problem. The user just presses the "red" button in the corner of the application screen and says "I've seen an opened hatchway". Then the last minute of the video is automatically extracted and is uploaded into the cloud. In this way the user can continue driving his car without the need for parking to make a call or type text. Besides, the user does not break the law by making a call while driving. The point of ergonomic usage is very important here. User's voice annotation and all the metadata like location and timestamp are also attached to the video and loaded to the cloud. This information is processed by city management services. After passing some automated filtering, the data becomes available to a special employee who decides that this information should be passed to the road service brigade of the current district. It all takes a few minutes before service brigade moves out to fix the problem. This feature can also be used to report about any city problems we can think off, for example, rude or dangerous behavior of other drivers, broken traffic lights, sewer breakthrough, water spills and much more.

The pseudo code for the "driver-initiated alert" scenario can be found below:

```
RedButtonPressedHandler(
    //First, make a recording of users voice annotation
    RecordVoiceAnnotation();
    //Make a file with last minute ( length
    //depends on settings) from recorded video
    //Wipe out original sound if needed
    CutLastMinute();
    WipeSound();
    //Load file and voice annotation to the cloud
    LoadVideoAndAnnotationToCloud();
    //get reported from the server and save report locally
    GetReportID();
    SaveMyReport(ID);
)
```

As it was already mentioned, the main principle of data acquisition is crowd-sourcing. Crowdsourcing seems to be a strong method of collecting data, but there are concerns about manual data processing. Though a lot of dispatching work can be automated, most of it has to be made manually and by professionals.

There are also a number of challenges that would arise in any crowdsourcing solution:

- **Redundant data.** An open hatchway can be possibly seen and reported by many drivers. All their reports must be linked to one and only one collective report to avoid redundancy. This can be done by showing all similar user reports to the employee who approves the report. The similarity can be found by comparing time, coordinates and key words that were detected in the users' voice annotations.
- **False data.** Someone's joke can become a waste of time for the service team. One of the solutions of this problem can be in storing user's credibility ratings in the database. These ratings can be made by giving marks to loaded videos by personnel who work with them. Requests from users, who had already produced false or

misleading data, can be blocked. On the other hand – users who provide reliable and relevant reports get credibility points, which can be later transformed into some incentives.

- **Feedback.** Users who send data want to understand what happens next. If they don't receive an acknowledgement that their request was processed and their work is needed, they will not send reports any more. Citywatcher Android application has a form with reports on all shared videos, so the user can check if his/her contribution was used.

Designing, running and automating a processing center is also a big challenge. First off all we need some speech recognition mechanisms, so the system could get some semantics without human intervention. Speech recognition can be done both on the side of pervasive cameras and on the middleware side. We choose to make it on the middleware side, as it would be easier to maintain, update and tune. Besides, such mechanisms could be energy consuming and it is better not to produce extra load on user's devices. After speech recognition the system can try to apply semantic reasoned and make some decisions. These decisions include answering questions like:

- Is this report unique or is it redundant?
- How urgent is the problem?
- What district and what service are responsible for solving the problem?

At first, report processing can be done manually by experts. Later, when the business logic becomes computerized, many techniques can be used for process automation and reduction of the human involvement. Context reasoning techniques, which will be used in future releases of CityWatcher, can be broadly classified into six categories: (a) supervised learning, (b) unsupervised learning, (c) rules, (d) fuzzy logic, (e) ontological reasoning and (f) probabilistic reasoning. For example, supervised learning methods include artificial neural networks, Bayesian networks, case-based reasoning, decision tree learning and support vector machines [22]. Such methods must be supported by the middleware platform. We will discuss the choice and features of the middleware platform in the next section. The speech recognition engine is an important point for automatic report processing. The best way for getting results without having serious troubles with tuning and administering the engine is using a cloud service like Yandex. SpeechKit [23].

4   CityWatcher Architecture and Implementation

The proposed system is divided into three main parts: ICOs, middleware and client software as shown in Fig. 3. ICOs include the smartphones, VMSCs, smart cameras, cars video registers, etc. All participating ICOs record video via a special application.

The prototype is an Android app. Application features used in the discussed scenario include Video recording, Video annotating (GPS coordinates, time), auto register with middleware, constructing reports and sending them to the cloud, viewing the information about reports that were already sent. Screenshots of CityWatcher application for Android are presented in Figs. 4 and 5. It is a working prototype app.

The design of user-friendly interface will be included in future work. CityWatcher Middleware is based on OpenIoT Platform [24]. OpenIoT project is a new open source middleware platform for intelligent IoT applications. It is an extension to cloud computing implementations and provides functions for managing IoT resources. In this way users can get IoT services including Sensing-as-a-Service. OpenIoT platform is discussed in [24–26].

The CityWatcher project relates to urban crowdsensing. Therefore, the city administrations are to become service providers and a host to an OpenIoT platform. Using an OpenIoT platform gives us an efficient and advanced way to fusing data sources. Client software located in Utility App Plane is a web-based application, which allows an authorized user both to make requests to the system and to process reports.

One of the technical problems needed to be solved is identifying the device, on which video is recorded and stored. Firstly, middleware has to be aware of all participating ICO's in the system, as it has to broadcast/multicast a request to all of them, register that the task has been sent and match the answer with the device ID. Secondly, middleware needs to have information about user personal preferences, as the user obtains some incentives for participating and sharing his/her videos. Besides, having information about the ICO owner makes the video fragment more legal in the court. We must also bear in mind that one user can have several devices and one device can be used by different users.

We propose to use the following scheme: every user gets an account in the City-Watcher system. It is a classical login/password pair. With this account a user can start the CityWatcher app. On the middleware side login is linked to full user description/profile, so the user can get his/her incentives from city services. As the video is stored on the users' devices and one user can have multiple devices, we need to uniquely identify every device. To solve this problem a unique device ID can be generated following the CityWatcher installation. It is like a license number for software. Then, all users of one device use this unique ID, but log in with their own accounts. This enables the middleware to distinguish devices for video searching possibilities and also, distinguish users for incentive purposes.

When the video fragment is loaded into the cloud, it should be stored and registered in the database. Additional information about the fragment includes task ID, on which it was found, user ID, device ID and obtaining time. Besides, some information about device like camera resolution and record format is also attached. OpenIoT middleware with CityWatcher Application and their connection with city authorities are shown in Fig. 6.

We use SQLite as an engine for storing data about timestamps and coordinates. The CityWatcher app instantly adds record to the database. When a task arrives and there is a need to understand if there is a video on local storage – a request to the database is made.

The table structure of the local database that is used for both scenarios is shown in Fig. 7. For the content search scenario, when the request is made, we search not exactly the same time and coordinates, but add delta values and perform range search. For the "driver-initiated alerts" scenario needed data is derived from the same local database, before sending it to the cloud service. The middleware database structure is omitted in this paper due to space limitations.

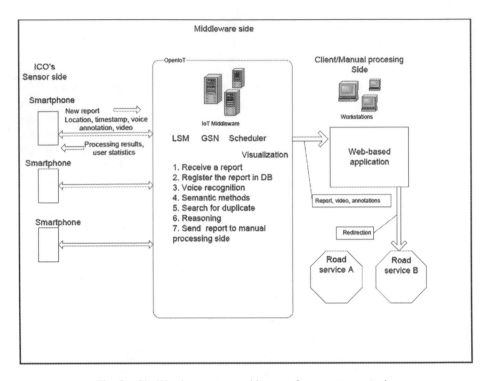

Fig. 3. CityWatcher system architecture for reports processing

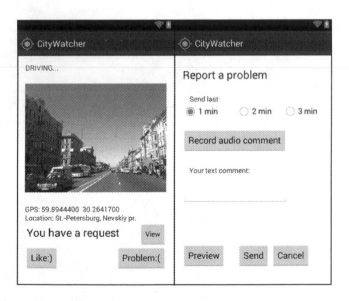

Fig. 4. Main screen, reporting a problem

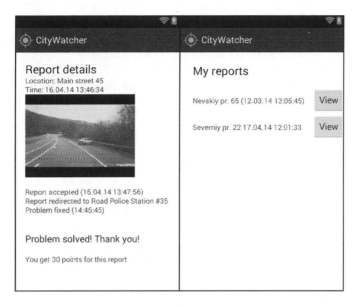

Fig. 5. Report list, report details

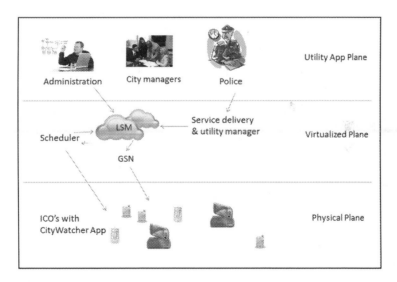

Fig. 6. OpenIoT middleware with CityWatcher application

We use Global Sensor Network (GSN) to provide middleware functionality for registering and finding ICOs. x-GSN (Global Sensor Network) is a part of OpenIoT platform and is used for managing virtual sensors and wrappers, processing classes, distributed processing storage and services [27].

Linked Sensor Middleware (LSM) is a central component of OpenIoT. It takes data from virtual sensors and transforms it to Linked Data format like RDF. If ontologies are provided – then data is annotated accordingly. Data can be loaded into LSM with pull-based and push-based methods. Both mechanisms have advantages and disadvantages and both are used in OpenIoT depending on a use case [28].

Scheduler formulates the request from user inputs. Scheduler performs the following functions: sensor and ICO selection, virtual sensor "indirect" activation, request storing and activation, service status update, access control [29].

Implementation of the storage facility for video fragments is subject to further analyses and discussion. The decisions regarding what, when, where and how to store should be based on the needs, relevance, capacity constraints, preservation of evidence etc.

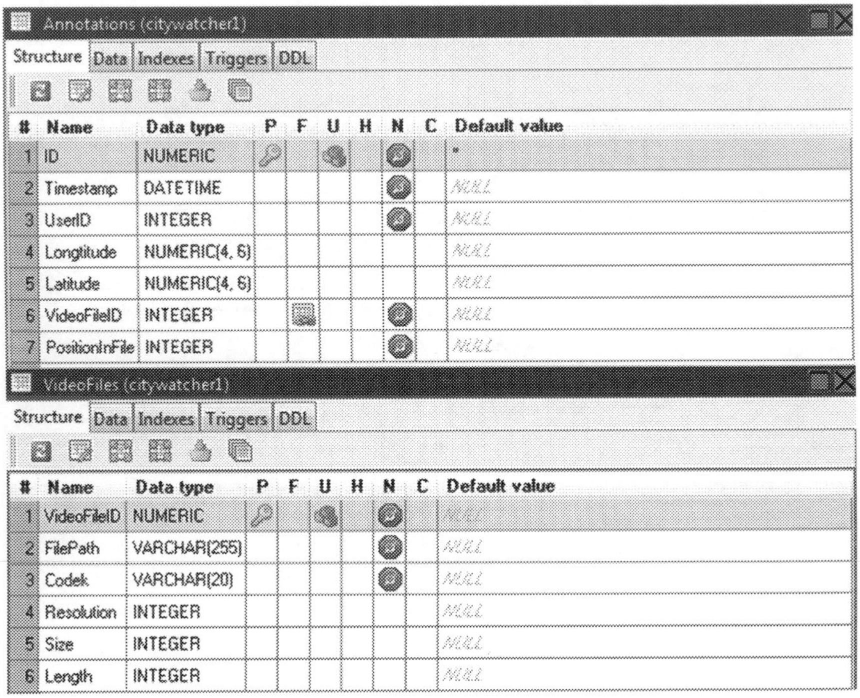

Annotations (citywatcher1)

Structure | Data | Indexes | Triggers | DDL

#	Name	Data type	P	F	U	H	N	C	Default value
1	ID	NUMERIC							
2	Timestamp	DATETIME							NULL
3	UserID	INTEGER							NULL
4	Longtitude	NUMERIC(4, 6)							NULL
5	Latitude	NUMERIC(4, 6)							NULL
6	VideoFileID	INTEGER							NULL
7	PositionInFile	INTEGER							NULL

VideoFiles (citywatcher1)

Structure | Data | Indexes | Triggers | DDL

#	Name	Data type	P	F	U	H	N	C	Default value
1	VideoFileID	NUMERIC							NULL
2	FilePath	VARCHAR(255)							NULL
3	Codek	VARCHAR(20)							NULL
4	Resolution	INTEGER							NULL
5	Size	INTEGER							NULL
6	Length	INTEGER							NULL

Fig. 7. Table structure of SQLite DB

5 Conclusion and Future Work

We can think of a scenario, where people not only report problems by pressing the "red button", but, in addition, they press a "green button", to appreciate things or changes they like. These "likes" can be marked on a map, aggregated and analyzed to understand, which locations in a city produce positive emotions. This can be a little step towards improved and enhanced services and possible connections to social networks. Moreover, creating such a "map of feelings" in future can be automated by gathering and analyzing statistics about users' heart rate variation and other parameters that can be obtained via different wearable devices like smart watches or fitness bracelets.

Research in this area will be highlighted in future papers. Besides, we are confident that it is possible to extend the CityWatcher application with pervasive object search options. It is hard to imagine a location where ICOs cameras can't reach. ICOs can be deployed anywhere and anytime. This reinforces the motto of the IoT "anywhere, anytime, on any device and over any network". While it might still be hard and expensive to put surveillance cameras everywhere, with the advent of mobile computing we can assume that users carry their ICOs/smartphones everywhere they go. ICOs become more and more powerful and video recognition algorithms also are becoming more advanced. For example, we can include some library for car number plate recognition [30]. An ICO can receive a request from the police, searching for a stolen car. ICO analyzes all car number plates that it detects on the road. If a match is found – an alert can be sent back to police.

As video recognition algorithms become mature, we foresee more and more scenarios of pervasive object search. Present day smartphones are able to record and store a large amount of video content with location and timestamp annotations, as well as other diverse context. The proper use of sharing this information can help in improving how the smart city runs and functions.

Acknowledgement. The research has been carried out with the financial support of the Ministry of Education and Science of the Russian Federation under grant agreement #14.575.21.0058.

Part of this work has been carried out in the scope of the ICT OpenIoT Project which is co-funded by the European Commission under seventh framework program, contract number FP7-ICT-2011-7-287305-OpenIoT.

References

1. Caragliu, A., Del Bo, C., Nijkamp, P.: Smart cities in Europe. In: Proceedings of the 3rd Central European Conference on Regional Science, Košice (2009)
2. Hu, M., Li, C.: Design smart city based on 3S, internet of things, grid computing and cloud computing technology. In: Wang, Y., Zhang, X. (eds.) IOT 2012. CCIS, vol. 312, pp. 466–472. Springer, Heidelberg (2012)
3. Smart city. http://en.wikipedia.org/wiki/Smart_city. Accessed 18 April 2014
4. Giffinger, R., Fertner, C., Kramar, H., Kalasek, R., Pichler-Milanovic, N., Meijers, E.: Smart cities – Ranking of European medium-sized cities. Smart Cities. Centre of Regional Science, Vienna (2007)
5. Intelligent transportation system. http://en.wikipedia.org/wiki/Intelligent_transportation_system. Accessed 24 April 2014
6. Ki, Y.-K., Lee, D.-Y.: A traffic accident recording and reporting model at intersections. IEEE Trans. Intell. Transp. Syt. **8**(2), 188–194 (2007)
7. Chae, K., Kim, D., Jung, S., Choi, J., Jung, S.: Evidence Collecting System from Car Black Boxes. School of Electronic Engineering, Soongsil University Seoul, Korea
8. Huang, T.: Surveillance video: the biggest big data. Comput. Now **7**(2) (2014). http://www.computer.org/portal/web/computingnow/archive/february2014?lf1=929719755f161316415 589b16868896
9. Schuurman, D., Baccarne, B., De Marez, L., Mechant, P.: Smart ideas for smart cities: investigating crowdsourcing for generating and selecting ideas for ICT innovation in a city context. J. Theor. Appl. Electron. Commer. Res. **7**(3), 49–62 (2012)

10. Georgakopoulos, D., Baker, M., Nodine, A.: Event-driven video aware-ness providing physical security. World Wide Web J. (WWWJ) **10**(1), 85–109 (2007)
11. Chatzimilioudis, G., Konstantinidis, A., Laoudias, C., Zeinalipour-Yazti, D.: Crowdsourcing with Smartphones. IEEE Internet Computing **16**(5), 36–44 (2012)
12. Vondrick, C., Patterson, D., Ramanan, D.: Efficiently scaling up crowd-sourced video annotation: a set of best practices for high quality, economical video labeling. Int. J. Comput. Vis. **101**, 184–204 (2013). Springer Science+Business Media LLC
13. Improve My City Webpage. http://smartcityapps.urenio.org/improve-my-city_en.html. Accessed 17 June 2014
14. Tsampoulatidis, I., Ververidis, D., Tsarchopoulos, P.,Nikolopoulos S., Kompatsiaris I., Komninos, N.: ImproveMyCity: an open source platform for direct citizen-government communication. In: Proceedings of the 21st ACM International Conference on Multimedia, pp. 839–842. ACM, New York (2013)
15. Buiten Better Webpage. http://www.buitenbeter.nl/English. Accessed 17 June 2014
16. FixMySreet Webpage. http://www.fixmystreet.com. Accessed 17 June 2014
17. King, S., Brown, P.: Fix my street or else: using the internet to voice local public service concerns. In: Proceedings of the 1st International Conference on Theory and Practice of Electronic Governance, pp. 72–80. ACM, New York (2007)
18. RosYama Webpage. http://rosyama.ru. Accessed 17 June 2014
19. RosZKH Webpage. http://roszkh.ru. Accessed 17 June 2014
20. Medvedev, A., Zaslavsky, A., Grudinin, V., Khoruzhnikov, S.: Citywatcher: annotating and searching video data streams for smart cities applications. In: Balandin, S., Andreev, S., Koucheryavy, Y. (eds.) NEW2AN/ruSMART 2014. LNCS, vol. 8638, pp. 144–155. Springer, Heidelberg (2014)
21. Amazon EC2 Webpage. http://docs.aws.amazon.com/AWSEC2/latest/UserGuide/concepts. html. Accessed 17 June 2014
22. Perera, C., Zaslavsky, A., Christen, P., Georgakopoulos, D.: Context aware computing for internet of things: a survey. IEEE Commun. Surv. Tutorials **16**(1), 414–454 (2014)
23. Yandex Speech Kit Webpage. http://api.yandex.ru/speechkit/. Accessed 17 June 2014
24. OpenIoT Architecture Webpage. https://github.com/OpenIotOrg/openiot/wiki/OpenIoT-Architecture. Accessed 12 April 2014
25. OpenIoT Webpage. http://www.openiot.eu. Accessed 12 March 2014
26. What is OpenIoT and what does it can do for you? http://academics.openiot.eu/. Accessed 24 April 2014
27. X-GSN Webpage. https://github.com/OpenIotOrg/openiot/wiki/X-GSN-Use. Accessed 17 June 2014
28. LSM Webpage. https://github.com/OpenIotOrg/openiot/wiki/Data-platform-(lsm). Accessed 17 June 2014
29. Global Scheduler Webpage. https://github.com/OpenIotOrg/openiot/wiki/Global-Scheduler. Accessed 17 June 2014
30. Buch, N., Kristl, V.S.A., Orwell, J.: A review of computer vision techniques for the analysis of urban traffic. IEEE Trans. Intell. Transp. Syst. **12**(3), 920–939 (2011)

Author Index

Printed in the United States
By Bookmasters